LEADERSHIP EDUCATION

The Phases of Learning

THIRD EDITION

LEADERSHIP EDUCATION

The Phases of Learning

THIRD EDITION

Oliver and Rachel DeMille

Check out edits, updates and upgrades
to this book and download a free audio!
TJEd.org/New-7-Keys

WWW.TJED.ORG
AN EDUCATION TO MATCH YOUR MISSION

The Leadership Education Library

Volume 1: *A Thomas Jefferson Education: Teaching a Generation of Leaders for the 21st Century*

Volume 2: *Leadership Education: The Phases of Learning*

Volume 3: *Hero Education: A Scholar Phase Guidebook for Teens, Parents and Mentors*

Volume 4: *Thomas Jefferson Education for Teens – and Every Adult Who Wants to Change the World*

Volume 5: *The Student Whisperer: Inspiring Genius*

Volume 6: *19 Apps: Leadership Education for College Students*

Published TJEd.org.

Edited by Michele Smith

Book and cover design and illustration by Daniel Ruesch Design
Alpine, Utah
www.danielruesch.net

ISBN 978-0-9912240-0-5

To W. Cleon Skousen

(1913-2006)

who inspired us off the conveyor belt

Contents

Introduction

The education of tomorrow's leaders determines the future. Throughout history, this pattern has been repeated again and again. The largest educational shift in the history of the world occurred with the advent of the Industrial Age nearly two hundred years ago. The Industrial Age delivered education to the masses, as well as the privileged, through a conveyor belt model of learning which continues to be prevalent in both public and private schools today. We are all beneficiaries of these momentous educational developments.

Today we stand on the brink of an even bigger transformation. The Information Age is changing everything and education must also evolve. The parents, teachers and educational leaders of our day will determine society's future because they hold the education of the next generation in their hands. What kind of future will they give us?

This is perhaps the most important question in the beginning decades of the twenty-first century. But it does not get fully to the heart of the matter. The education of tomorrow's *leaders* will determine the future, rather than the education of the masses. Leadership determines destiny. Leaders select the goals of nations and generations and determine which paths to take in pursuit of those goals.

The biography of great leaders is the history of the world. Consider the format of the scriptures of the world's major religions, or secular histories such as Thucydides, Plutarch or Durant; the stories of great individuals are the basis of history. To know the leaders of the past is to know the past. Sometimes the leaders are good and sometimes they are not. In the twenty-first century, it falls to us to choose which type of leader we will produce. In our era leadership, and the education which informs and nurtures it, is no longer a function of blood lines or birthright. The wisdom of the ages is available to anyone willing to pay its price. Becoming a leader capable of impacting our civilization's future is now a choice available to more of the earth's inhabitants than at any other time. It is *your* choice.

Parents, teachers and educators who choose to become and mentor leaders will construct the future. Our purpose in this book is to invite you to be one of these pivotal figures. Our goal is to help those who have chosen to educate tomorrow's leaders do so not only effectively but *greatly*. Greatness is the second indispensable trait of true leaders; goodness is the first. Both are the function of education. Indeed, separation of intellectual learning from moral development most characterizes the modern conveyor belt educational system—from pre-school through post-doctoral studies. It is precisely this separation that parents and educators of our generation must overcome if we are to educate a generation of leaders with character and competence, who are both good *and* great.

Such leaders are desperately needed in our world today. Fortunately, we have met thousands of parents and teachers who are up to the task, and we are sure there are many others. This book is for them. It is also for the rest of us who want to be up to the task, who worry that we are not, but who try anyway because we know our children were born to make a positive difference in the world.

Three Traditions of Education

In the recorded history of the world, there are three major traditions of education. First, conveyor belt education trains the masses in basic literacy, lifting generations from poverty toward better jobs and lives. The emphasis is on "what to think" as dictated by others in order to get "right" answers, be "good" students, and most of all, "fit in" with an externally imposed structure defining worth. Those who are able to navigate the playground politics and jump the requisite hoops receive the rewards of conformity to the academic and societal norm.

Second, professional education trains experts in fields including medicine, law, business, accounting, engineering and many others. Professional education uses a competitive conveyor belt methodology to establish a standard that our society depends upon for safety, efficiency and order. Those professionally trained in their fields become experts who are compensated to the degree that they effectively apply the model of "when to think." Professional education creates an "expert class" whose explanations, recommendations and standards are trusted and valued by conveyor belt educated masses that have been trained to act and think according to the expertise of others.

Third, Leadership Education trains thinkers, leaders, artists, inventors, citizens, entrepreneurs, and statesmen. It educates individuals "how to think" and teaches them why it is important. As Robert Hutchins put it, this type education is "the education of free men in the knowledge and skills that are needed to remain free."

Leadership Education prepares leaders who motivate individuals, communities and nations to greater good in an environment of liberty that allows all that is best to flourish. Though the problems civilization presents may be new, the process of solving problems is not. Leaders taught in this manner act according to ageless principles of success. They are taught that the accomplishment of their mission in their homes, communities and societies will create impactful and uplifting change. Their vision, capacity, tenacity and involvement inspire and motivate others to worthwhile purposes that elevate society.

Leadership Education is Vital

Nearly every system of education in history and modern times fits into one of these three categories. We believe the most important of the three types is Leadership Education. Without an effective system for training leadership, the other two vital systems (and the free society that fosters them) cannot be perpetuated. Without Leadership Education, no nation maintains its liberty or its prosperity. Without Leadership Education, the other two traditions of education ultimately decline, creating a "dark age" of learning.

Without Leadership Education, nations are forced to assign *experts*, instead of *leaders*, to fulfill vital leadership roles in the community, family, education, business, media, entertainment, economy and government. Eventually, without Leadership Education, great and powerful nations decline and lose their influence for good in the world. Without Leadership Education, the future is bleak.

The United States of America led the world into the twenty-first century. The Berlin Wall had fallen, the Cold War was over, and the economy had experienced an unprecedented explosion of growth from 1987 to 2000. Democracy and capitalism were both on the rise around the world. On the surface, everything looked bright for world freedom and prosperity—but only to the blissfully ignorant. The student of history knew better. History revealed that the bright present was the result of past efforts. Increased liberty and wealth were the natural results of an economy and society forged fifty years earlier. History's most thoughtful students saw that present affluence was undergirded with a very different foundation.

For the last three decades, our society has been setting the stage for economic, cultural and political decline. At the center of this change are the schoolrooms of our homes, neighborhoods and campuses. E.D. Hirsch's *Cultural Literacy* and Allan Bloom's *The Closing of the American Mind* both warned in 1987 that our modern educational format could not deliver on its promises to the future. Both suggested that only a return to great education, rooted in a deep understanding of history and the classics, would allow us to prevent decline and build that future of promise. Twenty years later, their warnings are still applicable.

History shows repeatedly that the strength, wisdom, and foresight of one generation creates peace and prosperity for the three generations that follow. The third and fourth generations, born in peace and raised in relative luxury, seem committed to ignore the lessons of history. They assure themselves, "we're different from past generations," while plunging headlong into crisis. The structures which come crumbling down during these fourth generations are rooted in widespread poor education and high levels of expert training for "the few"—the lethal historical combination of ignorance and arrogance.

The only historically proven solution capable of averting this danger is high quality Leadership Education. The liberty, prosperity and stability of future civilizations are dependent upon the leaders of tomorrow getting a Leadership Education today.

Providing a Leadership Education

Try a brief exercise. Picture the face of each of your children or grandchildren. Look into their eyes and see what potential is there. If you are like most parents, you will see and feel that they were born to be special, to make a difference. This is not just because you love them; it is because it is *true*. The leaders of the twenty-first century—not only the generational "icons," but the parents, educators, business owners, artists, scientists and church and community service leaders—live in our homes. They will find their voice in service and accomplishment in their own field. They deserve the highest quality of education, and it is our responsibility to help them get it.

Leadership Education has a long and successful history as an essential part of any successful nation's educational offerings. In our generation, ever increasing numbers of young people are seeing Leadership Education as the best path for their life and education. More and more parents are setting the example for and empowering their children by getting a Leadership Education themselves.

One challenge is that few adults in this generation had the benefit of receiving in their youth a classical education such as Leadership Education provides. We often feel that we must re-invent the methods and systems of Leadership Education. We will find much help as we apply principles of success that parents and teachers of the past used to train leaders.

Another challenge lies in the fact that children learn developmentally, moving through stages according to a unique individual timetable. The perfect thing for the education of one three-year-old may not be at all right for another, and definitely wrong for the same child as a nine-year-old. Indeed, it seems that just when we start to get the hang of teaching a child at a certain age, the child grows into another phase. Also, each child approaches the same developmental task differently, so we have to be continually creating and innovating as we parent and mentor.

Finally, many parents struggle with a lack of confidence, wondering if they can actually do it. In fact, we do not know of any parents raising their children with (or without!) the model of Leadership Education who do not express doubts, anxieties and concerns. We certainly have many such moments. It is easy to ascribe our feelings of inadequacy to the inherent challenges in our Leadership Education agenda. But could it just be that parenting is such a high stakes endeavor that we are constantly in awe of the magnitude of our responsibility? It helps, if only a little, to know that we are all struggling with an impossible task of being a perfect parent. Having lofty goals can make that task seem more difficult, but we believe that if we keep things in perspective—that is: learn the principles, apply them and trust the process—it actually leads us to greater confidence and success. This is all true of teaching as well.

Parenting and teaching are challenging, and educating ourselves and our youth will always be difficult. But at the end of the day we are still the parents, and it is our responsibility to do our best. No longer is it the obvious choice to delegate that role to someone else without deliberation. The parents of this generation are reclaiming their duty to make considered choices regarding education for their families.

So we keep at it. Over time, we see ourselves and other parents getting better at it, and having little "paydays" along the way. We doubt parenting or teaching can ever become truly easy or routine, but by applying principles of success, we have found that parents can consistently and even drastically improve. Today's children were born to serve and make a huge positive difference in the world, to really lead. We simply must help them get the best possible education.

Part of our personal journey as parents and mission as educators has been to catalog and codify the principles of Leadership Education as expressed in the lives of those who shaped history for good, and also as observed in remarkable families of our acquaintance. We have spent more than fifteen years developing and teaching Leadership Education. The response has been wonderful! It has often been voiced in a two-part reaction:

"This is just what we've been looking for! It feels so natural! It's so obvious!"

Followed by:

"But...*how do you really do it...?*"

It seems strange that something so "natural" and "obvious" can leave us feeling so unsure of how to act. We believe it has to do with the fact that it is difficult to put something into practice that we have not internalized. It is nearly impossible to communicate with conviction something we have not experienced. The answer to this is also natural and obvious—the change has to begin with the teacher, and the parent. Like the difference of knowing a place from looking at a map as opposed to actually being there—as parents and teachers gain a Leadership Education themselves, they will have walked the path. Understanding the journey, they will be able to serve as enthusiastic and experienced "tour guides" to their own children and students. With few exceptions, those who struggle most to find success with their children in Leadership Education are those who are still focusing on educating *their children* with little or no *personal* experience with Leadership Education.

Leadership Education is based on two key assumptions. Many great educators in all of the systems have discovered these principles for themselves; however, the conveyor belt models of education do not foster or reward these conclusions. First, Leadership Education presupposes that each individual was born with a unique and important individual mission and a vital role which he or she can do like no one else. Leadership Education consists of discovering, preparing for, and fulfilling this mission. Of course, such an education must be personalized.

Second, Leadership Education recognizes that every person is a genius—literally. Each and every person, not merely a predetermined upper echelon, was born with the natural talents, passions, desires, interests and abilities to fully accomplish his or her mission. True, some people choose not to develop their genius or are stunted in an environment that does not nurture their optimal growth; but it is inside each and every person you have ever met or will ever meet. The ultimate goal of Leadership Education is the development of the inherent genius inside each student.

All truly great teachers taught this—from Socrates and Plato to Confucius and Buddha to Turnbull, Wythe, Witherspoon, C.S. Lewis and others. Leadership Education is not for a few elite; it is for everyone. Every person has a mission and the potential genius to accomplish it. It is the role of Leadership Education not to fill students with a pre-determined set of facts, beliefs, or processes, but to "draw forth" from each student the amazing potential and abilities that he or she alone possesses. Great leaders throughout time were educated in a manner that prepared them to make unique and essential contributions. These educational principles still work.

Most of the current population of the United States is educated according to a conveyor belt model of education. In contrast, the great leaders of our Founding Era and leaders throughout history received a Leadership Education. Leadership Education is a compilation of leadership principles and practices by which great men and women throughout history were educated. It is time for another generation to get a Leadership Education.

Getting the Most Out of This Book

Leadership Education occurs in several general phases, each vital to superb learning. *Leadership Education: The Phases of Learning* is designed to help the reader study these phases of Leadership Education as they naturally unfold in human development.

An overall introduction to and survey of the Phases of Learning is provided in Part I, A Philosophy for Life: Why the Phases Matter. We examine the philosophies of leading educators in modern times and the influence they have had on the current educational model. We explain the essential lessons of each Phase of Learning and the Seven Keys of Great Teaching. We provide a road map of the progression of families who choose a Leadership Education and are able to implement a powerful Eighth Key. The Life Paths that result from the educational model we choose are presented.

In Part II we discuss the Foundational Phases of Core and Love of Learning. We discuss fifty-five ingredients of a Leadership Education home environment and include insights on applying the list based on your unique circumstances. Transition to Scholar provides thirty-five skills that will help you guide your child's Transition to Scholar as well as important suggestions for relationship and discipline. Three Indispensable Choices parents must make in order to facilitate an effective transition to Scholar Phase and common concerns addressed in a question and answer format conclude this Part.

Part III explains the Educational Phases of Scholar and Depth. You will learn how to parent and better teach youth in Scholar and Depth Phases to truly meet their potential in the face of very different societal norms. Included in Part III is a discussion of our nation's past and present higher educational offerings and the attributes of an ideal Depth Phase university environment.

Part IV contains new understanding of the Applicational Phases of Mission and Impact with a Coda discussing the crucial and influential role Grandparents (a title denoting status or function in *community* as well as family) have in Leadership Education.

We suggest that readers study and understand all of the phases. For example, if your children are in Scholar Phase, you may be tempted to skip directly to the Scholar Phase chapter and focus your studies there. This could be a serious mistake. Unlike the conveyor belt system, where grade levels proceed in a linear fashion (e.g. from the fifth to the sixth grade), in Leadership Education you never actually leave Core Phase, or Love of Learning Phase, or the others, once you have reached them. Students in Depth Phase still apply the lessons of Core, Love of Learning and Scholar.

If you have children in Core Phase only, you still need to carefully read all of the phases, since knowing where your children are headed will significantly influence how you teach and guide them as toddlers. Teachers of every level will want to know how the level they teach fits into the whole pattern.

Understanding all of the phases is also crucial while your family is young because many people in the early stages of child rearing have not yet fully achieved their own Scholar and Depth Phases and the time is ripe for obtaining such an education. In short, a vision of the whole is necessary to proceed with confidence and to be effective. You will undoubtedly have experiences that we have not; our anecdotes cannot possibly answer all of your questions or concerns. A thorough understanding of the underpinning principles will be your refuge when such questions arise. You must be your own expert.

With all of that said: if you are inclined to start with one chapter out of sequence, read the chapter on Scholar Phase. It is the crux of the Leadership Education model. The fruits of Leadership Education planted and nurtured in childhood begin to be abundantly harvested in Scholar Phase. Once you have completed reading this chapter, we feel sure you will see the need and will want to study the other chapters as well.

With a good overall understanding of all of the phases, you will know where to turn to find principles tailored to the specific needs of your children (as well as yourself and others you mentor) in each phase. We have formatted this book by phases so that a parent or teacher can read and study one phase at a time, learn the basics, and apply principles of success for that phase. As children (and parents themselves) grow into new phases, the section on that phase can be revisited and principles relating to it implemented. Understanding and continuing to educate ourselves on the phases presented in this book will give us a starting place for determining what is needed for each child, when it is needed and how to optimize the educational opportunities of each phase.

We know that in trying to truly get "off the conveyor belt" and onto the leadership path, real and living examples are needed. In addition to our own experiences, we have included in this book many answers to questions and examples from our children as well as from the lives of parents, families and teachers who have established and continue to create Leadership Education homes and classrooms. We are grateful to those who have allowed us to use their stories; the overall work is richer for their contribution. We don't consider the way we do it, or the way anybody else does it, as perfect. But we will share many examples of families and teachers who are trying to apply the principles of Leadership Education, and hopefully you will benefit from their efforts.

A note on usage is in order. We will routinely use male and female pronouns (he, she, him, her, his, etc.) interchangeably; sometimes the female and other times the male. Also, though the personal anecdotes used in this book were written over the course of ten years, we have decided in most cases to keep the ages of the children cited the same as they were when the account was originally written. This will allow the reader to see how a given person progresses through the phases. It may be confusing when one chapter notes that a child is six while another says she is eight, so please be aware that we have done this on purpose to maintain the integrity of the commentary on each phase.

There are so many people to thank for their help on this work. More than anyone, we especially thank Michele Smith for her hours of work in preparing this book and in urging us onward toward its completion. Her expertise and ideas have made this book better. Additionally, we would like to extend our sincere thanks to the tens of thousands who have attended our seminars and corresponded with us over the years. We have learned from your examples, your struggles, your questions and your discoveries as you have taught your children and positively influenced your communities. We have learned directly from you as you have challenged our assumptions and shared your stories of difficulties and successes. If you are one of the many who consider themselves "off the conveyor belt," thank you so much for your leadership. This generation needs you.

Part I

....

A Philosophy for Life: Why the Phases Matter

CHAPTER ONE

Two Views Of Childhood

The conveyor belt and leadership models of education disagree about how to educate most effectively. Indeed, they are based on totally different assumptions and have very different goals. Knowing these differences is essential to anyone trying to get off the conveyor belt, since it is not enough to merely change behaviors; you must also change paradigms. If you try to implement Leadership Education with a conveyor belt mentality, you will constantly find yourself in the frustrating position of trying out new methods and techniques but applying them in the same old ways—without getting the hoped-for results! Getting off the conveyor belt is much more than behavior modification; it is a shift of underlying beliefs and assumptions about education that brings values, vision and action into integral alignment.

At the root of the decision of how to view education are two divergent views of childhood. The opposing views of childhood and the educational assumptions they promote are drastically different; indeed, they are in conflict. Both had influence on the modern conveyor belt school system, from kindergarten to Ph.D. studies. Both are also used by various non-conveyor belt private, home, charter, prep, elite and non-traditional educational entities.

The first view rejects the notion that there are distinct learning phases; assuming that children, youth and adults learn the same way. This view arranges its curriculum and educational methodology accordingly and drives the public conveyor belt and the elite competitive professional conveyor belt. This educational view treats all people of any age virtually the same, so that young children are molded into an adult-type system.

The second view affirms that children, youth and adults actually learn differently and that this must be taken into account in the setup of their educational environment and in the approach of their parents, teachers and mentors.

This is the phases approach discussed in this book.

The debate between these two views has a long and interesting history. But the most striking thing we noticed as we read the writers on both sides of this discussion is the gap between what great educational pioneers *said* and how their words were *applied.*

The childhood researchers with perhaps the most impact on our current American school system are: John Dewey, Lev Vygotsky, Erik Erikson and Jean Piaget. Most of these names are known to professional educators and many of their ideas are utilized in all three educational models. However, having been trained in typical conveyor belt fashion, many educators learn about these influential thinkers and their ideas from textbooks. Few educators have gone to the original sources to read in context what these four founders of modern education actually wrote.

Our era is not unlike a "dark age" of education where certain experts (professors) train practitioners (teachers) about the "gospels" of the educational canon. Like the dark ages, the teachers have not personally studied the canon in much depth, if at all. And where extensive studies of these writers by the experts has occurred, it has most often led to specialization in a narrow expertise that can tend to preclude complete understanding or relevant application.

We recommend that you closely read the writings of these four very influential men, and a number of others we will list below, and draw your own conclusions. Then read textbook commentaries and summaries of what they supposedly said. We do not mean to say that the textbooks purposely misrepresent the facts and philosophies. We will give our own summaries which are undoubtedly also lacking in some measure. But the best use of commentaries is as further consideration of ideas by those who have read the original work.

To carry on with the historical analogy: to the uninitiated (those who have not read the originals), commentaries are often mere indoctrination. To those who have read and closely pondered the originals, the same commentaries are valuable conversation. Do not be one who is content to rely on indoctrination. Read the originals, draw your own conclusions, and then dig further into the commentary and become part of the dialogue.

John Dewey

John Dewey taught that education must be student-centered and personalized. He also taught that it must be both active and interactive. The active part comes from doing that which interests you—which for children usually means playing. The interactive part of learning comes in two ways: first, by doing activities with others, and second, by doing things directly with and under the direction of professional teachers. It was to this latter application that he spoke when he outlined what the public schools should offer.

There are two main areas of emphasis in Dewey's writings: the teacher's role and the nation's role. Dewey said that first of all, teachers should have a strong base of general knowledge from a good overall general education. Next, teachers need to know the specific needs of each student in their care. Third, teachers should build on students' home values. Fourth, teachers should observe each student, consider his needs and guide the student toward fulfilling those needs. Dewey considered a major part of the teacher's role to be helping the student make sense of the world, by asking and answering questions and discussing the reasons behind things. Dewey also taught that a key part of the teacher's role was to plan, structure and document.

On the issue of the nation's role, Dewey promoted national systemization of education at all levels so that each person would have the opportunity to get the education she needed for her part in society. He differs in various specifics from Jefferson and Washington, but generally agrees with them on this point.

Dewey taught one concept which seems to have eclipsed all his other teachings—at least in actual application. He said that learning is more influenced by the structure, environment, and the model of education than by its actual curriculum. Montessori said the same thing, and we agree with this. But note that such a structure can be used for good or for bad: to break down class barriers or to reinforce them, to promote morality and religion in learning or to marginalize or even banish it, to encourage learning in order to become a productive adult or to focus on career productivity in school while neglecting to educate. The list could go on.

In short, Dewey is great reading for teachers from any educational model. There are certainly many things to disagree with in Dewey, but there are also many things of merit. At the very least, his writings are food for thought, and invaluable in the dialogue on educational ideals.

Dewey's ideas on good teaching and personalized curriculum were not adopted or applied as much as his structural model; and the application of the structural elements was perhaps not exactly as he intended. This is a tragedy, and has led to much of the failure of modern education. In the chart below, we will compare the teachings of Dewey that have been implemented and those that have been ignored:

DEWEY VS. DEWEYISM	
DEWEY'S MODEL THAT WAS APPLIED	DEWEY'S MODEL THAT WAS IGNORED
• The structure, model and environment of schooling teaches more than curriculum content • Factory-like buildings • Halls, lockers, bells • Classes segregated by age • Experts who are also "rulers" • Rewards and punishments to prod learning	• Parents are the primary instructors • Teachers should reinforce and build on the child's home values • Teachers should individualize learning to each child • The best way for a child to learn is to play • Teachers should guide rather than demand

The differences are distressing. School buildings modeled after factories instead of homes are Dewey's legacy; not teachers who closely observe each child and help him make sense of the world while remaining rooted in the values of his home life. The class system is reinforced from kindergarten on, with the higher grades serving as the higher classes. We have an aristocratic oligarchy in the middle of most American neighborhoods: a public school structure where the masses are kept in by fences and the Homecoming King and Queen are elected by "clique" or "mob" popularity. And out of this, we expect children to grow up to be truly informed and autonomous adults! We have applied all the wrong lessons of Dewey, or at least, all of his lessons wrongly.

In the school system built upon the applied principles of the Dewey model, everyone is expected to fit in. Babies and their parents must follow the day care and institutionalized health care rules; toddlers through college students spend countless hours in line to get bureaucratic stickers, stamps, passes and IDs; their parents and grandparents do the same in the factory, corporation and community. Remember Dewey's original point was that learning occurs more from the structure of our education than from the curriculum.

In modern America's Deweyland, nearly everyone learns the same lessons: life is about how you fit into big institutions, success depends upon pleasing the expert-rulers who run them, and if you are doing anything different than the norm you must justify yourself and get permission. Plato's Republic is here, and Dewey gets the credit. Of course, it is easy to overstate this. But we are concerned that greater danger is evident in the understatement, as most people refuse to admit that we now have a nation of schools that train followers rather than leaders, and bureaucrats rather than independent thinkers and citizens.

The lasting impact of Dewey (and we believe he would regret and even resent this) is *sameness*—of expectations, of educations, of lives. As a final insurance of sameness, drugs are prescribed for and administered to many of those who do not fit in. The differences between the first and second views of childhood reveal themselves here. In this system, children are expected to behave and learn like adults rather than act and learn differently because of their young age as depicted in the following vignette:

> *"After all, the little guy wants to run and play and jump and shout. That just can't work in our 'hallowed halls' of learning. He must sit down, be quiet, and act like an adult. You know, he is six years old now...he has got a career to think of, college entrance, status and income, his place in the world...make sure he gets those pills every day."*

This is obviously an extreme view (though, we believe, too prevalent). We hope to cause no offense to those for whom medical intervention is truly warranted. We are not medical experts. Nor are we the experts on your family. You are, and we respect the sovereignty of your home. We believe that gifted and inspired people developed medications in the same manner as innovative, life-changing developments have taken place in every other field. We have certainly seen great benefits from medical science in our own family. We are surely not saying that nobody ever needs to be medicated. But we *are* most definitely saying, from the perspective of parents and educators whole-heartedly endorsing the second view of childhood, that a six-year-old who has a hard time sitting still, listening, and fitting into the conveyor belt might just be showing all the signs of a healthy young boy or girl.

All ages are not the same. Childhood should be a time of beauty, passion, excitement, learning and lessons. For example, compare the educational method taught by Jesus to that of Socrates. The teachings of Jesus Christ honor the special state of childhood. It seems to us that Jesus really meant to communicate that children were different and described these differences as recorded in numerous scriptural references. He told us to become "as a little child" (which makes no sense if we already are). He said "suffer the little children to come unto me," and at times focused on them instead of adults. We recommend further study of the unique experience and characteristics of children as provided in this example from Christianity. Such teachings are also to be found in religious, philosophical and cultural writings and traditions throughout the world.

Contrast this second perception of childhood with how Plato treats little children in *The Republic*. Perhaps he wrote in satire (we believe he did), but so many in history have taken him at his word and set out to apply his teachings. Children were treated the same as adults in Plato's model—considered more pliable perhaps—but taught and trained the same. As we said, this debate has been going on for a very long time.

Socrates and Jesus Christ were both great mentors, but their approaches were very different. One looks you in the eye and invites you to make necessary sacrifices while recognizing your right to choose, as in Jesus' interchange with the wealthy young man who seeks his guidance. The other grabs you by the neck and holds you under water, as Socrates reportedly did with the young man who asked him for mentoring. These two examples provide the contrast of two divergent theories of education: leadership versus the conveyor belt. Leadership Education recognizes the need for freedom in education and encourages self-motivation and personal mission accomplishment that result in feelings of inherent self-worth, leadership and compassion for others. The conveyor belt enforces sameness and aims to foster feelings of societal interdependence, based upon feelings of personal inadequacy and dependency on experts as the norm.

In Dewey's modern institutions, the teaching of seven-year-olds in a public classroom has the same structure and environment as the training of forty-year-olds in a corporate auditorium. The curriculum is different, yes, but the real, "Dewey" lesson—taught by format, structure, environment and model—is the same. We do not want to be misunderstood on this point. There is a period of education in which the classroom setting plays a vital and perhaps central role. It is a great place for part of the education of a youth or an adult. But we affirm that children are different—inherently different—at distinct stages of development, and their exposure to adult-ideal settings should be considered and limited. Children are impressionable, accountable and capable at different levels and should be educated accordingly.

Lev Vygotsky

Lev Vygotsky was a Russian educational and psychological theorist who came to the United States in the early twentieth century. Though he is lesser known than his contemporary, John Dewey, his ideas are almost as influential. Where the modern schools adopted Dewey's *structural* model of the conveyor belt, they turned to Vygotsky for the *methodology*.

Vygotsky taught that learning occurs when people play—period. He said this was true of all ages, even adults. This has been applied in modern society, yet (ironically) the application is precisely backwards of what it should be. While youth and adults are forgiven for avoiding any scholarly pursuit that is not "fun" and entertainment is seen as an entitlement, children are allowed to play less and less. Some of the activities that pass for play (soccer leagues, special lessons, etc.), are essentially high-pressure obligations. These environments of organized play have rigid guidelines and huge time commitments. They do not allow freedom to explore, create and enjoy. Much of the application of learning through play in schools is actually just thinly veiled academics, such as math manipulatives and the like. Even these token concessions to children's developmental and psychological needs are under fire by political conservatives who consider them frivolous "play-games" learning.

Schools and parents foster far too little play for youngsters (who cannot effectively stage a protest and who are more inclined to seek approval through conformity) and indulge way too much play for teenagers (who intimidate us with their personal power and have no scruples about using it to get what they want). Youth who have finally escaped the regimented learning of their early years have no intention of submitting themselves to a demanding Scholar or Depth Phase. Nationwide, teens and their families spend a king's ransom on home theaters and all the gadgetry technology will permit, from smart phones and palm pilots, iPods and MP3 players to complex gaming systems. Each new year brings a host of upgrades and renders last year's models obsolete. None of these are inherently bad, and perhaps in some cases they can be an advantage in carrying out a life's mission; but no one can deny that they can be a serious distraction from studying. Not one person in a hundred has the discipline or the desire to continue to educate himself at scholarly levels under such circumstances. Society's trends take us further and further from the ideal as time goes on.

If Vygotsky had limited his prescription to learning through play in the early years, we would promote him as one of the greatest educational thinkers ever. But his first major point is applied inversely in modern educational institutions and in society at large—children's education is work and adult education is, too often, play.

Vygotsky's second point is that the highest levels of learning occur when students are in the ZPD, or Zone of Proximal Development. This is the zone *above* the most difficult task the person can do alone and *below* the most difficult task they can do with help. To re-phrase and clarify this: learning occurs when an individual is pressured to do that which he could not do alone. Think of it as a ladder against a wall. Without the ladder, there is a natural limit to how high one might reach on the wall; the ladder extends that reach considerably. The range beyond natural, unassisted reach that is accessible from the ladder is the ZPD.

Vygotsky taught that teachers should observe students playing and intervene at a sign of interest to push them beyond their comfort level. We think Vygotsky was right on—for adults. We call it mentoring. We have used it in college courses, simulations, in hundreds of adult seminars across North America and in corporate trainings and workshops.

This model is wrong *for young children*. Most of modern education—public, private, home, primary, secondary, college and adult—has adopted the ZPD model. It works great for young adults and their parents and grandparents. But children are different. Childhood is special. Children are distinct from adults. They have different motivations and they have a different optimal learning environment. This is especially true before age eight, where modern educators do the most pushing, and before twelve, where they also manipulate and over-program. Anyone who has been on the conveyor belt has been taught for years and years, by the curriculum and even more by the structural model, that if you do not push a child he will not learn.

Childhood is when a child's assumptions of basic truths are formed and acquired—not through pedagogy, but through experience. Young children learn most not from what we say, but from what they feel and infer. In short, the application of ZPD learning in the early years is a disaster. As we enforce academic drills and Zone of Proximal Development learning in a little one, here is what many, if not most, children learn:

1. Learning is what I am forced to do by others when I'd rather be enjoying what I discover myself.
2. I will not learn unless I am subject to being put on the spot and made to feel stressed, annoyed, stupid or at least vulnerable because I am out of my comfort zone.
3. Learning is so complicated that full-time teachers are needed to walk me through it (or a homeschool equivalent: Mom has to neglect the younger children/house/personal grooming, etc. and give me her full attention and line-by-line directions or I am incapable of learning).
4. I do not know anything unless someone certifies to me that I do.
5. I am probably wrong about a lot of the stuff I think I know.
6. I have to master this stuff now or I will be behind for the rest of my life.
7. The things I am really interested in are not very important.
8. Learning is one thing and what I feel and experience is another.
9. When I am a Mom/Dad I will worry and "beat myself up" about what I am not doing and wonder if I should be doing what I am doing.
10. When I am a Mom/Dad I will say I know something is the "right" thing and then constantly second-guess my decisions.

The list could go on. Even for children who do not have a patently "negative" experience with early academics, the lessons can have detrimental effects:

1. I am really great because I know how to read (subtle lesson: self-worth and comparison evaluation is based on

academic achievement and timing rather than truth, right choices, service, repentance, etc.).

2. ___________ is dumb because he/she cannot read.
3. I'm cooler than ___________ because I am reading before him/her.
4. We work hard on my reading/math/??? because Mom and Dad want to prove to Grandma/neighbor/etc. that they are "good" parents.
5. The most important thing I can learn right now is skills (displaces the more crucial moral childhood lessons of good-bad, right-wrong, true-false).
6. The faster I grow up, the better (this is a huge one, overlooked by most educational analysts with long-lasting implications and impact on young lives).
7. Once I am a Mom/Dad I will not have time to study anymore.
8. Once I am a Mom/Dad I will not need to study anymore.
9. Once I am a Mom/Dad I will not have to study anymore.
10. I really need to fit in, or…
11. I really need to stand out.

None of these lessons is a terrible thing to sort out as a young adult. They define that period of life and a youth's identity and mission. But lessons such as these become negatively scripted in the psyche and on the heart of very young children (of about ages three to thirteen). In most cases, the pressure for young kids to perform is based on either their parent's fear or ignorance—often both. Unfortunately, pride is sometimes a factor as well. The misconception is that without pressure and "guidance" (a euphemism for running the little one's time to the hilt and taking every spark of curiosity and turning it into a theme unit to force-feed them) they will become bland, anti-social, and completely devoid of personal development or accomplishments. This is false!

Ignoring the principles of Leadership Education out of expediency is not the answer!

There does come a time when "pushing" is extremely valuable (we would say indispensable) and when a mentor saying just the right thing at the right time or demanding that you dig a little deeper than you thought you could or wanted to, or insisting that you buck up when you want to quit, makes all the difference. But in the realm of academics, this comes after the age of eight, and very, *very* sparingly before puberty.

The natural desire to grow up and a natural inclination to exceed one's limitations come with puberty. Before then, the anxiety to go faster and quicker too often results from a pushy and usually insecure (or at the very least, well-intentioned but ignorant) parent or teacher, or a child who is not in sync with her time of life (a syndrome that does not just go away with the passing of time). Continual pushing of a child in scholastic achievement throughout childhood most often results in a rebellious teenager who digs in his heals and refuses to be pushed any more—particularly educationally.

Childhood is different. Read Vygotsky and let the kids play. Read him and apply the ZPD concepts in youth and adulthood, not childhood. One way to read Vygotsky is that you push everyone according to their ZPD, and the ZPD of little children is such that you should not push them. If you read him this way, fine. But it should be said that this is not how he has been widely understood or applied.

As we have stated before, the greatest irony in modern education is that we will not let children play when that is practically *all* our teenagers do. What if children played and worked with their parents more and were lovingly taught about good and bad, right and wrong and true and false? What if youth worked very hard and put in long hours getting a great education and preparing for their life mission? What amazing results could come of making such a reversal in our society!

So what is a parent to do? Just turn the kids out to pasture until his voice starts to change or until you are buying her bigger shoes and longer jeans every two months? Doesn't that feel like you are not parenting? Like you are being irresponsible? How are the kids supposed to feel good about themselves if they are not accomplishing anything?

The answer is much, much harder than keeping thirty kids in a classroom progressing or running a homeschool for multiple children with varying learning styles and ages while balancing home maintenance and other responsibilities. It is this: be inspirational. Be inspirational. BE INSPIRATIONAL. So much is encompassed in this mandate, and it is the answer to almost every insecurity and complication that arises in the process of having a great classroom or a great home. *Be inspirational*. We will cover some of the "hows" of this later. But first, let us look at two more of the most influential child development researchers, Erikson and Piaget.

Erik Erikson

In contrast to the modern schools of Dewey and Vygotsky, highly regarded psychologist Erik Erikson taught that children are distinct, and that to teach effectively, one must understand their differences. Please take some time to study and ponder Erikson's teachings on the following two charts:

ERIKSON ON HOW PARENTS/TEACHERS CAN HELP CHILDREN SUCCESSFULLY NEGOTIATE EACH STAGE		
AGE	HOW TO TEACH	ATTRIBUTE DEVELOPED
0-1	• Lots of physical contact • Respond immediately when they cry or fuss	• Trust vs. Mistrust • Hope
1-3	• Give simple choices • Do not give false choices • Set clear, consistent, reasonable limits • Be relaxed with mood swings	• Autonomy vs. Shame/ Doubt • Will Power
3-12	• Encourage independence • Focus on gains while ignoring mistakes • Individualize all expectations • Do things together • Support individual interests	• Initiative vs. Guilt • Purpose • Industry vs. Inferiority • Confidence
12-18	• Help expand exploration of everything, learn about self • Individualized study • Group interaction	• Identity vs. Role Confusion • Fidelity

As you spend time reflecting on each stage, you are sure to consider some very profound ideas. For example, review the details on ages zero through twelve. Look at the strengths that are developed if the child gains the desired lessons during the Initiative vs. Guilt stage or the Industry vs. Inferiority stage. We have spent literally hours talking about this chart and what it teaches us about ourselves, our family, and our philosophy of education.

ERIKSON'S STAGES OF PSYCHOSOCIAL DEVELOPMENT		
0-1	Trust vs. Mistrust	Hope
1-3	Autonomy vs. Shame & Doubt	Will Power
3-6	Initiative vs. Guilt	Purpose
6-12	Industry vs. Inferiority	Competence
12-18	Identity vs. Role Confusion	Fidelity
18-40	Intimacy vs. Isolation	Love
40-65	Generativity vs. Stagnation	Care
65+	Ego Integration vs. Despair	Wisdom

Erikson taught that in each stage a person has a fundamental challenge or choice, which makes up the central conflict of that stage of life. The young person's ultimate decision in each stage is very important, including such choices as whether to be trusting or distrustful, independent or doubtful, to take initiative or feel like a victim, and so on. Note that usually these decisions are not conscious, but they are still very real.

You may be inclined to just keep reading instead of taking time to study, ponder and personalize the charts. After all, really putting in the effort to think about these two charts and how they apply to our children and ourselves is hard work. But it is worth it. If you did not stop and analyze these charts in detail, personalizing them to yourself and your family, we encourage you to do so now.

Getting the positive lessons at each stage of development is very important for each student. Erikson says that a person who makes a bad choice during a particular stage can go back later and renegotiate it. But he also taught that once a person chooses the negative in any stage, he will not be able to choose the positives in later stages without first backing up and renegotiating his earlier choice.

Instead of us giving further commentary on this (we suggest you read directly from Erikson), spend some more time studying the first chart, which lists our summary of Erikson's specific recommendations for parents and teachers of children and youth at each stage. Erikson's emphasis is on giving the child what he or she is developmentally ready to receive. What a great concept! This idea definitely represents the second view of childhood. Whether you agree with Erikson on the specifics or not, the idea of giving the student what he is ready for results in superior learning to Dewey's structural-institutional one-model-fits-all or Vygotsky's ZPD, in which manipulation and external pressure is the name of the game.

Jean Piaget

Jean Piaget (Zhahn pyah-ZHAY) is perhaps the most influential developmental psychologist, and his research solidly establishes that children are different and should be educated accordingly. It is astonishing that as much credence as Piaget's work is given in the curriculum design of modern schooling, Dewey's structural model still has more power over what is actually learned in most schools.

Piaget disagreed with both sides of the old debate about whether learning is intrinsic (coming from within the child) or extrinsic (based on things outside the child, including her parents, teachers and environment). Instead, Piaget discovered that learning is "constructive," or intrinsically driven in response to extrinsic factors. He is often remembered for the phrase "Construction is superior to Instruction."

Piaget taught that children only learn when their curiosity is not satisfied. Parents and teachers of young children should spark curiosity and then back off—this is their whole role. We have referred to this process elsewhere as the "right kind of vacuum." It is certainly not ignoring the child or her education; and yet it is the polar opposite of Vygotsky, who jumps in and meddles or manipulates whenever he sees curiosity. Piaget warns the parent and teacher not to instruct in a force-feeding way, but rather to incite interest and then leave the child to the wonder of experimentation and self-discovery. We can not think of a more apt description of one of the Seven Keys of Great Teaching: "Inspire, not Require."

How will you know when the child is curious? Piaget would likely answer that when a child is playing, she is curious (substitute the word "interested" for "curious," with fairly good results). If she is not playing, consider a way to spark curiosity and then retreat again. Piaget warns that it is not possible to pour knowledge into young children—only to encourage interest or demand behavior. If you demand behavior with enough pressure, the child will give into it, but he will not learn what was intended. He may respond when the pressure is on, he may get the "right" answers, but it will not really get through because he will turn it off as quickly as possible once the pressure lets up. Pressured behavior can help him pass exams, but very little knowledge will be retained or used in life; understanding and application were never the objective. Many readers may share our experience of cramming for exams—could you pass that same exam today?

If you spark interest, on the other hand, children will "construct" their own learning and retain the lessons learned throughout their lives. Piaget says expressly that academic instruction is wasted until the child is twelve years old. We would editorialize here that chronological age is not as important as developmental age.

"Developmentally twelve" might be defined as the onset of puberty. The following two charts illustrate some of the child development principles Piaget introduced.

PIAGET AND PARENTING STYLES	
PARENTS	CHILDREN
Authoritarian (dictatorial)	Withdrawn, low in vitality, mediocre social skills, prejudiced, low cognitive skills in sons
Permissive	Vitality, sunny moods, poor social skills, poor cognitive skills (especially in sons)
Authoritative (firmly governing but democratic)	Self-assertive, independent, friendly, high social skills, high cognitive skills

PIAGET'S STAGES AND GUIDE TO TEACHERS			
AGE	STAGE	BEHAVIORS	TEACHING GUIDE
0-18 months	Sensory-motor	• Learn through the senses • Learn through reflexes	• Keep safe & interested • Comfort as needed
18 months-8 years	Pre-operational	• Learn through perceptions • Learn by focusing on one thing at a time • Learn by over-generalizing	• Large blocks of free play time • Open-ended activities • Open-ended questions
8-12	Concrete Operational	• Learn through self-reflection & reasoning, but limited to things concrete and familiar • Learn through internal self-dialogue and exercise of will • Learn by beginning to sort through contradictions in their worldview—to come to moral values	• Example • Conversations • Projects—trial & error • Field trips • Wide exposure

PIAGET'S STAGES AND GUIDE TO TEACHERS			
12-17	Formal Operational (not everybody achieves this stage)	• Conceptual & hypothetical thought, formal categories • Feel the need to improve world • Desire beauty, religious truth, logical consistency • Begin to establish character—the full expression of personality	• Study hard • Ideas challenged • Work redone

Once again, we encourage you to take the time to ponder and really think about the material in these charts, and to study Piaget's writings on your own.

Both Piaget and Erikson treat children differently than adults, and recommend teaching them according to their developmental level. We have seen the specific ages listed in several different ways in their works, so study them in the original and draw your own conclusions.

The Four Gospels and the Essays

Dewey, Vygotsky, Erikson and Piaget could be called "the four Gospels of modern education." These could be followed up by a collection of essays from other great thinkers, educators and teachers. We think all parents and teachers should read Francis Bacon, John Holt, Maria Montessori, Charlotte Mason, Jacques Barzun, Thomas Jefferson, Mortimer Adler, E.G. West, Glenn Kimber, Howard Gardner, Robert Hutchins and Josiah Bunting.

What is needed is a printing of an educational "bible" (or library) that contains both the original writings of the four gospels of modern education and essays from other authors in a format everyone can read. A "Reformation" will certainly follow. We are not arguing that Dewey's writings are akin to Matthew's or Luke's of the Bible, but to consider it in this manner certainly makes a poignant analogy. The world was transformed when individuals were able to read the gospels and letters of the Bible in their own language rather than relying upon the interpretations or summaries of others. We believe the educational world will likewise be transformed as the unfiltered wisdom of these great educators is recognized and implemented.

As we will further discuss later, we recommend that readers apply educational principles within the context of the phases and the Seven Keys of Great Teaching (these will be discussed in detail in Chapter Two). Many educational applications that would be excellent in one phase can be extremely detrimental in another.

In summary, great mentors know that children are different than adults in some very important ways, and they organize and implement their methods and content accordingly. The Leadership model of education is counter-intuitive to the conveyor belt approach. Most parents educated on the conveyor belt try to apply it in precisely the wrong way. To apply Leadership Education successfully it is necessary to listen closely to those who have mastered the system and work hard to duplicate both the content and, especially, the methods of experienced leadership mentors.

For most educators, the hardest part of getting off the conveyor belt is getting their own Leadership Education. The second hardest thing is backing off from a "require, require, require" view of education when children are young. If you do these things well, your fourteen-year-olds will beg for a Leadership Education like Thomas Jefferson got and you will be ready to help them attain it. They will get a superb Leadership Education, and the future of the world will be changed—one home and one classroom at a time.

CHAPTER TWO

The Phases

With a better understanding of what children need and how they learn and gain optimal development and education in childhood, we are ready to press forward in understanding how to raise the leaders of tomorrow with a Leadership Education. We have examined and hopefully challenged some faulty assumptions about the educational process. This will allow us to see and apply education in a new way. In answer to the many questions we receive on the particular points of Leadership Education, we will now focus our discussion on the Phases of Learning of Leadership Education.

In the Leadership Education model, the six phases are grouped in the following fashion: the Foundational Phases consist of Core Phase and Love of Learning Phase, the Educational Phases are Scholar Phase and Depth Phase and the Applicational Phases are Mission Phase and Impact Phase.

Rather than picturing the phases on a time line, moving chronologically from birth through adulthood, they are more accurately understood spherically (as described by Tiffany Earl and Aneladee Milne), like a planet or an apple, with the vital Core at the center and the additional phases or layers building out from the center. Others connect with the image of a pyramid, where the later phases must build upward as they rest firmly on top of their foundation. Core Phase is always part of any other phase, and its neglect negatively impacts the student's whole education and life. By the same token, the succeeding phases include the lessons, attributes and skills acquired in the earlier phases, and cannot be successfully carried out unless the groundwork has been laid.

Integral Relationship of Phases

The Foundational and Learning Phases are the most basic of Leadership Education. Each is vital, and they must come in the right order—Core, then Love of Learning, Scholar, then Depth. Older students who do not love learning—who see schooling or study as a chore or a negative—will usually need to start back in Core Phase. Each parent and teacher who desires to raise leaders needs to understand all of the phases, and how to implement them with their children and students. Viewing the phases as an overall integrated system helps us appreciate and make the most of each individual phase.

Each of the phases is important; but the Foundational Phases do come first, and they continue to animate the whole process and set the tone for later successes or failures. It is virtually impossible to overstate the importance of the Foundational Phases. As Erikson taught, older students and even adults who skipped or had negative experiences with stages presented from birth to age twelve (i.e. trust vs. mistrust, autonomy vs. shame and doubt, initiative vs. guilt, and industry vs. inferiority—see Erikson's chart in Chapter One for review) are able to back up and re-negotiate them; but it does take focused effort, hard work, and a real time commitment.

While it may seem that too much time has been wasted and one cannot afford to slow down and cover lost ground, the opposite is actually true. More time is wasted by limping along out of phase with little hope of happening upon a magical cure. The time spent to go back and start fresh is actually measured in weeks and months, not the years the original plan would have indicated. Once the choices are rescripted there is a miraculous domino effect that seems to propel the individual into his natural phase of development.

By contrast, if individuals with insecure foundations neglect to renegotiate the Foundational Phases, the Educational and Applicational Phases are forever skewed and usually do not come to full fruition. This deformity of the latter phases occurs in at least two ways. First, without quality Foundational Phases, the latter phases are always anemic because they lack an intrinsic drive toward learning, a foundation of truth and right, and a love of knowing. Sick later phases can still accomplish much, but only by replacing the wholesome with the artificial, such as substituting for the love of learning a love of money (or status, security, approval of others, "success," etc.). While artificial motivations may help a number of students through law, medical and other graduate schools, they will seldom result in happy accomplishment of an individual's life mission.

Second: without healthy Foundational Phases, "cancer" inevitably sets in during the Applicational Phases, as even those few who achieve a quality education put it to use on things other than the central purpose of their lives. Sometimes a mid-life crisis during this period sends such people reeling back to Core Phase. Re-starting and creating positive life change will only occur by getting in touch with what religion calls "truth," popular psychology calls "the inner child" and Leadership Education calls Core Phase. Those lucky enough to take this route can then move on to Love of Learning Phase, which replaces the Hate of Learning they passed through so many years before and have carried around like a dormant tumor. The renegotiated path is usually *greatly* accelerated once the necessary corrections have been made.

Sadly, few people take the time to fully regenerate; and too often it is not with the healthy guidance that early childhood should afford. Without direction, the individual often is left to make reckless and self-centered choices. Thus, the bad rap of "mid-life crisis." It is typified by broken commitments, broken hearts, broken lives. It is much better, of course, to have healthy Foundational Phases in the first place—or at the earliest possible moment if you are already past your youth.

Indeed, this is one of the great wonders of the universe: parents who parent diligently get to apply the wisdom of adulthood to the recurring experiences of being a child as their own children progress through stages and phases. Hate of Learning may be more easily purged by doing a really excellent Love of Learning Phase with your nine-year-old than in perhaps any other way, but it requires courage for the parent to do it in the face of social opposition, and discipline to follow through in our busy twenty-first century lives.

Sometimes the normal progression between the phases is compromised due to traumatic experiences, interrupted progress (such as protracted drug use or chronic illness during a period of life), or abuse or neglect. In such cases it may be helpful to carry out an enlightened rescripting of the traumatic events.

Without the principles that Leadership Education provides, there are far too many examples of parents delivering a hollow Core experience, and then a Hate of Learning Phase, all in the guise of "conscientious parenting." For such parents, the natural tendency is to push younger children academically and then unwittingly deny youth a Scholar Phase in order to pursue fun activities. This sometimes occurs because the only Love of Learning many people in the current generation experienced was in adolescent clubs, bands, plays and teams and they naturally try to reproduce their positive experiences for their own youth.

In addition to increasing one's understanding of each of the phases, those who seek to provide an ideal educational environment also need to deeply understand how to apply the Seven Keys of Great Teaching. Though we have discussed them extensively elsewhere, because of their fundamental importance and their relevance to the topic at hand, we will briefly review them here. Following this review, we will introduce the concept of an eighth key that results from family or school progression in leadership education.

Check out edits, updates and upgrades to this book and download a free audio! TJEd.org/New-7-Keys

The Seven Keys of Great Teaching

Each of the Seven Keys of Great Teaching is based on principle, rather than expediency. When they are applied, learning occurs. When they are ignored or rejected, the quantity *and* quality of education decrease. These principles can be applied to complement unique interests or learning style. Application of the Seven Keys will significantly improve your effectiveness and success in any teaching environment. Each of the Seven Keys stands alone; if any of them is applied, the educational model will improve. Together, they form what Shawn Ercanbrack has called Reinforcing Cycles, a full system of principles which support, augment, improve upon and synergize with each other.

Our use of these principles or keys needs to include the understanding that different applications are necessary during different phases. This is *extremely* important. In general, the Keys are applied in a holistic, family-oriented way in the earlier years, with ever-increasing rigor during the student's youth and young adulthood (this is in keeping with the philosophy outlined throughout the first section of this book). How to apply each of the Keys within the different phases will become more obvious as you study each phase in depth in the chapters which follow.

1. Classics, not Textbooks

Virtually every subject is most effectively learned directly from the greatest thinkers, historians, artists, philosophers, scientists, prophets and their original works. Great works inspire greatness. Mediocre or poor works inspire mediocre or poor learning. The great accomplishments of humanity are the key to quality education. The twin conveyor belts (mass public education and the competitive conveyor belt of the professions) emphasize textbooks that are often just "dumbed down" summaries of long lists of rote knowledge. A "classic" is a work worth studying over and over again, because the student learns more each time. There are classics in each and every field from history, science and literature to computer design, gene-mapping and the digital age, and even surfing, cycling, gardening and so forth.

2. *Mentors, not Professors*

The professor or expert tells the students what they need to know, invites or compels them to conform to certain ideas and standards, and grades or otherwise rewards or punishes them for their various levels of conformity. In contrast, the *mentor* finds out the student's goals, interests, talents, weaknesses, strengths and purpose, and then helps him develop and carry out a plan designed to effectively develop his genius and prepare him for his unique mission. Let us here clarify that there are many who bear the professional title of "Professor" who are truly quality mentors.

3. *Inspire, not Require*

This is perhaps the least understood and most neglected of the Seven Keys. Yet it is vital to all great teaching. There are really only two ways to teach. You can inspire the student to voluntarily and enthusiastically choose to do the hard work necessary to get a great education, or you can attempt to require it of him. Mediocre teachers and schools use the "require method"; great teachers and schools pay the price to inspire. Instead of asking, "what can I do to make these students perform?" the great teacher says, "Something's not working! I must not be truly inspirational. What do I need to do to spark their passion to do the hard work to get a superb education?" If this one change were duplicated in schools everywhere, education would be dramatically improved!

4. *Structure Time, not Content*

Great mentors help their students establish and follow a consistent schedule, but they do not micro-manage the content. Indeed, micro-management has become one of the real poisons of modern Dewey-Vygotsky education. In contrast, great teachers and schools allow young students to follow their passions and interests during their study time and inspire them as needed to take on areas they may not initially recognize as interesting and desirable. Interviews and mentor meetings can be invaluable tools to facilitate and inspire effective study, but a certain level of detachment is necessary to accomplish this effectively. Tiffany Earl applies Adam Smith's maxim here: students must have the freedom to fail in order to truly take responsibility for their own progress. They must *know* that their education, their life, their mission, will hinge upon *their own* choices. When they truly own this responsibility (and some do not until the reality of negative consequences begins to threaten) they begin to make the hard choices.

Of course, no one really wants to fail. We may trust that in a supportive, healthy, inspiring environment students will set worthy goals, will have successes and setbacks and will, on the whole and over time, learn to make and keep commitments and progress in character and competence. Parents and teachers who trust this see the successful results in their students, while educators who do not trust this see very few successes. When the students do take responsibility for their lives and education with the inspired guidance of a mentor, they will accomplish incredible things and exhibit their own true and unique genius.

5. *Quality, not Conformity*

In the early phases, this key refers to personalizing experiences to address the needs and accomplish the fundamental objectives of the student's particular phase. Parents who did not receive a classical education in their youth feel a pull as relentless as gravity to duplicate their own experience, and that of the societal norm, for their own children. Having a vision of the lessons of each phase helps one to make considered, deliberate choices about how to lead in a self-educating home, and how to inspire the individuals to accomplish their purpose for their time of life. This is "quality, not conformity" for young ones.

Once the more mature student (in Scholar Phase) is inspired and working hard to get a great education, the mentor should give appropriate feedback and help. But the feedback should not take the form of rewarding conformity. Great teachers and schools expect and nurture quality work and quality performance. Great teachers inspire and demand quality, ever urging their students to higher levels of excellence. They shun mere conformity and expect their students to think and perform to their ever-increasing potential.

6. *Simplicity, not Complexity*

The more complex the curriculum, the more reliant the student becomes on experts and the more likely the student is to get caught up in the requirement/conformity trap. This is to say nothing of the "dumbing down" and overstressing of the parent or educator who attempts to facilitate a rigorous and uninspiring curriculum. This leads to effective *follower* training, but is more a socialization technique than an educational method. Education means the ability to think independently and creatively, and development of the skill of applying one's knowledge in dealing with people and situations in the real world.

Great teachers train great thinkers and leaders by keeping it simple: students study the greatest minds and characters in history in every field, write about and respond to what is learned in numerous settings, and apply it in various ways under the tutelage of a mentor. Find a great thinker and leader in history and you will nearly always find this method in their educational background.

7. *YOU, not Them*

If you think these principles are primarily about improving your child's or student's education, you will never have the power to inspire them to do the hard work of self-education. Focus on *your* education, and invite them along for the ride. Read the classics in all fields, engage mentors who inspire and demand quality, structure your days, weeks and months to include study time for yourself, and become a person who inspires great education.

A parent or teacher does not have to be an expert to inspire great education (the classics provide the expertise), but he *does* have to be setting the example. In fact, if in the selection of a mentor one had to choose between someone very knowledgeable but low in vision or passion, and one who is just getting started on an aggressive learning curve with a mentor of his own, we would personally prefer the individual who is exemplifying self-education over the one who seems dormant, if accomplished.

Time and time again we have seen that relatively inexperienced parents with a personal commitment to study and individual transformation are extremely effective at communicating passion and commitment to their students. Of course the effect is so much the better when a mentor is not only passionate but prepared, and constantly expanding his ability and repertoire. Such a mentor is worth more than words can say.

Applying the Seven Keys

We recommend that the reader apply the principles of the Phases of Learning and Seven Keys to whatever educational works he studies, since many education systems (for example, intensive trivium-type memorization) work wonderfully in Scholar Phase but compete with the key lessons of Core and Love of Learning, or things that would be great in Core Phase (like Unschooling) can be inferior choices for Scholar Phase.

Parents often find it easier to apply the content portions of the Seven Keys of Great Teaching (classics, mentors, structure time) but ignore the leadership methods (simplicity, quality, inspire, YOU). This keeps parents and children stuck on the conveyor belt. Upon objective consideration, we assert that "Sergeant Mom" or "Dictator Dad" can be as bad as Gatto's public school "Seven Lesson School Teacher"!

We have found that in order to internalize, comprehend and successfully apply the Phases of Learning, a family must have been working on the process of getting off the conveyor belt for about a year or more. It has not been very successful for us to teach this advanced material to an educator or family before this elapsed time. The "detoxification" period is too critical, and some questions can only be answered after individuals—and this is important—*have formed the questions themselves*. This applies not only as we set about to facilitate the education of the children under our stewardship, but also as *we* seek to progress personally from phase to phase.

Nearly all development occurs in stages or phases. This is also true of education. We believe it is important to take advantage of each phase of development to its fullest. Some things are best taught during a particular phase; it not only goes against nature to work on a different schedule, but very important opportunities might be missed, and this can impact the development of the individual. It is difficult to learn something before its time, perhaps *more* difficult to gain things missed that should have been mastered previously and worst of all is trying to *unlearn* what should not have been learned.

Having said all this, note that children are resilient and all of us benefit from positive changes in our lives no matter what stage we are in. There is no need for someone just now learning of these ideas to feel like a failure, or worry that it is too late to make a difference. One of the major points of emphasis in Leadership Education is that parents must lead out and change their own approach to education. Certainly if we "old dogs" can learn "new tricks," it is not too late for our children!

The Eighth Key

An important Eighth Key of Great Teaching is "Secure, not Stressed." It seems that the disease of the twenty-first century is being overwhelmed; almost everyone has caught this illness, and most people communicate the contagion to their children. The solution is to find true security, by knowing (1) that what you are doing is right, and (2) that you are doing it effectively.

Whatever your means of knowing what is right, it is essential to use it so you are truly secure about seeking a Leadership Education. If you don't have an effective system of finding out what is right for you, you might consider Benjamin Franklin's common sense method of listing all the pros in one column and all the cons in the other, and then analyzing the two lists using both your head and your heart. In our day, emotions are often seen as less worthy than logic, but it has been our experience that the best choices are made when we employ the wisdom of both our minds and our feelings.

As for the second part of being Secure, not Stressed, it is vital to know that you are doing Leadership Education well. Otherwise, you'll always feel doubts and fears about the future results. There are two very effective ways to get good at Leadership Education. First, you can just keep trying for years, learning from trial and error what works and what doesn't. We have seen this work for dozens of families, but it takes a long time—and it's stressful.

The second way is to learn what works from those who have already done it successfully—in the classics, in books such as this one, in seminars and conferences specific to Leadership Education, or directly from friends or acquaintances who have successfully applied Leadership Education for some time. We highly recommend this second approach, and the fact that you reading the book means you are applying it.

Being secure instead of stressed about whether Leadership Education is right for you and knowing that you are doing it effectively will not remove all stress from your life, but it will immediately and significantly bring you peace and focus in your educational endeavors. This is worth almost any price. Indeed, those who apply the Eighth Key will find that they more happily and effectively apply all seven other keys.

With the background of the Keys of Great Teaching in place, we are now prepared to move on to a survey of the Foundational and Educational Phases.

Foundational Phases

The Foundational Phases, encompassing both Core and Love of Learning, are vital. They simply must succeed, or the other phases will always be ill until corrected through perhaps painful detoxification and healing crises in adulthood. The ideal environment of the Foundational Phases include the setup of the home and the presence of the ingredients or elements of which a Leadership Education is composed. These ingredients will be discussed in depth in Part II.

Children are typically in Core Phase from birth through age eight or nine, but in truth, each person at each age should be continually refining the important lessons of Core Phase. Utilizing the analogy of the planet for a model, the Core must always be active in order for the planet to sustain life. Even when we move on to later phases, we should still keep in practice the lessons of Core Phase. Core Phase is the basis of a life. A good Core Phase naturally provides the foundation for a good life, a great Core Phase for a great life, and so on.

Core Phase is also the basis of an education. It is the basis of a family, and its generations. It is the basis of a society's culture, politics, economy, art, law, government, etc. It is, in short, the foundation of a person—who he or she is and what he or she can and will become. We cannot overemphasize this point. It is true that we can rise above our foundations, but only by, at some point, expanding, deepening, or otherwise improving upon them. The foundation itself must be solid. During Core Phase, we lay the foundation for all learning and service in the child's life. The "curriculum" is simply:

- right and wrong
- good and bad

- true and false
- relationships
- family values, especially spiritual culture
- family identity, including family history and mission
- family routines and responsibilities
- accountability
- the value and love of work and play

Any attempt to over-program the Foundational Phases with lessons on skills acquisition can create conflict in the child's mind. Little children are impressionable and eager to please, and will conform (at least mentally/emotionally) to the models and rules given them in this phase. Children in this period should be instructed and trained in gentle, loving, constructive and positive ways. Always remember that during these phases, children learn more by what we are and the environment and feelings that surround them than through the explicit teachings or activities we provide.

Crucially important life lessons are taught during these phases including abstract lessons and answers to deep questions such as: "What is success?" "What is maturity?" "How do I resolve conflict?" "What is home?" "What is my relationship with God?" "What is my relationship with others?" "What is my duty?" and so forth. When we give inappropriate attention to academic achievement during these phases, it can teach our children that they dislike academics because everything is hard and boring, and/or offer our children an alternative source of self-worth that is inferior to a genuine and positive self-concept resulting from living according to true values such as faith, good works and accountability.

Ask yourself: if my child could do or know only one thing, what would it be? Your answer might be something like: "that she is a child of God," "that her life is precious" or, "that she has the power to be happy." What is the second most important value you would want your child to internalize? Lessons and learning priorities that come from these questions are what constitute *Core*. You could continue the exercise for some time by prioritizing your values for your child's life. Invariably such a list grows quite long before academic achievements begin to appear.

The beauty of such a grounded list is that it is virtually identical for a child who is blind, gifted, brain injured, precocious, developmentally delayed or emotionally traumatized. Which is another way of expressing the same concept: these values and lessons are part of the Core experience and they trump any other and should take first place, both chronologically in a child's life and in terms of the attention, emphasis and value we place on them.

The lessons of the Core Phase are best learned through daily experiences in home life, uncomplicated by the secondary goals of pressured academic achievement. The best efforts of the parents will be in nurturing healthy relationships and modeling an active spiritual and scholarly life. Socializing outside family without the rest of the family should be limited and carefully considered. This is an ideal time for reading and discussion of good books, listening to and discussing good music, watching and discussing good media programs, playing at art or math and building with Legos or Erector sets and other similar activities.

The tools for academic learning are present, as are the tools for cooking or making home repairs, and little children use them more in the context of tagging along or *playing* at the work of *adults*. There is no adult skill that children are obligated to master at this stage. The assumption is clearly conveyed that through frequent exposure (as in our reading to them or on our own) and later instruction (mostly by trial-and-error, with a loving mentor to answer questions and help avoid disasters) they will gain that facility as a matter of course.

Lessons in self-discipline, perseverance and pursuit of excellence are modeled by the parents, and experienced by the young child in mostly physical ways. These might include: household chores, caring for animals and gardens, helping in a family business and cooperating in a daily routine. Little children start to internalize the virtues of excellence and perseverance as they do their part with family duties and in service to others. During Core Phase, children are taught the fundamentals of the family's faith and how to arrive at and recognize truth. Most importantly, during Core Phase the child should be prepared to make choices, heed her conscience and know in her heart when she is being inspired.

Let us reiterate here, and the reader will note in later chapters, that a successful Core Phase is not devoid of exposure to the tools of academic achievement or the body of human knowledge. A mother plays at learning with her children in a core-appropriate fashion such that her children are exposed to great ideas; indeed some children will, with such exposure, naturally pick up academic skills.

We would not expressly discourage academics—quite the contrary. However, our experience has made us much more wary of the mother who (with the best on intentions) leads her young children right into the ZPD and thereby displaces critical core lessons than of the mother who provides a cocoon of simplicity and nurture and waits until the last minute to teach her youth scholar skills.

Love of Learning Phase naturally follows the establishment of a solid core. During the Love of Learning Phase, the student falls deeply in love with learning, studying, knowing and learning even more. For many young people this naturally occurs between ages eight and twelve. If a person is forced in pressured formal schooling or assignments during this phase, she can develop a hate of learning attitude or even just a dislike of studying.

Ideally, however, each young person has the opportunity to freely fall in love with the joys of learning and to experience first-hand how wonderful learning can be. These are the years when children dabble with learning, getting to know "what's out there." If they have come from the Core Phase in good order they are usually fearless, feel almost everything will be interesting and believe they will be able to do whatever they set their minds to.

During Love of Learning Phase, parents should provide opportunity for children to make and take responsibility for personal decisions. Personal accountability should be stressed and respected. During these years, children will start to become aware of gifts and interests that will help define their life goals and mission. Parents should encourage the child to orient himself by this inward sense of direction, and model the same in their own lives.

Peer involvement should continue to be carefully filtered and is ideally either an extension of whole-family relationships or, by design, grows into them. In other words, the young child's companions should be from that group of families that the parents trust and identify with. For example, if one of our children discovers a significant friendship from outside our circle of influence, that new friend's family would become the object of outreach so that a whole family relationship can be developed and the new family can be invited into the fellowship of our family's community of friends.

Children in Love of Learning Phase can benefit from some positive peer pressure in making and keeping goals and achieving excellence. During this phase, the skills and tools of learning such as reading, writing, math skills, experimentation, library research, and oral persuasion (what kid does not practice that?), that will enable later scholarly habits, are practiced according to the student's level of interest and desire (cue the inspiring, non-manipulative parent who trusts the process) and a fair level of competence gained. A certain amount of time should be set aside on a regular basis for study, e.g. daily, every other day, M-Th, whatever schedule suits the needs and style of the home, parent and child or the classroom. The content may be flexible and vary from day to day or even change several times during a study period; or, it may be a concentrated, passionate pursuit of one area for even weeks or months. It will vary from child to child, from year to year, and will commonly be some combination of these approaches.

Reading together as a family, and the child reading alone and discussing with the parent (once the skill of independent reading has been acquired), are two very common activities during this phase. Teachers reading to the class can be very motivating. Writing skills are developed by the keeping of a personal journal, thank-you notes, birthday cards, correspondence with friends and loved ones, and creative writing. These skills may be fostered by the parent asking the child to write a shopping list for him while driving, or to take down a phone number or address, etc.

The parent and teacher should be imaginative in offering opportunities to relate every day life with books read, historical events and the operation of scientific and mathematical principles. Projects requiring integration of a variety of skills and resources should be encouraged. For example, a child might want to build a birdhouse. Preparation could include:

- research on the nesting preferences of the targeted bird
- drawing up plans
- listing materials needed
- contacting suppliers for price comparisons
- reviewing safety rules for power tools
- consideration of finishing products like paint that would not harm the bird
- planting certain bushes or feeders and other things to attract the particular bird

The use of project learning is an incredible way to encourage the child to venture into new areas of study. You can start with almost any subject of interest and with enough ingenuity arrive at any other discipline from music to science to math, or economics to biology or history, or world religions to future trends, and so on. We encourage the reader to analyze the above examples for the various skills and disciplines touched on.

The need to relate the child's daily experiences and study with the rest of the body of human knowledge and achievement makes obvious the need for the parent to put a great deal of energy into his own education rather than making the child "the project." This is more consistent with natural law: one can only change one's own self and—bottom line—it is much more effective to *lead* than to *force* such an enterprise as the education of a child. The parent and teacher should be diligent in self-education so that the child cannot help but internalize the value of self-improvement and the obligation of the individual to be serviceable to his God, community and others.

The increasing intellectual demands of the child in Love of Learning Phase upon the parent require that the home life and family's time be kept as uncomplicated as possible. Too many outside activities, no matter how valuable or interesting, can be over-stimulating for the child and draw him much too soon away from the ties that bind him to the nest. Too much "stuff," either as clutter in the home or as entertainments and possessions that rob time from the necessary "right kind of vacuum" (that space of discomfort/boredom that impels a young person to exert himself to accomplish something worthwhile) can derail a family's education. Many times we find that a parent that seems to "get it" and is trying to do everything right is not seeing the expected results because of this problem. Teachers can apply these same lessons in the classroom.

Project learning usually begins when a child sits around for a while wishing for something to do, as taught by Erikson. Thus we see the problem with filling up his time. This can be difficult to avoid, especially when parents are unprepared for the peer pressure (not the children's peers so much as the parent's) that may be leveled at them. When "every" other boy and girl is in soccer, dance, little league, (you fill in the blank!), it is sometimes hard to justify a decision to use that time to do relatively "nothing." This is not to say that any of those or other similar activities are inherently wrong for the child. But the time spent at home in simple, "homely" (a word that has lost too much of its charm in the progressivist evolution of culture) activities is irreplaceable, and needs to be held in greater esteem and higher priority against the more stimulating activities that society insists should fill our children's and family's lives. It is okay to stay home! It is okay to just play sometimes! We need to take responsibility to fill our homes with wholesomeness, warmth, light and learning and provide the time for family members to benefit from this ideal environment. Consider the experience and thoughts shared by Ana Veciana-Suarez that appeared in the *Miami Herald* and *Reader's Digest* some years back:

> Last fall was a first-of-its-kind season. For better or worse—I did not register my children in after-school activities. No swimming. No music lessons. No play dates. Nada.
>
> Once they finished their homework, they were free to do what they pleased, with a simple caveat: only one hour of TV. In the beginning, my sons, Ben, 11, and Nick, 9, were anxious about this sudden, unplanned freedom. I had to push them out the door with a ball, a bike, a scooter. "Play!" I ordered.
>
> I learned that deprogramming takes time, patience and a lot of faith in the theory that having a stellar resume by the end of elementary school isn't necessary. Truth is, we stopped the activities because I was stressed out. Too frantic to smile. Too exhausted to floss. The children weren't much better.
>
> When my older kids, now in college and high school, were young, I bought into the rules of modern parenting. They're unspoken, but followed zealously. First, you must expose your child to a variety of activities. After all, you never know where you'll find a prodigy. Second, if the child shows the slightest talent, the activity must be pursued with lessons, private coaching and several days a week of practice. Every minute has purpose. Heaven forbid you have blank spaces in the calendar. The kids might be missing out on the one class, the one talent that will get them into Harvard.

> Providing opportunities sounds wonderful, but when taken to an extreme, the concept snares the family into a frantic pace where time for hanging out, the essence of childhood, is completely squeezed out.
>
> Not last fall. Double-shift dinners were gone. We told stories. We relaxed. Once we watched some crows dive-bomb our cat. The kids played with bikes, balls, scooters. Nobody kept score.
>
> In fact, the boys played outside so much that the lawn is worn down to the soil in places. They've made friends with kids who come from all over the neighborhood to play in pickup kickball games. And I've caught up on my reading, my sewing. Why, I've even organized my recipes.

We will see great strides in our young childrens' education (and the peacefulness of the family and home) when we re-enthrone free play to the prominent place it should occupy in a child's life. Play is one of the chief educational curricula of the Foundational Phases of Core and Love of Learning. This can be very difficult to adopt in the classroom setting, as the market demands high test scores and measurable results. Still, the greatest teachers learn how to do both.

As the student gets close to Scholar Phase, she goes through an advanced Love of Learning period which we call the Transition to Scholar. It is a part of Love of Learning, but it makes all the difference in effectively preparing the student for a great Scholar Phase. Indeed, the Transition is so important that we have given it its own chapter in this book. The key to the whole Leadership Education system is to have students who are absolutely head-over-heels in love with learning. When this occurs, they will naturally proceed at some point to the Educational Phases. This progression will occur as parents and teachers become effective at inspiring young minds to study and learn.

The Educational Phases

After the Foundational Phases come the Educational Phases. The Educational Phases consist of the Scholar Phase and Depth Phase. During this period, the bulk of a person's "book learning" takes place—at least up to that point in her life. In the past sixty years, fads in education have swung back and forth between a focus on emphasizing learning that takes place outside the classroom versus using the classroom to train for nearly everything. The truth is that both are needed—classroom learning and outside experience.

During the Educational Phases, classroom and intensive scholarly study ideally take up about 70% of the learning time, and are supplemented by field experience, simulations, internships, travel with mentorial support, practica and projects, clubs and lessons, etc. In the later Applicational Phases, these percentages are about 80% project and 20% classroom study, reading, etc., depending on the individual's personal mission. Parents seeking to gain a scholar education as they simultaneously raise their young families will also benefit from honoring the percentages of Mission Phase (details presented later). Parenting the unique souls who have been entrusted to our stewardship is a very important mission in and of itself.

The Educational Phases form the foundation of one's intellectual education, and as such, are vital to success. Without a high-quality Scholar and Depth experience, a person is not really *educated*. Although each person is different and each education should therefore be personalized, there are also some basics that we should all learn as part of the Educational Phases. Our place in history and the cycles of society help define our generation's role and the critical body of knowledge for our time. John Adams alluded to this point when he said, "I must study politics and war that my sons may have liberty to study mathematics and philosophy. My sons ought to study mathematics and philosophy, geography, natural history, naval architecture, navigation, commerce and agriculture in order to give their children a right to study painting, poetry, music, architecture, statuary, tapestry, and porcelain."

Important skills for the Educational Phases include: history, science, mathematics, literature, etc., along with basic skills of writing, public speaking, business planning, using technology, etc. Our generation, and that of our children, will find that an understanding of the principles of freedom and prosperity, and the type of civilization and culture that perpetuate them, will be critical. And the present crisis of education and leadership should make obvious the necessity of each generation giving due diligence to the arts of citizenship and statesmanship even in times of relative ease.

Educational Phases provide the opportunity to gain vitally important knowledge and necessary skills in an environment where we can make mistakes, refocus and keep learning—all under the guidance of a great mentor. Nothing can compensate for not getting this great experience.

During the Scholar years (roughly twelve to seventeen for most girls and thirteen to eighteen for most boys), the young person begins a rigorous, disciplined survey of classic works and real life application. At first, the new scholar may study only a few hours at a time, but as the student matures and his studies gain breadth and momentum, his thirst for knowledge, self-mastery and discipline keep his nose in the books for many hours at a stretch. By the end of Scholar Phase, most students are studying well over forty hours a week. Scholars cover every subject imaginable and go from one subject to another with rigor and passion.

In an established Scholar Phase, students typically study six to twelve hours a day (increasing as they get older), five to seven days a week for ten to twelve months a year. Scholar Phase for youth usually lasts five or six years, while adults who did not get a Scholar Phase when they were young may spend up to ten or even more years getting a Scholar Phase by studying one or two hours daily. While Scholar Phase students study whatever interests them, their parents, teachers and mentors should help inspire them to see the value, relevance, and excitement of studying other important subjects (like history, math, writing, science, the arts, etc.) along with whatever topics they naturally pursue due to interest and personal mission.

The mentor or parent should be deliberate in seeking inspiration on what projects/studies to promote; remember our tendency to default back to the conveyor belt. The mandate and trust of mentorship is that we pay a price to *know* what is right, not resorting to knee-jerk conformity. If we are never surprised at what we do or do not emphasize in our interactions with those whom we mentor, we are likely being too formulaic in our approach and need to be much more conscientious in taking a personalized approach and paying the price to receive guidance and inspiration.

Peer involvement and interaction are not only *desired* by the student, but also *desirable* for his progress through Scholar Phase. Group discussion of classic works and review of original works by the students are invaluable in expanding the young scholar's horizons. He learns to articulate his thoughts and is brought face-to-face with the present limitations of his accomplishments, thus inviting him to challenge himself to greater excellence and motivating him to more disciplined study. While all of this sounds very grown-up, it should be remembered that the Scholar is still a work in progress and frequent interaction with and accountability to the parent, teacher and/or mentor are imperative. He still needs nurture and affection as a child, and respect and responsibility as an adult.

During Scholar Phase, it will probably be appropriate for most students to be involved in some type of formal arrangement such as a public, charter, private school, Commonwealth school or multi-family cooperative that follows the Leadership Education model. The need for mentors in addition to the parents will probably arise as the student progresses toward his personal goals and shows leanings toward the areas in which he will pursue a deeper education, especially during the later scholar years. Indeed, in our own case, we have utilized both parent-mentoring and "aunt/uncle-mentoring." One mentor we engaged perhaps had little edge on the two of us in terms of what he has studied; but the chemistry between him and our Scholar youth was just right for the time. With them accountable to *him* for their academic commitments, we were merely facilitators, sounding boards, confidantes, and of course, parents. Their mentor had a relationship uncomplicated by how clean their rooms or their ears were, or whether or not they were grumpy or helpful with a sibling. He dealt with them strictly as their academic mentor, and as such had special power to influence them on this plane.

At the time of this writing our three scholar-aged youth are participating in a class that meets once a week, hosted by Rachel with two other mission-phase mothers who also have youth in the class. A handful of other teens have joined for a dynamic group culture, and the result has been phenomenal. The Scholar youth are studying harder than ever. It has also had the effect of a deepened trust and respect between Rachel and our young scholars, and the community of families involved is experiencing a renaissance in learning and cooperation.

During Depth Phase, mentors assess student strengths and weaknesses, help students fill in gaps in their knowledge, go into real depth in their areas of strength and passion, and otherwise lead young people in preparation for their life mission and focus. During Depth Phase, the mentor plays a most important role in the student's life.

The first mentor for most children is likely a mother, followed by other teachers and/or mentors as they get older. Ideally, a father is one of the key mentors during Scholar Phase. As a student leaves home and pursues Depth Phase, his mentors become his *Alma Mater*, which means "the soul's mother." Most young people go through a period of subjecting the lessons of home to new scrutiny; they typically reject part of what they learned at home, while idealizing and seeking to emulate the views of the new mentors they encounter as they move away from home. Indeed, not only colleges serve as the alma mater, but whomever or whatever becomes the new mentor or new mother of the young person's new life on his own. Since you are literally helping young people choose a "new mother" in their life during Depth Phase, make sure to educate them on the critical impact this important transition to adulthood will have on their lives and help them choose wisely.

It is incredibly valuable to have a clear understanding and vision of the phases and the ability to communicate that vision to your children. Helping your child to expect this re-orientation in Depth Phase, and the realization that you predicted and prepared her for it, will help your young adult to stand firm on the foundation that you helped her lay in her core years, and to evaluate effectively the peers and mentors that come her way when you are no longer constantly by her side.

Depth Phase is most often accomplished at college and it is important that students and their families choose the best available environment for college level studies. Students in Depth Phase should continue to learn and apply the important lessons of Core, Love of Learning and Scholar Phases during their Depth studies. Parents and students should be aware that few colleges or universities emphasize Leadership Education. Students must either specifically choose a college where they will get a Leadership Education or they need to seek out special mentors and get a Leadership Education in their personal "outside of class" studies while at college. And it should be noted that more and more it is not neccessary to go to college to find excellent mentoring and a great education.

The Applicational Phases

The two Applicational Phases are Mission (building the two towers of family and organization) and Impact (changing the world to be whatever it should be for your grandchildren and their children).

The importance of the Foundational and Educational Phases can be clearly seen when we contrast the life path indicated by conveyor belt education with the life of service and impact pursued by students of Leadership Education. The purpose of education is to prepare children and youth for life. It helps to bluntly ask the question: "What kind of life are you preparing your children for?"

During later periods of life, the conveyor belt encourages conformity of thinking and then performance based on one's abilities and innate potential. Note that in this model each person is assumed to have a basic level of potential, often detectable by experts (teachers and counselors), and measurable by testing. Upon retirement, the conveyor belt abandons the person, expecting him/her to quietly allow those who "still have potential" to run the world. The convalescent home is often a mirror image of the conveyor belt elementary school—but without the energy and hope. The economic prospects and societal norms of the conveyor belt virtually preclude families caring for elders (both the young and old in the conveyor belt life path view this option as unacceptable). This deals the final blow to family culture and individual worth.

In contrast, the Leadership Path follows moral education with a superb, broad scholarly education, and then intensive and in-depth expertise and, if desired, professional education. The Leadership Path assumes that our potential is rooted more in our choices and actions than in a pre-set genetic, social class or otherwise-scripted fate.

Leaders build things. Adults on the Path of Leadership are expected to build two important entities: a family and an organization that edifies their community. Both of these should be built to last, with a solid foundation and a leadership worldview.

Later in life, leaders own their obligation to family and society to grandparent, that is, to be an elder statesman and mentor, to communicate the long view, to communicate hope in adversity, to warn of unheeded pitfalls, to exhibit public virtue, to have the moral authority to act as patriarch or matriarch of their clan with revered wisdom. They impact the world with clarity of vision borne of learning and experience.

Let us make plain that the leadership model does not preclude any particular vocational choice. Rather, it liberates the individual to do what he desires without the limitations that such commitments might otherwise place on him. A landscaper can also be a successful investor; an auto mechanic can be an inventor; an author can be a special education volunteer. Having a leadership education gives the individual an edge that helps him to successfully and independently live the life of his own choosing.

We recently met a tow-truck driver who rescued us from a breakdown far from civilization. On the 100-mile journey to where we would leave the car for repairs, we marveled at the truly amazing depth and breadth of his education, and the way he approached his work as a servant of humanity. He left such an impression on us that we spoke of him countless times in the following days, and still from time to time revisit the memory of our encounter with this remarkable man. Can you imagine a world, a community, where every function from plumber to politician, trash collector to track coach, was filled by an individual who loved his work, who loved the people he served and who had a leadership education? What a magnificent future to bequeath to our children.

Life Transitions

For the process of leadership to occur effectively, each leader on the path must face and overcome challenging "life transitions" which are common to all. Each of the four typical life transitions is difficult for most people, but nature has provided us with a guide to help us through them. The key to success in each life transition is to focus on what you are transitioning "toward," instead of looking backward. The transitions can be both physically and emotionally challenging. This is why a guide or mentor can be so helpful.

The first major life transition is the move from childhood to young adulthood. This typically occurs just before or at the beginning of puberty. During this transition, parents (or parent-figures) are our guides. In our current culture most people see this first major life transition, somewhere around age twelve, as a change from child to teenager. This conveyor belt misconception causes a great deal of frustration. Parents often tell their children how hard the teenage years will be, based on their own difficult adolescence. This message frequently becomes a self-fulfilling prophecy. Children follow their parents' and peers' pattern without realizing that there are other options.

A parent on the leadership path, in contrast, will help the child understand that the transition is not toward being a teenager, but rather toward doing the hard work of Scholar Phase and earning a truly world-class education. Thus the transition is not something that *happens to you*, as in the conveyor belt model, but a choice you make to become more and prepare yourself for greater things to come. It is a choice wherein parental responses to adolescent challenges need not leave our youth feeling disenfranchised and impotent, but are seen as an opportunity to create experiences of lasting meaning. A leadership view of this important life transition replaces the conveyor-belt search for identity and peer community with a quest for vision and mission.

Where lack of confidence is the symptom of the conveyor belt transition to being a teenager, the Leadership transition to scholar is filled with hard work and fun. Parents and teachers are not the enemy on the Leadership Path, but close mentors and trusted guides. Parents in most cases have nearly all of the say about which path the child takes, belying the murmurings of the past two generations and their legendary exasperation with "teenagers" and "generation gaps."

When youth go through their second major life transition, leaving home for college or work, the conveyor belt promises libertine pleasure-seeking along with an academic major for career preparation. In contrast, the leadership student transitions toward a truly excellent Depth Phase education accompanied by a mastery of self-control, the development of virtue and personal character, and in many cases, a life-time commitment to a spouse and creation of a family. The two paths could not be more distinct. A young person's college-level mentors either inspire a whole new level of excellence built on the moral teaching of home and hearth or a narrow conveyor belt expertise with its attendant disdain of "quaint" but outdated parental values and influences.

The "mid-life crisis" and "retirement" transitions follow the same pattern, with conveyor belters transitioning toward upcoming retirement and old age, and leaders toward community influence and then societal statesmanship and impact. In short, these four life crises are lived differently by leaders than by the rest. Each one of us can choose the Leadership Path. While we can make this choice at any point in our life, the most influential point is in our early transition during puberty—to either become a teenager or seek a Scholar Phase. Parents make all the difference in how their children approach this decision. Indeed, without parental vision, few children in our modern society even know the choice is available.

FOUR LIFE TRANSITIONS

Time of Life		**Conveyor Belt**	**Leadership**
Puberty (around 12)	Transition	to teenager	to youth
	Influence	peers/pop culture	parents/mentors
	Goal	popularity/ belonging/fun	scholarship/ education/ mission prep

Time of Life		Conveyor Belt	Leadership
Adulthood	Transition	to college major/ job/family	to mission/ building two towers of home and organization
	Influence	peers/pop-culture/ professors/boss/ experts	mentors/great ideas and minds of past and present/integrity to belief system
	Goal	money/status/ spend money	financial independence/ personal mission achievement/ leading others
Midlife	Transition	to midlife crisis	to Impact
	Influence	peers/popular culture/market	God/spouse/ family/continued learning/the great debate
	Goal	cope/escape/play/ job changes	mission application/ impact
Elder	Transition	to retirement	The Roles of an Elder: Grandparent, Mentor, Scholar, Citizen, Entrepreneur, Sentinel, Philosopher, Philanthropist, Disciple, Artist, Statesman, Healer
	Influence	peers/popular cultures/others	
	Goals	relax/play/earn money for old age	

It is unfortunate that our society has so few contemporary examples of the true and natural progression of the phases, at least as corresponding to the ages. The result is that a very remote few ever reach Depth Phase before having to take on the responsibilities of homemaking and breadwinning. These consuming and primary responsibilities have precluded all but the most determined from achieving the full extent of their mission and reaching their leadership potential while in their prime.

But it is important to remember that it is never too late for anyone who chooses to do the work required to create dramatic and effective change in their lives—adults as well as youth. It is because of adults making choices like these that more and more of our children and youth are on track to be ready for Depth Phase by their early twenties. This bodes well for the impact they will have later in life, at a time when much will be required of their generation.

Getting Off the Conveyor Belt

Thousands of parents, in numbers growing larger each day, have fourteen-year-olds who beg to study ten-hour days and follow through. These parents are full of testimonials about Leadership Education.

At the same time, and usually with much sacrifice, Leadership Education parents themselves set the example by getting a quality Scholar Phase education. Such parents are frankly not surprised when their fourteen-year-olds beg to study and love doing so. They are not shocked that they have young adults instead of teenagers, nor are they amazed at the quality, depth and breadth of the education of their college-ready young adults. None of this surprises them because they led the way—they have done it themselves, and naturally expect the children to follow. Fourteen-year-olds like this do not wake up "ready made" the morning after their fourteenth birthday. They had years of Core and Love of Learning mentoring, nurtured and inspired by parents who set the example, taught them the phases and what was ahead, and consistently led out.

Parents must get off the conveyor belt twice: once, mentally/emotionally and the other time, physically/behaviorally. Unfortunately, many people attempt to do the second one first, and then wonder why their results are not what they hoped. In other words, they teach the concepts to their children but fail to fully live and exemplify them. They say and do things that undermine the phases and other important principles of Leadership Education because they do not intrinsically trust the process, and are not fully implementing it. Knowing the Phases of Learning in more depth can help. This is one reason for the advanced material of this book. The chapter which follows will answer questions parents, specifically homeschool parents, often have in the process of establishing Leadership Education in their homes.

Part II

....

A Recipe for Success: The Foundational Phases

CHAPTER THREE

Core And Love Of Learning: Ingredients 1-12

Introduction to the Ingredients

Leadership Education is more than just a collection of ideas. It is a recounting of a process by which scholars such as Thomas Jefferson, Isaac Newton, Marie Curie and Winston Churchill achieved excellence in scholarship and personal development. And we do not consider ourselves the authors of this process as much as its biographers.

While we whole-heartedly endorse this philosophy because it gives us a vision of how to accomplish our goals for our family, we do not suggest that it is what everyone else wants or should want for their family. We simply say that if you decide to put meringue on your pie, there will be egg whites. You may decide against meringue, it is true. But as soon as you commit to meringue, you cannot argue on the point of egg whites. One cannot modify the details of Leadership Education without also modifying the outcome. The principles we enumerate below do not pretend to be everything to everyone, but they are what they are—A Leadership Education.

Our purpose here is to introduce a recipe for success in raising children and upholding families with a Leadership Education. Combining the ingredients of this recipe will result in the creation of an environment that is ideal for accomplishing the Phases of Learning: particularly, the Foundational Phases of Core and Love of Learning. Additional ingredients must be added to achieve Scholar and Depth Phases, but even these latter phases still require the early ingredients. Knowing this ideal equals understanding the recipe of success in a Leadership Education home.

No recipe will work without basic ingredients. The cook may improvise here and there—and in fact that is exactly what the great chefs do—but the basic ingredients remain ever present. It takes "off-the-conveyor-belt" thinking to understand this process. A great Core and Love of Learning environment is created by parents who understand all the ingredients and apply them as best fits their unique home and children.

We hope that nobody will follow a dogmatic application of these ingredients, but we also know that ignoring, leaving out, or putting in too much of any one ingredient may well doom the entire recipe. If you want cookies, the right ingredients must be used—and isn't it wonderful that there are so many kinds of cookies? We know many families applying Leadership Education in their homes. There is a fundamental harmony in their application, and yet no two have exactly the same flavor.

You are the expert on your home, and you were given your children, your position and your authority directly from God. It is hard to imagine better credentials. Learning the skills for creating an ideal educational environment and educating yourself on the essential ingredients which make your family recipe work can be considered a component of your own Love of Learning. As you spend time personally doing Scholar Phase, you will know how to apply the principles and how to mix the ingredients.

If you have not done Scholar Phase (or are not progressing toward it) you simply cannot pass on what you do not have; you cannot inspire principles that you are not living. You can try—you can even teach them—but the inspiration will be fatally lacking. That is not to say you should leave the educating of your children to someone else. Frankly, you would be hard-pressed to find a person with a Scholar-level education who could apply these principles with as much success as you can in the environment of home and family. It is virtually certain you will not find anyone who meets these qualifications who has more potential than you have to love and inspire your children. And even if you should delegate the actual academic mentoring of your children to someone else, *your* example will remain, and will largely make or break their success. You must lead out yourself, get a superb liberal arts education, and show your children what to do by example as well as precept.

Nobody has to choose between giving their children great Foundational Phases and being a model of Scholar Phase—they naturally fit together. To do one well is to do the other also. But to apply them, you must know the ingredients. We often hear of mothers of large families who exhaust themselves trying to meet the needs (physical, emotional, intellectual) of so many individuals. They protest that pursuing their own education under the circumstances is impossible and that the prospects of them continuing long into the future with their children's education are equally bleak. If this applies to you, pay close attention to these ingredients. There are many large families applying Leadership Education with great success. In our case, it has become increasingly easier and more effective as the family has grown—as a direct result of having more children and all the phases represented. This is not to say that it hasn't been hard. We have eight children, and parenting them has been and continues to be the hardest challenge in our lives. We can not imagine how hard it would be without applying the ingredients of success covered here.

To sum up: schooling can be a great tool to cause friction, frustration, disharmony, tension and a basic feeling of inadequacy in the roles of all family members. Or, it can be a source of uniting opportunities for service and growth which strengthen the family unit and support each individual in his personal development. The focus of these chapters on Foundational Phases will be on families rather than classrooms, simply because of the age of the students we are discussing. Most professional elementary teachers will tell you that the most important factors for the academic success of the students they teach are found in the children's homes. While these chapters are about the home, they should have great impact on parents raising and educating students regardless of where they get their academics.

Your success here depends so much on your vision and your expectations. To quote Ruth Hailstone, a friend who has children in the same ages and phases as some of our own: "Maybe one day in ten is perfect!" If you expect every day to fit a mold, you will be disappointed and frustrated. If you expect the *process* to work, you will be richly rewarded. Immerse yourself in the principles, live a life that is inspirational in its simplicity and commitment, and have a vision of what you are trying to accomplish that informs your choices along the way.

Be confident and joyful! Being "conscientious" is not a good excuse for being fearful, paranoid, controlling, other-centered (seeking validation from anyone or anything but the Highest source), or in any other way unprincipled. What our children learn during the Foundational Phases is how to be us—or at least, how we feel about being us. Internalize that and consider how our attitudes and habits can inspire or hinder them. This does not mean being perfect as in never making a mistake. This means repenting perfectly when we make a mistake, being consistent in our effort to achieve, inspire and promote excellence, and using simple, high-quality, everyday home life as the starting curriculum for greatness.

These ingredients have been used by many of the great parents of history, but unfortunately are too infrequently discussed in our day. Enjoy this introduction to the ingredients. Study and ponder each of them, and use inspiration to start with working to apply the ingredients that are currently the most crucially needed by your family in your own home. While you likely will not apply all of them right away, knowing and thinking about them will influence how you do the most important work being done in our world today—parenting. We hope you will have as much fun learning about and applying the ingredients as we have!

Ingredient #1: Sundays

Sunday is the day that makes it all work. Each Sunday we hold our Family Executive Committee (FEC) meeting. The family members who attend this meeting are Mom and Dad. Both are full voting partners, and we consider our unanimity in prayerful decisions to constitute a vote from God. We strongly believe that He has an interest in the process for any family that includes Him. It is amazing to see the times that a decision discussed and agreed upon by us will be reconsidered and overturned due to a prayer. In this sense, there are three voting members on the committee and all decisions require a consensus of the three. The FEC establishes long-term family policy including assignments and rules, and is the highest authority in the family. By assignment of our FEC, Dad presides at the meeting. He is responsible for announcing and convening it, preparing the agenda, and keeping the meeting running smoothly.

The following agenda items are usually included and discussed in each weekly FEC meeting:

A-Schedule the Week.

This includes discussing all events for each member of the family, which we correlate on a central family calendar. We also discuss any events we feel need to be included (i.e.: "Sara needs some time alone with you" or, "We really ought to get those bulbs planted" or, "The car needs to be detailed" or, "Let's spend some extra play time with Hyrum this week," or, "The leaves in the canyon are changing and we'll miss it if we don't go in the next four days"), and plan them. We make the assignments needed to effectively accomplish the family plans for the week. When we give an assignment to someone who is not in the FEC, we write it down and inform them later. We very often say "no" to things vying for a place on the calendar. Guilt doesn't earn anything a mark in ink on our calendar. Nothing is untouchable. With so many people's priorities to consider and so many young ones to look after, hard choices are made every week and our youth have come to trust and respect the FEC's decisions, even when they might be disappointing. We have had experience with fudging on FEC decisions and regret has always followed—and it wasn't lost on anyone. There is a "consent of the governed" with respect to FEC.

B-Structure Time.

Next, we decide how we want to structure school time for the week, and we write it on the calendar. We have an overall structure which changes little from week to week, but we always go through it because almost every week includes some variations.

C-Discuss Problems.

First, Rachel brings up her concerns, if any, and we discuss possible solutions and make plans and assignments. Rachel tries to limit her entries on the agenda to issues specifically within her stewardship. It may refer to Dad's stewardship, but only as it affects her ability to do hers (e.g. "On the mornings we miss family prayer I have a really hard time reining in the kids for chores and school time." Note: because of Oliver's irregular schedule the FEC ultimately assigned Rachel responsibility to call for morning prayer).

Any concerns that she has that actually fall under Oliver's stewardship she prefers to take to God in prayer, and He and Oliver tend to work it out. She likes to call this "The Tevye Principle," referring to Tevye's conversations with God in "The Fiddler on the Roof." Tevye was gentle and respectful with his wife Golda, while his relationship with God was transparent and unrestrained. This has worked miracles in our home as either Oliver's heart or Rachel's (as the need turned out to be) was softened and inspiration was received that made all the difference.

After Rachel is done, Oliver brings up his concerns, if any. This is not a complaining session, but a time for making decisions, commitments, and policies. Any decisions that are made require a unanimous vote. If it seems consensus is not forthcoming, we may table or postpone an issue to be discussed at a later meeting. We usually set a time limit on this part of the meeting. We have noticed that on items of controversy there is a point of diminishing returns for discussion. Thirty minutes is about right for us, but couples with different communication styles might decide on more or even less time. If more than the time allotted is needed for a timely or urgent decision, we schedule a special meeting on the calendar. This can require discipline and trust, but we have found that an orderly approach to such matters is almost always more successful. Other couples have stories of how they have made similar systems work for them, and undoubtedly the readers of this book will find a preference for their own particular application.

FEC has also been helpful in conflict resolution. If a disagreement arises during the week that could lead to an argument, either of us has the prerogative to "refer it to committee," meaning the Family Executive Committee. This means that further discussion must wait a minimum of 24 hours and must take place in the context of an FEC which can be convened especially for this issue, if necessary. We have agreed to use this sparingly (not as a weapon of passive aggression) and to honor it unfailingly. The times that we have "referred" an issue to committee and been privately prayerful in anticipation of the discussion—well, honestly, the discussion has never yet come. In *every* instance it resolved itself without further repartee and the meeting was subsequently cancelled.

This does not mean that we foresee no discussion on such issues in the future; just that when we apply this technique our answers thus far have come as a result of a commitment to not arguing and being prayerful about the solutions. This pattern has become so pronounced that it has been a couple of years since we have even referred anything to committee. This process has taught us new skills in communication and fostered more trust between us so that we do not get so anxious or defensive or critical when solutions are not immediately forthcoming.

D-Discuss Children.

Finally, we discuss the children individually—including concerns, needs, opportunities, problems, struggles, hopes, fears, doubts, talents, any particular impressions one of us may have regarding them, etc. We start with the oldest and talk about what we can do to help each. This is the first and most important step to mentoring a child in any phase.

In single parent homes or other situations with a non-traditional FEC, the FEC still benefits greatly from a formal weekly meeting where decisions are made prayerfully and planning is done in advance. Oliver recalls a story he read in a magazine about a young man who was doing a service project with his church group. They were taking gift baskets to the widows in their congregation. The youth was confused when they dropped one off to his mother. Although his father had died several years before, he had never thought of her as a widow. Whenever an issue of discipline or conflict arose in the home, Mother would excuse herself, "to go talk it over with father." She would then kneel beside her bed with her deceased husband's photograph nearby and pray until she knew what to do. She would return later and proceed confidently with the solution she had arrived at. This woman was participating in an FEC, even in her difficult circumstance.

After FEC each Sunday, we hold parent/child interviews. Each interview covers areas of concern, opportunity, etc. (as just discussed in the FEC) and gets the child's input. Interviews are used to give assignments, review past work or performance, coach, suggest changes, review how the child is using his structured time, inform him of events in the upcoming week, ask deep questions, resolve problems, and so on.

If Dad is out of town, Mom may hold the interviews. Sometimes Dad holds them alone even when Mom is home, but usually we both participate in the meeting with each child. We ask how they are living the tenets of our faith, how they are fulfilling their family stewardships, what worries or questions they have and how we can help them in their lives. With our Core and Love of Learning children, we usually ask if there are any particular interests they have that they need our support to pursue. We ask specific questions regarding personal safety and relationships to ensure they understand how to protect themselves from molestation and reassure them that we are comfortable talking with them privately about sensitive subjects.

We may ask the Love of Learning and Scholar Phase students to bring their compass: a list they make at least every six months of things they want to study. The compass is an excellent source of topics for discussion both about what they have done and what they want to do.

It is not uncommon that the interviews have absolutely no academic content at all. We may feel inclined to just let the child talk, and talk, and talk; we may re-teach a basic principle. We may discuss in detail a relationship the child has, and how she might take responsibility for doing her part to make it a healthy one. Other times, lots of academics are covered.

In short, we hold the meeting and talk about whatever we feel impressed to cover. We structure a time for the meeting, and basically let the content take care of itself. Sometimes we miss a week; sometimes we even miss two in a row. As our family got bigger and Dad's travel schedule fuller, we started interviewing only one to three of our children per week. In Dad's planner, we keep track of who has had an interview and when. This way we feel comfortable taking as much time as is necessary with each child, with no pressure to "get through them all." But we try to interview everyone at least once a month. If you get in the habit, the children will likely inform you if you start missing. Our children like the attention and their weeks go better when we meet.

If Sundays work well, the whole system is on good footing. Sundays are the basic building block of the Leadership Education home, like flour in a recipe or the number "one" in math. For us, the FEC has to happen every single Sunday (or on another day if that is best for you) without fail. Over time, as the couple learns to depend on the FEC, the pattern of relating and coordinating becomes as much a daily procedure as a weekly meeting.

You can personalize interviews to your family needs, but in our experience, the FEC simply must occur weekly. The first ingredient—truly the most important ingredient—of successful Core and Love of Learning environments is the weekly FEC followed by quality interviews.

Ingredient #2: Weeks

Families and educations run in waves that are about a week in length. Planning on any other level gets you back on the conveyor belt. Days are too short—they are always interrupted by something. If you schedule your education by days you will seldom follow through. Conversely, days are not long enough to take on big projects and really get somewhere. Months are too long—those who schedule their education monthly find that the plan usually works for about a week and then it breaks down for a number of reasons; ditto for six month or annual plans. The week is the perfect length of time if you want to control your calendar, rather than letting it control you.

Each Sunday it is important to carefully plan the week. If you have big interruptions on Thursday, need to take advantage of the shopping sales on Friday and Grandma is coming on Saturday, the weekly schedule gives you time to plan for such events. For example, in such a case, Monday, Tuesday and Wednesday might become bigger than usual school days, where you refuse to be interrupted—you might even take the phone off the hook. Or, if you have few interruptions in a week, you could follow a more casual schedule and answer the phone whenever it rings.

The key here is to control the calendar. In each weekly FEC, it is important to decide what the calendar will be for that week. You are far enough from events to make allowances and close enough to have almost everything on the calendar at once. It is important to have an over-arching view of what you value and how you want to spend your time. If you want a beautiful vegetable garden and yet constantly allow other things to displace the time allotted for gardening, you will obviously limit your success. If you want to show your children the joy of service and yet have no discretionary time in which to attend to arising needs of others, you will teach them a different value instead. It is important to say "no" to things, and it is much easier when you can see what else is happening that week. If the whole week seems full and school or family will suffer, change it—right there in your Sunday FEC meeting. Weeks are the basic building block of a life, and of an education. They give real power to the parents, and the impact on the whole family is huge.

Ingredient #3: Mornings

The persistent lessons of morning time are the foundation our children learn. As we establish a "default" pattern that we follow when intervening circumstances are absent, all the things we value are taught and modeled over time. Mornings are the daily default, and if you set and manage the default schedule well, the family will naturally get up and get into the regular routine. It takes discipline at first to get the routine established, and again modifications may be necessary as children move through phases and seasons change. When our family was young, scripture study was the first thing in the morning. Now that our older children attend early morning classes, that part of our routine moves to evening. Chores, breakfast and grooming are all part of the early routine. Morning is, for most families, the best time for Kidschool (more on this later).

The morning routine is very important for Core and Love of Learning students. It establishes structure and order, and "incentivizes" learning. With structure and order come more natural cooperation; everyone understands what is expected of them and experiences the inherent reward of feeling fulfillment at having done their part. When this happens, they need less "bossing" and there is a sense of momentum and community as all are focused on the same intersections on a daily basis (family prayer and scripture study, the morning meal, reporting on chores and studies, reading together with Mom, etc.). There is a sense of confidence and personal satisfaction as accomplishment comes early in the day. In the morning, everyone is fresh. Educators have long known that this is the best time for learning. It is also more fun and is followed by less "academic" activities later in the day.

During the morning, Scholar Phase students should be studying; getting the highest quality part of their learning under their belt while the day is young. Love of Learning students should use the morning for academics—reading, writing, working on math and science, etc. By afternoon, it seems more difficult to limit interruptions or other obligations. It is natural both for mental clarity and rational scheduling to provide time for academics in the morning.

Currently, in our home, Love of Learning Phase Eliza (age ten) reads, works on projects for Young Stateswomen Society, helps Ammon (age seven) with a project, does math projects, draws, does science, cooking, art, or other projects with Mom, etc. We have historically set aside the morning for school, and this has few guidelines, mostly in the "not" category. School time is "not": friend time, video time or sit-and-look-at-Star-Wars-cards-time; just about anything else is fair game. Parental inspiration and individual needs are the ultimate guide as to what activities should and should not be included.

The older children are naturally more and more interested in academic activities, particularly as they near Scholar Phase. During mornings, it is wise to limit interruptions so that they can have a block of time to read or do creative writing, etc. However, structuring time for Love of Learning kids DOES NOT MEAN STRUCTURING CONTENT. As we have said in other instances, this phase is more about "Love" than Learning. This does not mean that the children do not learn. It means that we resist the temptation to define appropriateness of their explorations and the way they engage their time beyond some basic and simple guidelines.

Some of what we do at various times throughout the week to inspire their morning explorations include: "Kidschool" (extremely important—we will cover this in greater depth as its own ingredient), reading together as a family, starting to read a book of interest to the older kids and laying it aside for them to complete, having frequent opportunities for them to perform or recite to the family or when visitors come (fair warning), playing games together with "skills," "data" or "principle" content such as Scrabble, Math-it, Outburst, Scattergories, Pictionary, Cashflow, etc., holding family mini-recitals for poetry, music, karate, etc., playing the Bean-Counter Game (another ingredient to be covered later), afternoon visits to the library and other venues rich in classical materials like zoos, aquariums, art or science museums, historical sites, etc..

The effectiveness of freedom truly recommends itself. More people should try it. As the children are free to fraternize and cooperate on their projects and interests (i.e. older kids making forts with the littles, or younger kids memorizing Shakespeare), older children are left with more natural compassion and innocence and younger children are invited into the world of "mature" activities, such as reading, drama and math manipulatives, through peer mentoring without any pressure or stigmatization. It is sheer play—Vygotsky, Piaget and Erikson style. Nothing gives us more joy than the devotion our little children feel toward their sixteen-year old brother—or the tenderness he shows them. We consider this one of the great blessings of our decision to pursue Leadership Education in our home. And none of this could happen if their time or content were over-programmed. These happy scenarios only appear in the right kind of vacuum.

Perhaps a comment on intervening circumstances would be appropriate. It is our observation that there are a high percentage of idealists and even perfectionists in the population that pursues Leadership Education. For their benefit, let us articulate that there *will* be intervening circumstances. These do not constitute failure, but opportunity. Examples of intervening circumstances:

- Mom has a new baby and is up frequently in the night, her energy not fully returned and is definitely a little out of focus where details are concerned.
- Shakespearean Festival (or whatever you do in your area) has us out very late to theatrical productions several nights in a three week period and we do not feel like getting up early.
- Olympics are on and we bring in a TV to watch them whenever we are not otherwise committed.
- Our next door neighbor ruptured a disk and we are over there several times a day to keep up on the dishes, fix meals and provide childcare.
- Dad is out of town and we decide to make it a totally outdoor play time without much heed to schedule.
- A couple of days to do a semi-annual "purge" on our belongings.
- Houseguests.

Obviously none of these or any other particular circumstances *require* that we do away with the routine. It is often meaningful to continue the routine even with a guest in the home. They can get a feel for what we do, see the family at its core, and even have the opportunity to be a part of the children's education in a more formal, intimate setting. This can build relationships, respect and rapport.

We bring these examples up to demonstrate the prerogative we have to adjust, abbreviate or even dispense with the routine to meet the family's needs. We would do ourselves a great disservice to value routine over opportunity. Still, we must be very careful not to treat the morning routine lightly, for its benefits are truly necessary for the function of the home, the unity of the family, and the success of Leadership Education. Any deviation from the routine should be considered carefully, and almost without exception should receive prior approval from the FEC.

Most of the wonderful things that compete with our morning routine truly can be put off until another time or foregone without grave loss. The value of a repetitive morning routine should not be outweighed by every little event or situation that presents itself. Once a morning routine is established and its benefits are felt, certain members of the family will naturally long for those benefits and the sacrifices necessary to get back on track are well worth the effort. It seems that the world is designed to distract from mornings, and successful leadership homes have learned how to shield themselves from distractions and have high quality mornings almost every day.

Ingredient #4: Kidschool

"Kidschool" is what we do with our Core and Love of Learning children that looks like "school." Of this time, Rachel says, "That is when I teach what's ***mine***." She shares whatever is personal and important to her with the children during this time. The subject matter can vary day to day, and always consists of what she is excited about.

By way of routine, Kidschool begins with a song, a prayer, and the Pledge of Allegiance. Of course, you will want to personalize this to your own family's beliefs, nationality and traditions. The Core Phase children may choose to take part or not depending on their daily interest. Frequently, they will be asked to lead the song or the pledge so that they feel like they are a part of what we do and are welcome whenever their interest invites them. We may have a pattern we follow in this opener, like singing a new song every day or working on memorizing a poem. Kidschool is a great example of structuring time, not content. Some other ideas for this opener might be:

1 Recite the Family Mission Statement
2 Child presents a prepared theatrical vignette
3 Child plays on her instrument to accompany singing

After the opener, the floor is Rachel's. Sometimes, if Rachel is involved in a big project (like writing this) or has an appointment (like Hyrum's Physical and Speech Therapy class), the kids will move on to their own projects and books right after the opener, and they all come together again for "zone check" right before lunch. But usually she takes some time, anywhere from thirty minutes to all morning long, to teach the children whatever she is in the mood for that day, and then to read to them from the novel of the day.

She might use some workbook pages on phonics she purchased at the grocery store as a resource, or a music theory clapping game she found at a thrift store; she often recurs to a graduated collection of poetry prepared by her brother-in-law Keith Lockhart for his private K-12 school. Sometimes she and the kids will pull out the math rods, "Take Your Hat Off When the Flag Goes By" or "Safety Kids," by Janeen Brady of Brite Music, Musical Notebooks™ by Camille McCausland, WeeSing America, etc. Some interesting anecdotes from past Kidschools:

1. Navel oranges were passed around and after they were peeled, we counted the segments. I got twelve, as did Emma (actually the thirteenth segment was eaten for my convenience). Then I asked Emma to divide the orange in half. She did so; I asked the kids to count how many segments of a 12-segment orange made one half. "Six." I asked them to divide the half in half. "Three!" I explained that half of a half was called a quarter,

or one fourth. We fit the whole orange back together again and I asked how many segments there were. "Twelve." What do we call one segment then? "...One twelfth?" Right! Now separate the orange into three equal parts. How many in each? "Four!" What do we call that? "Four twelfths?" Good! Can we use another more common way? (I had to prompt them—one third) "Oh, yeah. Duh!" (Now they were totally on to me) How many twelfths in one fourth? How many in one sixth? How many sixths in one third? How many sixths in one half? In two thirds? We played this way for the better part of a half hour. Then I got out a piece of paper and showed them how to express the fractions in written form. I made a column of simple problems using conversion of fractions and addition and subtraction of fractions with same and different denominators. That's where I lost them. Emma had fun with it for a little while but soon tired of it, Sara hung in but got frustrated, and then I knew I was into the ZPD and got out quick. I shoulda' quit while I was ahead!

2. I said to the kids, "Here's a poem by Robert Frost: 'We ran out of water so we went to the creek to get some more.'" They stared at me in disbelief. Oliver, who was home for the day in anticipation of a scout trip, said, voicing everyone's sentiment, 'That's it??!!' I said, 'Naw, here's what he really wrote:

The well was dry beside the door,
And so we went with pail and can
Across the field behind the house
To seek the brook if still it ran;

Not loath to have excuse to go,
Because the autumn eve was fair
(Though chill), because the fields were ours
And by the brook our woods were there.

We ran as if to meet the moon
That slowly danced behind the trees,
The barren boughs without the leaves,
Without the birds, without the breeze.

But, once within the wood, we paused
Like gnomes that hid us from the moon,
Ready to run to hiding new,
With laughter when she found us soon.

Each laid on other a staying hand
To listen ere we dared to look,
And in the hush we joined to make
We heard, we knew we heard the brook.

A note as from a single place,
A slender tinkling fall that made
Now drops that floated on the pool
Like pearls, and now a silver blade.

(Robert Frost, Going for Water)

They looked at me as if to say, "Now, that's more like it!" Emma added, "I love authors! That reminds me of the place in *The Phantom Tollbooth* when he takes two paragraphs just to say, 'Milo woke up.'" I had made that point one time while reading aloud to the kids several months back. (They remembered!!!)

3. The Bible was passed around, and we had a Love of Learning scripture search. I call out a reference (or a page number, for the younger kids) and they all raise their hand once they have found it. After everyone found the appointed place (with some hints and helps passed around to the younger children), I asked someone (not the first one—just anyone) to read and explain it. Next, we did a teaching activity. We each opened our Bible at random to a place in the book and then took turns teaching each other from our own two pages. The kids

could take a second try to find a "good one" if the first time opening yielded nothing they felt they wanted to teach. They loved this! They have requested this activity many times since. Their earnestness in teaching was touching and the depth was at times surprising.

4- I asked the kids if they liked riddles. They all said they did. I invited them to tell a few riddles. They had a good time with this for a while; then I said I wanted to take a turn. I told them I had a riddle in the form of a poem, and that the answer was the name of the poem. Here is the poem:

He clasps the crag with crooked hands;
Close to the sun in lonely lands,
Ring'd with the azure world, he stands.

The wrinkled sea beneath him crawls;
He watches from his mountain walls,
And like a thunderbolt he falls.

We spent some time defining the new vocabulary and talking about the texture and word choice, the repetition of sounds, etc. Then I asked them what the answer to the riddle was. After some guessing and visualization, I shared the title and author: "The Eagle," by Alfred Lord Tennyson. After so much discussion and banter it was a breeze to have them memorize it and take turns reciting for Bean-Counter (explanation follows soon). They still feel really cool whenever they get a chance to present this one from memory somewhere.

Now, inevitably we will have some people saying, "But I just can't think of things like that! You need to make a book of ideas and lessons for people like me!" The temptation to do this is not hard to resist. Remember the initial premise of Kidschool: "This is when I teach what's ***mine***." Thus we see the importance of a mother pursuing her own education. If you do not have a "mine," someone else's list will not get you much closer to having one.

But honestly—you *do* have a "mine." Even if all you have is lap time and a great book to share, *you* can give of yourself in ways that are most meaningful for *your* children for *their* mission. And your "mine" can grow daily richer with the treasures of knowledge and experience that you gain as you pursue your education. The passion for learning, the legacy of service and the joy in family that you manifest by the way you live will be treasures for your own children's "mines."

Ingredient #5: The Bean-Counter Game

An integral part of Kidschool that finds its way into many other places in our day is The Bean-Counter Game. This little invention is a vestige of a class we did long ago called "The Love of Learning Supplement." We had a group of thirty to forty kids from different families and different ages (eight through thirteen). Some were able to read and calculate, some were not. Some were from very "unschooled" environments, some were fresh out of public school, and we had everything in between. It was a challenge to try to create an optimal environment for all of them. In such a mixed group, we wanted to reward effort and excellence without hurting feelings or creating inappropriate competitiveness. So we decided to create a game that was much like life.

While we would probably never again attempt such a class (without exception we determined that everything that worked well in the class would have been even better on a sofa with a mom and siblings), we have continued The Bean-Counter Game in our own home. The Bean-Counter is simply a jar of garbanzos, pinto beans or whatever you have (dry of course) and a nice vase or just another jar to put them into. Whenever someone does anything correct, noteworthy or admirable, beans go from the jar to the vase. When the vase is full, an agreed-upon reward is meted out.

We like to make it both a personal reward and a service reward, as in: going to the city pool and buying passes for the slide and serving a meal at the local soup kitchen. This way, their success not only rewards them but blesses others.

The intrinsic lessons here are myriad. When anyone succeeds, all benefit. The helpless are still rewarded by the labors of the strong. This refers not only to the needy souls in the soup kitchen, but also to the four-year-old who did not get any beans for spelling but benefits because others spell well and gets to go swimming anyway. No one is resentful or jealous that Sara has mastered her 8 times tables; everyone gets closer to the Bean-Counter goal because of her prowess and they cheer her on! Her effort to help others has a more altruistic flavor because they are truly supportive of her success and she can afford to be generous and humble.

It is fun at times to be totally subjective and capricious in the awarding of beans so the game is never taken *too* seriously. Beans can be awarded to a twelve-year-old for having his shoes on the right feet, or for clean ears. Beans can be awarded for "acts of service which shall remain nameless but have come to the attention of the Bean-Giver." Beans can be awarded for being not-as-grumpy-as-one-might-have-been after too little sleep. This can take off the edge of correcting someone and turn it into a smile and a reminder to give your best effort even if you're feeling out of sorts.

A particular success of the Bean-Counter Game is that it gives a context in which mastery of otherwise useless things (for a kid in Love of Learning) has personal value, such as:

- spelling
- times tables
- penmanship
- punctuality
- good grooming
- exactness in obedience
- etc., etc., etc.

There is no reason under the sun why children MUST spell well as a Love of Learning kid, but if they do, they will probably get more beans. You are not going to hang privileges on their times tables mastery, but they might get more beans. You can have your kids begging you for things to study to get beans.

The game, like Pollyanna's "glad game," also has the virtue of removing the conveyor belt negative that so often accompanies things like spelling and penmanship. Not getting beans is not a punishment; they are awarded in a totally capricious manner. Getting beans is a celebration! It's the perfect one-sided principle. All gain, no pain.

Ingredient #6: The Six Month Purge

Every six months, purge your house. Throw away or donate anything you do not need. Then, donate what you think you might need but are not sure, and store whatever you really need but have not used lately and will not be using this month. Just make yourself do it.

This is hard work, and if it is emotionally challenging to you, you probably really need to do it. In one of our earliest Six Month Purges, we carried off three truck loads of good things to donate. We both remember unloading the truck into the donation bins, as Rachel re-debated each item and kept trying to convince herself that she should keep it. Five boxes of curriculum were the hardest. "We just don't know what we'll need in the next few years," we kept thinking. But we drove home with an empty truck and "freed up" brain cells.

In the following weeks the curriculum appeared on the store's shelves and was quickly purchased (Rachel was actually tempted to buy it—our things can be so enslaving!). Because there were fewer "things" cluttering the home, Rachel spent much less time cleaning—the newly discovered time was spent on education, relationships and family. Rachel finished her master's degree and prepared three Core kids for the coming Love of Learning Phase. Years later she did wish she had one of those books, and we shook our heads that we had let it go. Yet we found four copies of it for a dollar each at the very same second-hand store within a short time.

The Sixth Month Purge is essential, even for those who do not struggle at all with keeping the house clean. It gives you the chance to review everything on the TJEd bookshelf and in the TJEd closet (details later), notice a book whose time has arrived to be shared with the younger children, reorder certain supplies, or notice a lack of materials in an area of study that one of the children is starting to pursue. Purging the rest of the house identifies certain DVDs which are not really classics, clothes that can be used in the upcoming Shakespeare play, things that need to be thrown away or stored, etc.

The Six Month Purge is an important family event, one that is always followed by a burst of educational, creative and relationship energy. It also sets the stage for Ingredient #7: The Six Month "No" and Ingredient #8: The Six Month Inventory.

Ingredient #7: The Six Month "No"

Along with The Six Month Purge of your physical belongings and surroundings, it is important each six months to look inside and compare your real values with how you are spending your time. Every six months, make a thorough list of all you do, and then stop doing about half of it. Just say "no!"

The three biggest enemies of most mothers who mentor are chauffeuring, cooking and cleaning. Ingredient #6: The Six Month Purge is your twice-a-year attack on the latter, and Ingredient #7: The Six Month "No," is the bi-annual war on the first. By "chauffeuring" we mean all the things you do just to get people places and wait in between things. Some moms spend two hours a day or more in their minivans or SUVs. That could be time spent studying, learning, teaching and building relationships! (By the way: to make the most of the chauffeuring time that remains on the list of to-do's even after the purge, get to know your library's selection of audio books. You'll be amazed what a treasure this time can become!)

We know that some of it simply cannot be helped. You have real responsibilities that require your time. We also know that even if you figured out the perfect way to fix this, a force as strong as gravity would just fill your time back up again in the next six months. We also know that you have the power to say "no." You may not think you do, but you do. Some years back, Rachel had to be forced to submit to a long overdue Six Month "No." A string of challenges had brought her to an all-time low of health and vitality. Her pregnancy in 2001 was very difficult both physically and emotionally, and the labor and delivery were her most trying. Complications in recovery left her on her back for a month, and just 9 weeks later our little three month old infant, Hyrum, was critically injured in a car accident. She spent almost six weeks by Hyrum's side at the Primary Children's Medical Center with Oliver and the children left to care for one another and accept the kind service of countless angels of mercy.

Upon her return home, the family breathed with a collective sigh of relief, "Mom's home!" She smoothed over the anxieties and put the home back together. But Hyrum's medical needs were stressful and extremely time-consuming for months to come. Slowly, the family began to trust that life was back to normal, and regular life resumed.

After another pregnancy we were thrilled to welcome America Esther to the family. Hyrum's needs still consumed much of Rachel's time and energy, and she was teaching classes, running clubs and trying to be Oliver's partner. Her health continued to decline to the point that for several weeks the children were in other people's care as much as they were in her own. At this point she was humbled enough to accept what Oliver had been urging her to understand: she had to say "no." It astonished her that she was willing to "kiss good-bye" things that only two weeks before had seemed like moral imperatives. We made a long list and just started crossing things out. Rather than losing opportunities, we found we were gaining something that had been missing—Rachel's ability to be a great mother and mentor to our seven children.

In retrospect, Rachel felt sorry that she did not care better for her physical well-being. She learned in a very concrete way that "it is better to obey than to sacrifice." Putting her health on the altar under the circumstances was a dis-service to all those she was trying to help. She worried that her poor example had been internalized by her children who had once been so health-conscious.

It is exciting to see that her recent "new leaf" is being supported and even modeled by the children, who are also being very conscientious about their nutrition and exercise now. The point of this story is this: Rachel had the power at several junctures to make changes in her outside commitments, but was not willing to let go of anything. When she was faced with literal exhaustion, she happily allowed Oliver to take her through an exercise—a list of commitments followed by a Six Month "No"—which resulted in meaningful changes in her schedule over several weeks time. She had done this routinely in years past, but The Six Month "No" is something that must be repeated each six months. It is regretful that we had to come to such a crisis before changes were made. You can perhaps benefit from our experience.

You do have the power to say "no." You cannot do it all. Be honest. Things suffer when you keep filling your time. It may be your family education, your personal study, your relationships, your health (we make different food choices under duress of over scheduling), your finances (we budget and spend differently when we are stressed and rushed) or your peace.

You have to be in touch with the hierarchy of duties that flows from you—personal, spiritual, marital, parental and intellectual. When the list gets very much longer, energy can be inappropriately diffused. There is a right balance, and one of the great challenges in life is to get the inspiration to keep things in balance as seasons change and needs evolve. When you have the foresight and courage to do a periodic evaluation, you can spot trends and clues to coming changes and adjust your commitments. Often in a family, one spouse thinks she can do everything, and one is savvy to limitations. Be trusting of the counsel of the savvy one, and utilize the FEC to set limits and make decisions.

It really works. In fact, it is hard to make things work without it. You *can* say no, and when you do, things change. And if you do it every six months, at the same time as Ingredient #6: The Six Month Purge and Ingredient #8: The Six Month Inventory, you will see real change. It will not last forever, and you will have to fight the same battle again. But you will win the war. You will cut things that you would otherwise just keep doing, and you will spend more hours doing meaningful things with baby, toddlers, youth and family members that you used to think you would never have time to do. Learning occurs. Not in years, but in hours; and if you gain two more hours a day for three months you have added a full public school year of study (averaging 54 minutes of study per day per a 180 day school year as did Adler in his study of public school students). That does not seem like much, but if you do it for six years, that is a Scholar Phase—and that is huge!

So make a thorough list, and start slashing things you think you just *have* to do. An hour is a powerful, precious, once-in-a-lifetime, never-to-be-repeated opportunity to do the work of God in your role as parent and statesman. Every six months you will be overdue for a big purge and a big "no" to about half of the time-clutter on your list.

Ingredient #8: The Six Month Inventory

Right after you do your Six Month Purge and cross off some activities in a Six Month "No," take an afternoon to do a Six Month Inventory. Find a peaceful place to sit alone where you can relax for a while. This may be your family room or bedroom or the library or a park.

List each child—and anyone else you mentor—at the top of their own page.

Then spend some time to ponder, consider, brainstorm, pray, question, plan, etc., concerning each individual. Do not make a list of assignments to give, but rather list things you can/should do. This "to do" list if for You, not Them. Consider the following questions for each child/youth:

- What are his/her biggest interests?
- What are his/her greatest fears?
- What are his/her fondest dreams?
- What are his/her top needs in the next six months?
- What should I do to help fulfill those needs?
- What else do I need to know?
- What else should I do?

Write bullet points filling at least one page per person that you mentor. Do not take time to analyze your thoughts, or even decide which are good and which will not work. Just write down everything that comes to mind. Then, go through each item and weave together an action plan for each person. This takes time, and it takes some hard mental work. But it is exactly this work that makes you a mentor.

To be honest, this will not do much good unless you are willing to do The Sixth Month Purge and The Six Month "No" and you will not use it much if you do not have Sunday FECs and interviews. But if you combine these most basic of ingredients, you have the makings of a powerful recipe for superb Leadership Education. Your children deserve it—they were born with important, world-shaping and universe-shifting missions. What a tragedy when their parents fail them by not situating family life so family members can pursue an education that is up to the tasks they have ahead.

Frankly, it is not part of our personal mission to improve the house cleaning of the world—there are other more qualified experts than us to help you with cleaning. What we are interested in is the education of the leaders of the future, and they live in your homes. We teach The Six Month Purge and The Six Month "No" so that The Six Month Inventory will happen, because when it does, a great education will occur and a leader will be trained.

Ingredient #9: The Annual Project

Each year, the whole family gets involved in a big project. One year it was a play—all our Scholar and Love of Learning students auditioned and were cast, the Core Phasers stayed home but loved home rehearsals, kitchen table discussions and attending all five nights of dress rehearsals and performances. By the end, even our Core Phasers could quote much of the play. One year it was Shakespeare's *A Midsummer Night's Dream*, another year it was a musical revue built around *The Wizard of Oz*. One year our family's annual project was a big family banquet and gala with over 300 attendees. All of our children from Core through Scholar participated in the arrangements, rehearsals, and sang in the two performance choirs, followed by a formal ball.

One young man we know did an excellent community fundraiser where he brought in over $9,000 for the internationally acclaimed Wheelchair Foundation. Our son, Hyrum, got to participate in the program by going out on stage to show off his shiny red wheelchair. This was done as an Eagle Scout Project, but as we attended, we could tell it had become a Family Annual Event.

There are many ways to do The Annual Project. One year Emma and Sara made performing at the local County Fair their project. They learned to sing and sign a song. The whole family got involved and everyone learned. Another young man we know trained for and ran a marathon with his father. Dr. Shanon Brooks took his kids for weeks of hiking in the high Rockies, down the Continental Divide. The planning of details and months of physical conditioning for this was considerable. Our brother, Alma DeMille, of Monticello, Utah, helped his daughter Ami win a national trail riding competition in her age division. The Goodrich family of Mountain Home, Idaho, went to Mexico to give humanitarian service. One year, we spent a month in Missouri giving our kids a real farm experience with their grandparents, hauling 22 tons of hay, freezing berries, making pickles, learning to drive tractors and ride horses. On yet another occasion, we organized an event for our private school, Colesville Academy, where over 160 individuals (grandparents, parents and Colesville students) went together to SeaWorld armed with marine biology workbooks and two months of preparation and marine life study.

The Annual Project needs to fit your family and be right for you, and it is an exciting ingredient in fostering a successful Core and Love of Learning environment. The Annual Project seldom impacts or competes with Mornings, but it can cut into Afternoons, Evenings and Weekends. That is okay as long as it does not become a "year-round" project. A once-a-year Annual Project is about right for most families. More than that is probably too much. The most important thing about The Annual Event is for parents to do things with the children, not just send them off to somebody else's tutelage.

Ingredient #10: The Annual Break

In agrarian times, schools naturally broke for summer so students could provide additional manpower to the farm. Most schools today still follow that pattern, though few contemporary children work much compared to agrarian standards. The Leadership Education model considers 180 school days far too few for Scholar Phase, and even too light for most Love of Learning students. About ten months of school is best for most families, punctuated by a big month-long break twice a year or a two-month annual break. Unless you live on a farm and need heavy spring and fall manpower from the whole family, almost any time of the year will work for the break. But it is best if it is planned and anticipated, allowing for a set time to catch up on things which might conflict with the more structured school routine.

If parents are doing it right, their Core Phase students will hardly know the difference between the breaks and the regular school year. They will still have a morning routine, Kidschool and morning play, games, manipulatives, reading time, and art and science projects throughout the summer. Love of Learning students will not see much change to their mornings either, but they will get to play more with friends in the afternoons. Scholar Phase students will see a real change, since they will be freed from challenging studies for the month. Often Scholars can be persuaded to lead activities and play times for Core and Love of Learners during the break. They usually find this really fun—a chance to share some of what they have learned and to revisit old interests.

It is interesting that in these breaks, Scholar and Depth Phasers usually keep studying some anyway, just for the fun of it, because they are learning things that really interest them. But it is also important that during such breaks they take more time to interact, work, play, and study with everyone else in the family. To get them to do this, it may be necessary to plan some specific events that get them away from their studies. For example, our family typically takes breaks the first two weeks of July and the last two weeks of December. There are so many holidays and parties during this time that Dad can not just read books all day—he has to go to events, fairs, parties, park activities and church get-togethers. And if he tries to get out of it, the weekly FEC helps him realize that he is shirking important fatherly duties (and by the way, the FEC solution works whether the "addiction" is books, movies, work, golf, hunting, cars, sports, or whatever it may be. Just remember the "Tevye Principle": shower love on the spouse and take concerns to the Lord. No nagging!).

Sometimes part of The Annual Break can and should include time away for Dad or Mom for a conference or seminar, a romantic getaway, hunting, a trip to an historical site, or something else they really want to attend. In our family, since we have only used four weeks of break total between July and December, there is time for smaller breaks as needed. We know a family that takes a break every May and December for basically the whole month.

Again, each family should apply this principle to their unique situation, but The Annual Break is a key ingredient to any off-the-conveyor-belt family. Students will study better when there is a natural flow from school to break time, and the breaks provide important mentoring opportunities which cannot happen in traditional academic settings. Camping is perhaps the most powerful mentoring environment possible because of the lasting memories it often creates, the removal of distractions, the necessity of family interaction and opportunities to work together and the virtually limitless supply of classical materials in the beautiful outdoors to ponder and learn from.

Ingredient #11: Afternoons

Afternoons are for setting the example. After a morning routine, a structured learning time, activities, lunch and clean up, the Core Phasers will be ready to nap or play. The Love of Learners will be involved in projects most days, but sprinkle the week with a couple of afternoon activities with friends, clubs or outside projects. Mom now has time to set the example of Scholar, Depth or Mission Phase, depending on where she is at. Once every week or two she may use the afternoon to be mentored (or mentor others, if she is in Mission Phase), another afternoon she helps a Love of Learning or Scholar Phase club, but most afternoons she is home studying or working on projects. Sometimes this means reading a book, other times she is writing an article or preparing a speech, practicing the piano or cooking dinner for a sick neighbor. Another day she plans the garden, a month later she uses the afternoon to plan a summer vacation. In between, she is reading and writing, often asking children and youth for their thoughts and input on whatever she is learning or the plan she is making, whether it be a church dinner or a 4th of July concert, for example.

This example is not lost on the children, who learn much more from what they watch us do consistently than from what we assign them. Some of the things our children and Rachel have participated in include: designing t-shirts for a youth conference, developing a catering plan for an upcoming executive retreat, making and marketing tamales for a community fundraiser, creating picture books for third world orphanages, making blankets for the regional pediatric hospital, compiling a collection of fully-stocked school backpacks for the local Family Support Center for children in crisis, and gathering a collection of reading materials for all ages for the Women's Shelter. Of course, these projects were taken on one at a time, with time in between!

Afternoons see wide use of the sand box and lawn, as well as the teepee in the back yard and an assortment of sticks that live in our yard—mostly by Core Phasers Ammon and Hyrum. When fingers get too cold from the snow or pants too full of sand, little feet trudge back into the house to find Mom reading from a current bestseller or with a worn classic in her lap, following up on family duties, studying Hebrew or French, researching current events online or corresponding with one of her many friends, or on the phone arranging a service opportunity. In such examples, lessons are taught. Afternoons are for setting an example, and interruptions from little people are welcome.

During Afternoons, we may have a family over to visit. We try to make friendships as family units where possible. We make choices about how we invest our time, and we nurture those relationships family-to-family where possible. If a child makes a friend that is a soul-mate, we reach out as a family to include their whole family in our community of friends. We do not often send one child to another child's home. Usually they visit in a minimum of twos and threes. When they were younger, it was almost always a visit that included Mom and this is still not uncommon. We find that after several years, many of these families are like family to us and our children.

One of the more difficult things we deal with is the transition from afternoon to evening. It is time to put the house in order and prepare for family time "just when we were getting to the good part!" as ten-year-old Sara put it. Nonetheless, the power of routine helps us achieve our vision for what we want as a family. At a designated time, we try to make sure the house is in order and begin preparation for the evening, doing meal prep and animal chores. If everyone is tidy and prompt, they can continue to "goof off" and enjoy free time until it is almost time for Dad to get home from work.

Ingredient #12: Evenings

Evenings are for inspiring. "Inspire, not Require" is the most challenging of the Seven Keys of Great Teaching, at least for those of us with a conveyor belt background. It is the most talked about and least applied of the Keys. It is also every bit as important as each of the other six. But inspiring greatness is challenging. It is the fundamental job of statesmen, religious leaders, teachers and parents. As C.S. Lewis taught, God does not want us to grow up to be just his servants, his gophers or errand boys. He wants us to be a different kind of creature altogether, one he can trust and give full stewardships and talents and then leave and come back to see that we have used, expanded and made them flourish. That is what Leadership Education wants out of education: real "men with chests" (read *The Abolition of Man* by Lewis to follow up on that thought) who stand with courage and wisdom and do what is needed, and real women who face the world with knowledge of what is right and the virtue and strength to bring it to pass. Such is the goal of educating boys and girls—to make them men and women of strength, virtue, wisdom, and courage.

American schools used to share this goal, and their curriculum and methods were designed to match. Washington and Jefferson wrote extensively about this. But in the 1930s this goal was eroded from two sides. The liberal agenda promoted a new goal of social change—more tolerant, less discerning, more caring students were to be the new crop of the schools. At the same time, the conservative scheme advocated job training as the new purpose of schooling—skilled, corporate-socialized, well-behaved workers were the esteemed products of the schools. Never mind that "virtue" already meant tolerant and caring, while "strength" already required skill and dedication. The new schools were to drop the training of great individuals, adults, parents, and citizens. Instead, tolerant voters and competent workers were the prize.

With these new goals, it appeared (wrongly) that inspirational teachers were no longer needed. They were replaced with those who best exemplified the new values of liberal caring and conservative certification. Most of today's parents were educated on the conveyor belt, and this is what education means to them. When they choose "alternative" education, this is all they know—so they attempt to duplicate it, albeit in a home or private setting.

The most damaging result of this is that few teachers or parents understand the central role of teaching—which is to inspire. Teachers are to educate themselves, and to inspire others. That is what teaching means; it is what teaching is. When teachers inspire, students study. When students study, they learn. This is not a complex formula. But it is a difficult one to teach to the third generation of people "educated" by conveyor belt "require" methods.

Indeed, it always amazes us when we read the public commentary and discussion about Leadership Education. Ironically, the two biggest complaints are that Scholar Phase is too hard and the Love of Learning Phase is too easy. But at a deeper level, there is a real flaw in this commentary. There is nothing more challenging in the entire educational world than an excellent Love of Learning Phase. Day in and day out, week after week and year after year, the parent-teacher's role is to inspire the child to happily, consistently and unswervingly study, learn, search, discover, enlighten, know and apply. The sad reason that people think Love of Learning is "easy" is that they have been brainwashed by the conveyor belt. When they hear "Inspire, not Require," their brains are so conditioned against combining "inspire" with "education" that they actually go home remembering something very much like "ignore, not require."

Nowhere in the Thomas Jefferson model do we advocate ignoring the student. There are two easy shortcuts (a misnomer, actually, as they do not actually result in arrival at the destination) to education: ignore or require. The third type of education, Inspire, is extremely challenging. The conveyor belt seems to have conditioned this generation to believe that if you are not requiring, you are neglecting, and to say "inspire" is just an excuse to ignore.

But that is the conveyor belt, not the Leadership Education, approach. There truly are inspiring teachers—thousands of them. And there truly are thousands of inspirational parents whose students study—hard—because they love learning. In the past fifteen years, we have personally seen thousands of families with parents who have gotten off the conveyor belt and become inspiring examples to their children and youth. In almost every case, the youngsters have followed their parents' example.

It all comes down to inspiring. And evenings are the Universe's gift to those who want to inspire. Have you ever noticed how many high-level political and religious addresses are offered in the evening? They may have morning events too, but through history and in our current world when statesmen or others want to really make a point, they do it in the evening. Oliver gives speeches at leading American corporate events, and invariably they do the training and socializing during the day and the important bonding events and paradigm-shifting speeches in the evening. They do it because it works, and yet the typical American family seems content to let television be its center of inspiration. That is both fascinating and tragic. The current degenerate and deteriorating state of the family is the lamentable consequence.

Those with whom we spend our evening are those with whom we bond. This is one reason we discourage "sleepovers." A friend told an account of a camping trip they took with several other families of like mind and wonderful spirit. The young ladies were allowed to have their own tent, and by morning they were off giggling and playing together, ignoring everyone else. The friend remarked that it felt a little strange to experience that distance from her daughter for the first time, but she supposed it was inevitable and even healthy.

We hope not. We believe that the bonding that took place might easily have been with parents and siblings, with a totally different outcome. Although nothing evil took place and the friendship was one the families were glad to encourage, the bonds might have been different, and the "centeredness" could have been different. Whatever your stand on "sleepovers," your family must make considered choices if you are training leaders, and evenings must be one of the things at the center. This is one of the great things for Scholar Phase scouts and other camps and youth conferences: youth bond with other admirable adults to reinforce, simulate and illustrate parental teaching.

Youth very naturally long for the passion of being inspired, although many would probably not say so or even admit it explicitly. This is one of the reasons they so often want to be away every evening, to do something fun, to feel alive, passionate, real. This is all the more reason that inspiring evenings for Core and Love of Learning kids should be the rule. Such evenings are numbered before youth will have other things competing with the family circle. If we have a legacy of evening inspiration, they will see wholesomeness as the norm. They will be much less likely to be seduced by the flash and sparkle of external offerings, and will have a more healthy appetite for worthy entertainment and relationships.

It is not too much of an exaggeration to say that in the evening we are all inspired—by something, to something. Sometimes the something is good—or not; sometimes it is planned and led by the parents to help the children—or not. Evenings are for inspiration; and we can be inspired for greatness or otherwise. If you have struggled to inspire, not require, and it just does not seem to work, look closely at your evenings. If there is something you really want to inspire, consider what evening event will best accomplish it.

Perhaps the easiest evening inspiration is just reading a great book together as a family. This teaches and inspires on so many levels. Board games can be good, trivia or quiz games, cookouts around the campfire with singing, working in the garden together in the evening dusk, sitting around outside and waiting to count the stars together, telling stories of ancestors by the fireplace or grill, "shooting hoop" in the driveway or tossing a football on the front lawn. A variety is good over the year. But in our opinion, the evening reading of a great book is still the best because it is simply the most inspiring. Finally, a caution concerning movies: they are certainly inspirational, sometimes for bad. The good ones, the classics, the ones you watch over and over like *Pride and Prejudice*, *It's a Wonderful Life, The Quiet Man, Pollyanna, The Robe*, should only be used occasionally in evenings; movies that do not inspire desirable sentiments are poor choices for evenings, if they are to be viewed at all. First run movies in the theater are often risky ventures, and we prefer matinees not only for the bargain rate but because they do not become "evening" activities.

The Hebrews taught that the day started not at sunrise, but at sundown each evening. Thus, the most important part of the day in the Hebrew tradition is the evening, since how you spend your evening has the most impact on your entire day. The Hebrews taught that we should start the day with making each evening wonderful. A good day will naturally follow. In the West, with our emphasis on morning and our use of the evening as entertainment, it is not surprising that we have lost touch with the inspirational, the heavenly and the eternal. Our pragmatic realism is an illness, one easily reinforced by our poor evening choices.

Evenings are inspirational. Be wise about what you inspire.

Applying the First Twelve Ingredients

Before going onto the next chapter, consider the following recommendations on applying the first twelve ingredients to your life based on where you are in your family. If you want to really increase the quality of your educational environment, look to Sunday planning, Morning routine, and Evening inspiration as the three most powerful ingredients. If you feel frustrated because you do not seem to have sufficient time or energy for Leadership

Education in your home, start with The Six Month Purge, The Six Month "No" and The Six Month Inventory. If family bonding and cooperation are in need of focus, or you are trying to break out of a conveyor belt mentality in your family, plan an Annual Project or Break for your family. Moms who feel competing pulls in seeking to nurture their Core and Love of Learning children and feeling the need for personal development of their own, would benefit by working on having a really excellent Kidschool in the morning, the Bean-Counter to encourage learning and good behavior throughout the day, and Afternoons for a book in hand, personal project or a family-to-family visit at the park.

We recommend the following sequence: Begin with a specific, achievable goal for yourself, implement change, experience progress, enjoy the fruits of your labors, repeat. But wait! There's more! Keep reading for even more great ingredients that will assist you in developing a leadership home that supports each family member in their progress through the phases.

CHAPTER FOUR

Core And Love Of Learning: Ingredients 13-30

So much more goes on in and about a leadership home than in those houses which predominantly serve as "quick stops" or "drop and runs." This chapter of ingredients focuses on how to organize the activities that occur on the inside and outside your home. Attention paid to the following ingredients will help you make your home and the living that happens within and outside of it supportive of the leadership goals you have for yourself and family members.

Ingredient #13: Winters

Winters are for stories. In our agrarian past, people worked hard from spring through fall, and took winters off as a natural time to share the learning of the past. Indeed, Scholar Phase was the norm in agrarian society. Much of a farmer's work was done for the year when the snow fell, and winter was a time of learning.

With modern technological advances, it is possible to hurdle some of the challenges posed by weather. We can sit comfortably air-conditioned in the summer and hardly notice the cold if we stay mostly inside during winter. But nature knows her business, and our learning cycles seem hard-wired in us. Winter is a time for stories and study.

Many Native American Indian tribes still carry the tradition that winter is a time to sit around and listen long into the night to the old stories, told by the elders of the tribe. Spring and summer bring hunting and moving and work, and fall is a frenzied push to prepare. Winter, on the other hand, is the time to tell the old stories, sing the old songs, and for the younger generation to learn the wisdom of the elder. Many other cultures share similar traditions, and even today most schools build their calendar upon the vestiges of the old agrarian school year. Any high school teacher (except track or baseball coaches; but then, those pursuits are consistent with their season, which we will cover later) can tell you that May is often a wasted month.

Winters are for stories. Not just any stories—but mainly the stories of family, ancestor, founder and pioneer past. In short, winters are when we pass on that which is classic.

Whatever your heritage, winter is the natural time to pass it on to the next generation. Morning routine changes little with the seasons, perhaps starting a little later in the cold, but following the same basic itinerary. Afternoon projects are more inside, as opposed to warmer weather activities in the sunshine. But evenings take on special importance in the winter.

Just as the Hebrews start their day with sundown, agrarian societies also started their year with spring and the new annual birth of earth late March to early April. Through the years as we have planned adult classes, the calendar always seemed short to the parents involved; but when April began they found their previous passion for the class waning as nature called them to move on to the next thing!

The activities of body in spring, summer and fall prepare the mind for yet another significant annual learning spurt from October through April. While mornings, afternoons and evenings can be used for learning year round, the natural time of significant paradigm shifts and great learning is winter. The stories anchor us to the important and inspire us to achievement in the months ahead—like seeds gathering strength to suddenly bloom with incredible speed once winter ends.

Winter is an annual seasonal return to Core Phase, where our vulnerability to the elements and the stark reality around us remind us of right and wrong, good and bad, true and false, play and work, home and love. Our absolute attachment to these most important things is easily forgotten in the warmth and sunlight of budding spring's love of learning, the heat and hard work of growing summer's scholar intensity, and fall's necessary depth in preparation for the test ahead. The farmer who was our ancestor surely felt these things—they were real and very corporeal—and so he probably understood them much better than we do from our abstract comparisons.

But the same genetic tendencies and natural rhythms still go with us to buy our school clothes, start the first day of a new school year, long to leave the classroom when the sun comes out for spring, and feel perpetually bored with our lazy summers—our body knows better and it will not let us enjoy anything less than the hard work we naturally crave.

Scholar Phase has a special expression in Winter. The first lesson of Core Phase is doing what is right; and at a certain age the right thing is to get the great education we each need for our powerful mission in life. Like the young man whose summer sweat starts early in the morning as he goes to work, the youth in Scholar Phase feels so much happier and better than the lazy boy sleeping in until ten a.m. who awakens to a day of Nintendo, or his educational counterpart who plays through high school and learns very little. Whether he gets poor grades or straight A's, he is still the boy rather than the young man.

Winters make men. Rome became the ruler of the world as long as she followed Alexander's example and only marched south, attacking nations with milder climates. But the men raised on the winters of the north countries rode through Rome like they were fighting small children. Napoleon missed this lesson in his studies and paid dearly for it. Montesquieu, the philosopher most quoted by the American Founders, was right when he noted that only nations with cold climates have ever bred cultures of freedom. There are no big exceptions in history—except the Israelites, and their freedom was born in the opposite extreme of the desert. The natural seasons are God's school bell, and he rings it with excellent efficiency.

If you live in a perpetually spring-like climate, there is still a need to respect the seasons and treat education accordingly. Even if the weather does not signal the old agrarian model, the length of the day usually does. Winter is a time of family closeness, especially in the inspiring evenings, a time for classics, stories and the sharing of that which is most important.

Ingredient #14: Summers

Summers are for family, especially work projects, evening work, and family activities. In the heat of the afternoon, Scholars read while Core and Love of Learners watch the example of Scholar and Depth parents and older siblings. Morning routine is basically the same as the rest of the year, but specific afternoon activities move outside while evenings are less about reading and more about work and play together. It is still a good idea to have a great book going, though perhaps only one to four evenings a week instead of six or seven like in winter.

In climates with four strong seasons, summer is like winter in that the afternoons drive us to our books. Indeed, in some locales where winter is play time, summer is actually too hot to be outside—so reading and learning is the norm for the afternoon. Travel and vacations are excellent opportunities for educational breadth, but this requires parents to do their homework beforehand. Most modern Americans drive right past historical sites without so much as slowing down and pointing. In contrast, the educated parent can teach much by telling the stories ahead of time, then stopping and taking the time to feel the place, to ponder the events which occurred there. Time can be spent afterwards discussing the experience.

In our modern return to nomadism, there is a real need for summer connections with extended family—especially grandparents, aunts, uncles and cousins. It is a sad circumstance of our modern lifestyle that families that once occupied the same residence now may scarcely see the inside of one another's homes. The multi-generational family with cousins and their parents being part of the immediate family is a thing of the past for most of us, but we can use summertime to forge those bonds and build relationships and experiences of inestimable value. These relationships need not be tenuous and transient.

In fact, the history of freedom admonishes families to follow the model of our great-grandparents and their great-grandparents. Great education and real freedom developed from our agrarian roots. Indeed, the past shows us real education and freedom occurring only in fundamentally agrarian societies, so it is culturally vital to find ways around our current society's nomadic tendencies. Nomadic societies were ever bastions of ignorance and tyranny, while industrial societies have proven to be mostly democratic, abounding in specialized training yet lacking in lasting freedoms and virtually devoid of ennobling education. This creates a class system—one where the under classes are unaware that they are being used, and the upper classes are prisoners of the system that leaves them without friends, family or freedom.

In our post-modern world, with its combination of the nomadic and the post-industrial culture, we desperately need the consistent connection with extended family, and summer is an opportune time for many people to make such connections. Whereas the conveyor belt pulls the generations apart by focusing on innovation and specialized training, Leadership Education naturally bonds the generations by emphasizing that which endures.

As recently as ten years ago, Grandma and Grandpa were likely to be quite antagonistic toward educational alternatives, but today they are probably excited to help. Try asking them to turn the summer vacation into an educational mini-school for the grandchildren, passing on their stories, skills, knowledge and values. Where grandparents are unavailable or unwilling, much the same might be accomplished with a good organization of aunts and uncles or other seasoned folks from your community.

Summers are a good time to sweat, something the last two generations have largely forgotten to teach (or been unwilling to learn). Some of this can be the "assigned" kind, where the young person has daily stewardships that require hard physical labor, but much of it should be done together as a family. If you outsource the care of the grounds and home, the children might be suffering for lack of meaningful work. A very important part of Core and Love of Learning Phases is to work together daily with parents. A vital part of Love of Learning is the mastery of skills which make one a confident and competent young man or woman. Those living on farms tend to find the phases naturally; those in other settings need to give work (work that the family really depends upon) to young family members. In our affluent society, we often think we are helping a child by not requiring him to do real work. In reality, we are stunting his development.

One family of our acquaintance has used day hikes as a metaphor for life and education. Apart from the physical exercise and family-bonding recreation, they have reinforced many invaluable principles. The young hikers get to learn many vital lessons regarding preparation—from the type of footwear and clothing chosen, to the physical conditioning, to the availability of water and food, etc. They learn lessons in courage and perseverance, and the thrill of doing what you thought you could not and half-way through were *sure* you did not really want to do. They learn about cooperation and sacrifice, as one takes on more work to help another on their way and so facilitates everyone's success. So many lessons have been discussed, and more importantly, internalized, as a result of this family's summer pastime.

One half of getting a Leadership Education is gaining the knowledge base of a true scholar, the other half is developing the skills, abilities and habits of action and impact, the type of skills used by a great entrepreneur or statesman. Where winters emphasize the former, summers are indispensable in training young men and women of action. A wide variety of summer activities is best during Scholar and Depth Phases, with different jobs, internships and projects taken on each summer.

In Core Phase, basic home chores and work with other family members is best. Love of Learners do the same and begin to master homemaking and other skills that prepare them to manage their own future home. Oliver James started gathering wood at age five and by age eight was in charge of keeping the wood boxes full, the fires built, and the house warm. This was real work the family actually depended upon, as the wood stove was how we heated the home. He started milking at six and by age nine had full charge of our little goat herd. At age eight, he started helping Dad with yard care each summer, which he then took over (okay, with some nagging) at age ten. The lawns, trees, flowers, fruit trees, garden and shrubs all depend upon him for life and summer beautification. Dad does the chores with Oliver James quite often, and continues to teach ways for Oliver James to improve the animal care. When it is time to haul hay, Dad does most of it with Oliver James helping more and more each year. Digging ditches and planting trees are part of the annual process, and of course the whole family takes part in planting, weeding, and harvesting the crops. Young Oliver is learning to manage the dual nature of his role as a scholar who leaves the home to study all day and as caretaker who manages home duties upon his return. Oliver James is now helping Dad to train Ammon to replace him in the years ahead.

One of the great things about the phases, especially in large families, is that each child gets a chance to come of age. In modern practice, we see families where older children are never released from family childcare duties, and the younger ones never have the respect of the older ones until late in life, if at all. In the Leadership

Education model, the transition to becoming a youth in Scholar Phase means the chores of childhood are passed on to the next family members coming up, or passed back to parents if there are no younger children prepared to take them on. The Scholar has new status in the home with special responsibilities (study all day and full charge of stewardships at home) and privileges (much less errand-running and childcare, more prerogative—though not absolute—over such personal things as nutrition and bedtime). The younger ones are primed and excited to be "bigs" instead of "littles," and come with a great attitude toward chores that the older children have mastered and are ready to pass on and revel in their new respect and responsibilities.

Emma and Sara have had bunnies which required daily care, Sara has a dog (affectionately named "Laddie" after Gene Stratton-Porter's exemplary character) and Ammon had two dozen chickens which older siblings took care of while he was being trained to be responsible. Emma started doing errands around the house at about age five, and in Love of Learning she was responsible for the order, cleanliness and beauty of the upstairs. As a Scholar, she is now in charge of the dishes and her studies, with a turn caring for Hyrum's needs several times a week. Sara, who started helping at a similar age, became in charge of the beauty and order of the downstairs and full charge of the laundry during Love of Learning. As a Scholar, she is now in charge of the downstairs. Rachel took the laundry back. When Eliza was just seven, she was in training with both Emma and Sara, but preferred doing the milking and outside chores with Oliver and Ammon. She was back and forth between not wanting more responsibility and being pleased with the status that gradually came to her as she became more able and more dependable. Now in Love of Learning, she has responsibility for the upstairs and all five bathrooms.

Mom is there all day, oversees it all, does most of the cooking and lots of the training for all the children. Sara and Emma consider it an act of service if she does a load of or dishes or works on the downstairs. Were it not for the additional load of caring for a disabled brother, the kids would probably have all the cooking and housework split between them with Rachel as manager, trainer and facilitator.

As our good friend Cherie Logan put it, "If you're still doing the housework, you missed your promotion!" Neil and Cherie Logan's family is a great example of everyone learning to do everything, regardless of their gifts or interests. The babies had a relationship with every child as their caregiver, and the bonding between the children and compassion and affection that abounds in their home is truly something to be emulated. Each child is competent in the kitchen, and the kids are quite adept at eating what is put in front of them as the young ones have had their turn to cook. All do laundry, scrub floors and bathrooms, etc. With nine kids to raise, Cherie had ample time to manage the household (note we said manage, not do everything herself), oversee the education of the kids, continue her own classical education, maintain a popular web site on mothering and homeschooling, hold classes in communication and learning styles, do a weekly class for teens, and research thousands upon thousands of genealogical names.

Neil and Cherie have been a great inspiration to us on many points of family culture. Their children are well-read, articulate, poised, accomplished, creative, active and independent. We remember wondering if our kids would be as nice to each other as they are, and love to study like they do. Guess what? They are, and they do.

Our style has been intrinsically "agrarian." We simply could not imagine how to have the kind of family culture our grandparents did without having the environment and activities that they had. So we chose to have a little farm. It may not be much by some standards, but it was just right for what we intended. The yard, the animals and the home required our attention as if the homestead were a part of the family. We had to take care of it so it could take care of us.

We have since moved to a different home that more specifically meets the special needs of our handicapped son. Rachel does much more of the housework and cooking than she would if he were not handicapped, because his situation requires that we all take turns giving him full-time care, and this is a considerable time commitment. With her contribution to the housework the kids have more time to study.

Our recommendation to those who do not live in a place where farming is possible is to manage their living situation and modify it, as needed, to attain the specific educational results desired. For some this may seem drastic, but in fact it is a huge national trend. Tens of thousands of highly trained middle-aged professionals are moving from the suburbs to the "exurbs" as a matter of lifestyle. Many are seeing increased salaries as they turn entrepreneurial, and even those who downsize their lifestyle are reporting that their quality of life is significantly upgraded.

One friend of ours left a seven-figure annual salary at a prestigious East Coast organization to live in a "hick" town in the Midwest. He reported that he now makes about $30,000 a year, forty percent of which is spent on family education. He spends many hours each day with his wife and children, bought their nice family home for a fraction of the amount he received from selling his urban town home, and is the happiest he has ever been. Over the last two years, he has written and published numerous articles nationally and a recent manuscript has been accepted by a top five publisher. He told us he is living his dream life, though he is not sure what to do with the extra money since he is doing fine with his reduced income.

Many, many other close friends have moved to small towns in the past years with such a plan, and we know of a dozen others who are making similar moves to places in the Midwest and Rocky Mountains. Indeed, this is part of two huge current national demographic trends—the exurban flight that has received so much national press under the title of "down shifting," and the re-populating of the nation's interior region between the Mississippi Basin and the Sierra Nevadas. The "Nine Nations" of North America are rapidly becoming the two nations—what David Brock called the Federal Class of Americans living on the East and West

Coast and the Flyover Class of people who live between. This is creating the most culturally split nation since Tocqueville noticed the sectional divide between North and South—with real impact on education, culture, lifestyle, and family.

For those who are in the *right* place for their family and mission in urban or suburban homes, the values of real work may not be as naturally available—but they are just as important. Home businesses, pets, yards, homes, neighborhoods, church service, and daily meals and living require hard work. Young people gain as much education from cooking, cleaning, laundering, mowing and helping others as they do from books and manipulatives. Indeed, the city has much to offer that the country can not, such as museums, concerts, art festivals, more extensive libraries, music and dance exhibitions and instruction, performance ensembles, university lectures, service work projects, etc.

Whatever the setting, rural to urban and everything in between, parents must be vigilant to maintain a leadership family culture in the twenty-first century. There is much that militates against it. In particular, the "teenage" culture is so prevalent that all ages, from children to adults, seem to consider it not only normal but preferable. This does not mean that a family cannot succeed in modern times; just that special precautions and hedges need to be diligently put in place and vigilantly maintained.

Each family can take advantage of great opportunities available in their areas; particularly during the summer. Above all, real work done together in families is a vital part of raising quality future parents and citizens, and Core and Love of Learning Phases are the time to do this well. If you do, you will have youth in Scholar Phase; if not, you will likely create modern teenagers in "Entertainment Phase"—a fate we would not wish on anyone.

Ingredient #15: The Weekly Club

About once a week is perfect for Love of Learners and older to spend time with a group of people in their same phase who help inspire them. In Love of Learning and later in Scholar Phases, this is often best accomplished in a group setting—a club. Interestingly, in Depth Phase it is best done in daily group discussions or a classroom colloquium with a great mentor.

Examples of clubs include scouts, church youth groups, service project groups, and Mom Schools such as the Young Stateswomen Society, Knights of Freedom and Liberty Girls. A Mom School is under the purview of the mother who takes responsibility for it, and the more she can include her children in the administration and leadership of the club, the better.

The dynamics of a club can be intoxicating—it can dominate the kids' attention and focus. By the same token, the club can be inspiring and motivating; the group dynamic and the social interaction can apply positive peer pressure in support of the family's culture and the individual's goals. It is important that clubs do not dominate the young person's week, except where the FEC and the family decide to make a club activity the Annual Event. More than one club a week is probably too much.

The consequences of too much of a good thing are that the kids tend to become peer-centered, it tends to deplete mom's energy (lots of chauffeuring and lots of responding to the demands of commitments to the club), it tends to diffuse energy away from the home front, and it creates a fast-paced lifestyle that is both addictive and nearly impossible to maintain.

We are calling this ingredient a "club," but organized classes or regular field trip groups and even some book discussion groups fit into this category and should be considered with the same type of restraints. The club is not the only thing those in the Foundational Phases do outside of the home, so it is important to keep the club activities limited. The natural tendency is, "if some is good, more is better." This can turn Mom into a minivan chauffeur and leave the home fires untended. It is very important that the FEC set boundaries to curb this trend.

While limiting club involvement is important, clubs are really valuable and indeed *vital* to Love of Learning education. No matter how great parents are at modeling self-education, there is something really powerful about peer modeling. It fills a niche the parent just does not. When our children see other young people who really love learning, who share what they are studying, who excitedly tell stories about the things they are reading, who amaze them with their imagination, wit, vocabulary and prowess, something happens inside them. Since leaders are inspired, not required, the club is very important and extremely helpful to parents trying to inspire. The key is for parents to be wise about which clubs to join, and to get involved as much as necessary in the actual content and delivery of the clubs. Where clubs do not exist or do not fully meet the needs of your children, create a Mom School (see ingredient #27).

Note that clubs should avoid competing with mornings; they should usually be structured as afternoon activities. Once in a while, clubs should hold special evening events that include the whole family and focus on powerful inspiration. Also, clubs usually have more impact during the winter than the summer—though there are some obvious exceptions such as sports teams or clubs that specifically focus on the outdoors.

The FEC needs to be especially wise in choosing clubs, since many require seasonal commitments and cannot just be skipped when the week is full. This can be a huge time eater when several kids' clubs are calendared. Still, clubs are a vital part of Love of Learning and Scholar Phases, and parent mentors should look for the best options for their unique children and get personally involved in club functions.

We do not encourage Core Phase "club" involvement; a simple weekly playgroup with like-minded young families will suffice for the family without older children. Young children in larger families can get ample outside socialization with occasional visits to friends. In general, the family is most content when they know how to enjoy one another and are not constantly looking for outside diversions. If your family is feeling the need to escape from one another's company, the solution will likely not be more outside involvement, but less.

Ingredient #16: The Binder

The binder has been called many things in history—the American founding generation called it a commonplace book, and our grandparents called it a scrapbook. In our day, it is simply a binder, preferably full of plastic sheet protectors, which each student fills as he or she progresses. Core Phasers put in early drawings and writing, and parents insert pictures they have taken of baby and toddler. Older Core Phasers will add all kinds of things, cut-out snowflakes or painted hand prints and simple depictions of things they have read about. Love of Learners can meet on a club day afternoon and use a hot glue gun to attach pretty fabric around padding and insert fancy ribbon bookmarks to upgrade their binders to heirlooms. They may add reading lists (finished as well as planned) and written summaries of science projects, journal entries, monthly calendars, art creations, etc.

Each binder should include the student's past and current compass—a six month list of everything they want to study, learn and do. A special pocket in the front can be made to hold the compass, with a slot for a pencil next to it. Each binder should also contain a monthly calendar, and the Love of Learner can be instructed on how to plan as well as to record. Each binder should contain blank sheets of paper along with empty sheet protectors, and a zipped pouch should contain pencils, sharpener, rulers, etc. A cover sheet inserted as the first page can have a picture of the student and the title of this first of their written creations. A timeline or an index might be in order.

For boys a binder can be less fancy, and should be accompanied by a nice box with a good clasp or fastener. The box can hold rocks, cards, scout badges, small plastic toys, fossils, rattlesnake tails and other important Core and Love of Learning educational materials. The boy's binder will still hold the compass, calendar, photos and finished work.

The binder is a very important part of Love of Learning Phase, and it is helpful to get it started during Core Phase. As a side benefit to all the educational purposes of the binder, it can also provide a quality source of long-term documentation. When students get into Scholar Phase, they add the Thomas Jefferson Planner to the binder they are already accustomed to using. When a binder is full, it is a fun project to make a new one—and a shelf of binders to show for years of education is a helpful asset later on. The Young Stateswomen Society has its very own binder insert many mothers utilize as a centerpiece of their daughter's education.

Binders should be housed on a shelf in the family room, easy to access for everyone at any time during the day—especially mornings and afternoons. Binders should also be reviewed by parents periodically, for example in a weekly interview and during a six month evaluation.

Ingredient #17: The Field Trip

The field trip should not be confused with the bigger annual event, but rather just an enjoyable outing that fits into the schedule of the week. Field trips are very important in Core and Love of Learning, and a large variety of possible visiting sites are available in close vicinity to your home. Perhaps the first field trip might be a research project to find out what's available. Field trips can be as complex as a day-long visit to a national park, or as simple as a walk to an elderly neighbor's house to hear stories of local history.

An important part of field trips is to really take time to enjoy the location, to sit and talk instead of just rushing from place to place. Conveyor belt field trips are usually over-structured, over-planned, and too busy. Sadly, most of us tend to duplicate this conveyor belt mistake when we plan a field trip. The important purpose of the trip is to have time to talk—to get children to open up and really communicate with their parents. So plan the trip accordingly. Remember that Core Phase children especially, and all of us in the right circumstances, learn through what we feel about what is happening to us. Take time to interact and experience together, and to "debrief" through gentle questioning and conversation so that the individual experience is shared and validated, and the group experience is anchored.

Another conveyor belt field trip mistake is to get all the children actively involved in activities while the adults sit around and talk to each other. Consider this from the child's point of view. If he or she is herded into the activity, and then looks over to where the adults are seated together talking, how likely is he or she to walk over, sit down, and start sharing important feelings, concerns or questions with an adult? Again, the main purpose of field trips is to get outside the norm and open hearts and minds. When this happens (during an opportunity such as when the parent is seated alone on a rock after playing hard with the children) the young person naturally wants to sit close and conversation naturally occurs. Such conversations are among the most important of our lifetimes.

Field trips are for paradigm shifts. If allowed to happen naturally, and if the trips are structured well so that there is ample time for just sitting together in silence, important discussions and heartfelt bonding will occur. The result is often a huge change in the studies, direction, interaction and focus of children and youth when they return the next day to their regular routine. The quality of their education makes a significant leap forward.

For all these reasons, we generally consider the event a field trip when one family goes alone. Other events might be called clubs, parties, cookouts, socials or whatever, but field trips are where a family goes to experience something new and takes the time to naturally encourage real communication between children and parents. Such field trips are powerfully important to successful Core and especially Love of Learning and Scholar students.

Once in a while a bigger field trip with several families involved is a fun experience. But it is important to make it a true field trip by planning "down-time" where the children naturally spend time just sitting and pondering or maybe talking with parents. For example, after a group field trip to a local television station where the students were fascinated by the equipment and the teaching of the guide, a parent might leave the group of chatting adults at lunch and walk over to sit by the swings where the children are playing. This simple action can change a positive but not life-changing conveyor belt type field trip into a world class leadership event. If the parent sits there long enough, most of his or her children will naturally take the time to "report in," and even other children and a few adults will drop by for a chat. The discussions will be much more powerful than the typical group banter around the "adult area."

Like most of the ingredients of Core and Love of Learning, field trips will lose their effectiveness if they are overdone. More than once a week would almost certainly be a mistake, and about once a month is probably a much better guideline. Again, personalize the frequency and content of field trips to your unique family and situation. When done well, field trips are a powerful opportunity for significant conversations and result in increased effectiveness of student learning.

Ingredient #18: The Library Trip

The library trip can happen often, probably not in the morning, and only on a very special evening where the goal is to really make an important point. Mostly library trips are for afternoons. Such trips should be scheduled with enough time that they actually meet the criteria for field trips—time to talk. Most libraries have reading areas, and spending time there reading to Core Phasers while Love of Learners browse is some of the best time spent.

It is valuable to let even very young Core Phasers check out books and bring them home. This creates a relationship between them and books, and them and the library and librarians. It also familiarizes them with the handling of books and turning of pages. Consider frequenting more than one library. For example, our children have library cards at the City Library in Cedar City, the City Library in Enoch and the County Bookmobile. Our Scholars, Oliver, Emma and Sara, also use the Southern Utah University library. Oliver and Rachel use them all.

It is valuable that the children see the parents study in the library and check things out. Thus library use becomes something we all do, not a kid's activity which is seen as something to end when one becomes an adult. Sharing what you learned from the books you checked out is a natural lead-in to asking what the children learned from their books. Indeed, if you openly share they will naturally begin to dialogue and engage in classical colloquia without ever having to suggest it directly. The best mentors inspire, not require, and do so mostly through example.

While we are on the subject of libraries, let us make an important suggestion. As a good mentor, you need to be personally active in the Great Debate. Mortimer Adler, compiler of The Great Books series, called it the Great Conversation and others have called it a Great Discussion. It is the current state of a debate that has been going on for as long as we have written records. Most people do not even know about the Great Debate, but it is perhaps the most influential thing going on in the world at any given time. It is not found in textbooks, but textbooks often reflect the conclusions of the Great Debate in the past fifty years. The Great Debate is found in the classics, and the purpose of Scholar Phase is to make us fully conversant in the language of the Great Debate. This is the language spoken by those who have led, currently lead, and will lead the world in the decades ahead. The Great Debate is the discussion leaders of the world at any point in history are having about what we all want as human beings and how we should get what we want. In our society, one probably has not done Scholar Phase effectively unless they have at least a subliminal awareness of the history and current dialogue of this debate and are actively taking part in impacting it.

Since the natural consequence of studying the classics is to look around at the current world and wonder what is really happening, we are often asked about the best source for current events. The truth may surprise you. First of all, most people get their news from the electronic media—radio or television. Such people are usually very opinionated and frightfully uninformed. They know very little about what is really happening, but either do not care or very strongly share their opinions when asked. They have no influence on what happens, and no idea why it is happening or what really is going on.

The second group of people is a little more studied. They either listen to the same newscast or radio program each day (thereby following events in more detail), or they read a daily newspaper or weekly magazine. They are less strongly opinionated, consider themselves basically objective, and know a little bit more than the first group. In short, they know little to nothing about what is really going on either, and have no influence on what actually happens—except perhaps locally.

Finally, a relatively small group of people are part of the Great Debate. They are continually pursuing a classical education, and when they go to the library they take time to read the latest articles from scholarly journals like Foreign Affairs, Foreign Policy, The Congressional Digest, Vital Speeches of the Day, etc. They may or may not also read the newspaper or listen to a daily television or radio program, but they do study the journals. When Leadership Education parents go to the library, they set the example by reading classics and scholarly journals. At first they struggle to even understand the journals, but they keep doing it just like they kept reading Shakespeare. Eventually they understand what is going on in the world—really—not just surface skimming, but deep understanding. This educational process is a natural precursor to becoming someone who influences world events.

Of course, all phases are benefited by the library trip. Core Phasers love the pictures, the intellectual and sensory stimulation, and learn to love books. The smells, sounds, sights and feel of the library are part of the foundation they are laying for life. Love of Learners dive into the books, excited to have shelves and shelves of possible worlds to enter, whatever their reading level. They also quietly and usually subconsciously internalize the fact that learning is for life, not something you begin in September, end in May and graduate from after so many years.

Scholar Phasers enter the Great Debate through classics and scholarly journals, rejecting the conveyor belt notion that there is a dogmatic list of classics somewhere. Instead, they test a book to see if it belongs on their own personal classic list. Depth Phasers set out to impact and change the Great Debate, quickly learning how far they are from the education they need and returning more teachable to great Liberal Arts mentors who can now really help them since they are finally humble (a step beyond their Scholar Phase when they thought they actually knew something). Those in Applicational Phase actually impact the Great Debate…but that is another subject, built around personal mission and best left to your personal mentor when the time is right. In short, the library trip is invaluable, should happen about every two weeks, and combines the phases in one place as do The Bookshelf and The Family Room.

Ingredient #19: The Bookshelf

The bookshelf should stand in the family room, the room where the family gathers each morning to study together. The Leadership Education bookshelf is unique compared to most bookshelves, in the same way that Leadership Education is different from other educational models. The fundamental difference between Leadership Education and the employee and professional models is their underlying theory. The main assumption of the conveyor belt is that all people learn the same way, regardless of age or individuality (rooted in the teachings of Plato, Vygotsky and Dewey). In contrast, the prime directive of Leadership Education contains the truths that people learn differently at different ages of life and that each person is unique (rooted in Judeo-Christian tradition and taught in modern times by Erikson and Piaget, among others). Strangely enough, even something as simple as a bookshelf can, by the way it is organized, either reinforce the conveyor belt or leverage a leadership-style education.

The Leadership Education bookshelf is very distinct. Your visiting mother-in-law will likely think it needs to be straightened. You know better. At the very top of this bookshelf, the books are arranged neatly on the shelves, organized by topic and arranged by subject, size and/or color. In short, the Scholar shelves would look good in an attorney's office. Scholar shelves are high and can only be reached by youth and adults; thus Leadership Education bookshelves are five feet or more in height. Core Phasers cannot even reach the Scholar shelves without climbing on something.

Below the Scholar shelves are the Love of Learning shelves, eclectically sporting books of all sizes, shapes and subjects, arranged haphazardly but neatly through the whole middle section of the shelf. When these shelves are cleaned, they are neatly dusted and all the books are turned to face the same direction, but no effort is made to sort by subject or content. In fact, if a well-meaning grandparent or housekeeper does arrange them in order, an early afternoon activity is made of dumping them all out on the floor and re-shelving them by random delight. This is very important.

When Love of Learners tell you they are bored, and you give them the very best Leadership Education answer ("pick a book off the shelf and let's start reading it together"), you want them to thumb through individual titles that all seem lumped together in one big subject called "Love of Learning." If the shelf is arranged by subject or any other categorization, "Love of Learning" will be replaced by something quite inferior.

The bottom two shelves of the off-the-conveyor-belt bookshelf are the most important. Here you find Core Phase books such as

Dr. Seuss and his natural companions, stuck in every-which-way like a good old-fashioned toy box. If the shelf looks like books, it will not draw the attention of the two-year-old toddling through the room while mom and big brother read, big sisters are writing a poem and baby sucks on his sock. If the shelf looks like books, toddler will walk right past, search for toys somewhere or bother Mom, who is not sure what he wants. Well, what he wants is to sit on Mom's lap and read books together, but who could possibly tell *that* from seeing a neatly organized bookshelf that looks like something to get yelled at for touching. "Maybe a drawer upstairs is the best target," he thinks. "Nobody's up there to stop me! But no, look at that bookshelf…yes, the bottom one, the one with all those shapes and colors sticking out in all directions. That one must be for me. Here…this is the one I want. It is a book. Wow. Just like what everyone else is reading. I'll arrange all of these in patterns on the floor…that looks good. But wait, everyone else is…is doing something different with these book things. I'll take it to Mommy."

The Leadership Education bookshelf can be beautifully handcrafted cherry or old pressboard with chunks missing, but it should be tall and it should be arranged top to bottom as Scholar to Core. There can be one in the room, or six, but each of them must feature this top-to-bottom arrangement. It is very important for Core Phasers to look up and wish they could reach the books above, and for Love of Learners to feel the reach as they peek into one of the top shelves. The bookshelf should be in the room where everyone sits and studies. This ingredient is essential for Core and Love of Learning success and for ensuring a Leadership Education learning environment.

Ingredient #20: The Closet

Materials must be close at hand, as Montessori taught. They must be ordered, adequate, safe for children, and in the same room where the family sits to study together. Ideally, a closet in the family room copies the organizational style of the bookshelf: Core materials on the bottom, Love of Learning in the middle range, and Scholar Phase items above.

To keep this as neat as possible, and to facilitate easy cleaning and orderliness, we recommend filling the closet or cabinet with plastic tote boxes. One box might contain Lincoln Logs, another Legos or small cars, another Play Dough, or lace-up cards. Items such as these should be stored at the bottom of the closet with easy pop off lids. On the middle shelves, tote boxes could contain dress ups, fabric pieces, craft materials, crayons and various types of paper and rulers, etc. Games such as Monopoly, Cash-flow, geography or math cards are on higher shelves. Certain items such as paints, scissors, markers, etc. can be in locked boxes on the highest shelves. The closet or cabinet should have a lock on it. It should be wide open during study times and locked when nobody is supervising. Having some times when it is off limits helps to build the value and intrigue of its contents, and promotes respect and conscientious handling of the materials inside.

The closet is a vital ingredient of success in Core and Love of Learning Phases, and without a quality, well-stocked closet, the Foundational Phases might be lacking. Finally, as we have already said, the closet simply must be in the same room as the bookshelves and the reading area if at all possible.

Homes are sometimes built with mostly big open rooms as if nobody intends to raise young children there. Instead, a number of smaller rooms allow parents to effectively segment and thereby organize quality family life architecturally. In some rooms a fort made of couch cushions can provide a week of high quality child play, while the rest of the home remains neat and orderly.

Ingredient #21: The Family Room

By now you already know a great deal about this room. It should be the central learning room in your home. It should contain chairs, couches and other comfortable reading seats where people of all ages enjoy spending hours and hours of time. It needs to be adequately heated and air conditioned. It must contain enough bookshelves, arranged in the Leadership Education way, to effectively educate your family. Each book on the shelves should be wisely selected. This is not a place for just whatever books you have around. The six month purge should rid you of everything except those books you have a lasting relationship with, that you return to happily over and over again and that older kids will gladly sit through again for the benefit for the younger ones. Public libraries are simply bursting with stuff of the other variety, and we delightedly avail ourselves of its offerings, but the Leadership Education bookshelf is just for "keepers."

It's our opinion that the Family Room should never, ever, under any circumstances have a television or computer in it—ever. There should be other places for these appliances. Couches and chairs should be arranged to face each other for comfortable discussion (more than, say, eight or ten feet apart might be too far away to encourage interaction). The space between the seats should be open and empty; not filled with a table or other decorations or furniture. The open space should be covered with a carpet or thick rug, so that babies and other Core Phasers can lounge in the middle of the study, discussions and teaching. This space should also be comfortable enough that older learners and adults naturally gather there to sit together around board games or while listening to reading. Big bean bags can serve as chairs here if desired, and extend the seating availability for growing families. In short, the area should be comfortable and uncluttered with excessive furnishings and decor; indeed, it should be the most overused, inviting place in the entire house. All ages study in the family room, often together at the same time. Sometimes Scholar Phasers may need to get away to a separate place to study—that is fine. The rest of the family can study much better together than apart.

Just as important as effectively setting up the family room is identifying what the family room is not. It is not a school room.

Indeed it always amuses us that while homeschoolers are trying to emulate the public school by setting up desks and an institutional-like setting at home, the leading private, Montessori and other high quality schools are re-arranging their classrooms to feel like home. The family room is a place to live in, since learning is inseparable from living and vice versa. The more holistic the learning environment is, the more holistic the learning will be.

The family room is not a babysitting room, or a toy room. The closet will contain special toys that can only be played with during school, and school will be a unique kind of fun. The toy boxes and toy room should be elsewhere.

As we said already, and it is worth repeating, the family learning room cannot be the same room as the entertainment room. A room with a television or a computer, even if they are turned off most of the time, is unlikely to boast a daily output of world class education at all levels.

Ingredient #22: The Entertainment Room

For many years we did not use a television. One can get a world-class education without one. For many families, a television with a DVD player can be valuable to family life and education. It is not essential to effective Leadership Education, but you may find it helpful if you observe several important guidelines.

First, house it in a room with the computer, and perhaps toys and other entertainment items. Second, put it next to a shelf of classic movies, using the Leadership Education definition of a classic: a work worth studying (watching) over and over and over again, from which you learn more each time. Third, password protect it. This is especially easy if you purchase your DVD player as part of your computer and use the monitor for viewing, with other options also available. The entertainment room is best in an open family area that everyone frequents rather than behind locked doors where young people can get into inappropriate activities unseen, or waste uncounted hours with emails and games.

The main purposes of the entertainment room are to separate things which attack learning from the family room and at the same time provide a setting for fun and bonding family activities. We have at times seen people who follow this plan organizationally, but it appears that they have spent three times the amount of money on the entertainment room as on the family room. In a leadership home this is reversed. The investment in quality is much more important to the family room where the whole environment impacts the education. This should be obvious in the selection of couches, bookshelves, art work on the wall, and so on.

Finally, this is one of those huge details that people like to ignore. Separation of entertainment and family rooms is vital to successful Leadership Education. Leaving out these two ingredients seems small but is like just skipping baking soda or never changing the oil in your car. Leadership homes must have an ideal family room, and since the television and computer will make their way back into most homes no matter how many times you remove them, make a place for them separate from the family room. Otherwise you will be one of those wondering why this system did not work instead of those who know it works through repeated successful experiences.

Ingredient #23: The Donation Box

Leadership Education homes need a donation box, a place to put unneeded or unused items to pass on to charitable organizations. As mentioned, the three great destroyers of motherly mentoring are cleaning, cooking and chauffeuring. We tried to find a way to say this delicately, but finally decided it was worth being blunt: some of us will need to choose between our stuff and our education. Too much stuff in the home clogs up the education of everyone who lives there.

Start by throwing away everything that is junk, and sending to second-hand stores anything you do not really need as discussed in Ingredient #6 The Six Month Purge. And then put out a donation box, teach the whole family what it is for, fill it at least once a month, and haul it away to people who really need it. This is a great way to promote non-materialism in your children.

By the way, it does not hurt to send some really nice things to charity along with stuff you know you will never use. The people who get it probably need it much more than you, and being a pack rat is a sure way to sabotage the Foundational and Educational Phases. Ten great classics on the shelf are better than a hundred, or even a hundred thousand, mediocre books. If you have not worn an article of clothing for two years, you are not likely to wear it in the next two. Give it to someone who will. Honestly, when that weight finally comes off, you're going to want the latest style anyway! Move on. You can lose weight right now, today, by lightening the load in your closets.

Managing your stuff takes time, effort, resources, space, and above all the brain cells to keep track of it all, even subconsciously. Unburden yourself and free up those brain cells. We need every one we've got! Of course, we are speaking metaphorically here rather than scientifically, but try it and we think you will agree.

In our family, we keep our donation box in the back of the van or right by the door to the driveway, so when we send something away it leaves the house immediately and can be dropped of the next time we drive past a good donation center. We did not start that way. The first few years, we needed the box right under our nose, in the way in fact, every time we walked down the hall. This kept it in sight and in mind. Whatever system works for you, get a donation box and keep filling it regularly. The freed-up brain cells, time, and energy will greatly enhance your family education and relationships.

Ingredient #24: The Storage Box

Next to the donation box sits the storage box. When you just cannot bring yourself to give an item away when you know you should, or have not used it for a long time, put it in the storage box. When the box is full, take it to storage. Every year or so, pull all the boxes out of storage and have a garage sale. Perhaps better still, just haul the old, dusty boxes off to charity without ever opening them.

It may seem like we are overstating the case, but this ingredient is very important. If you have already mastered it, wonderful! But many parents we speak with have not. There seems to be a high proportion of Leadership Education families who are the type to get the last value out of everything they own, purchase in bulk and on sale, and not waste. This type of individual tends to store their belongings and not part with them when the time is right and to acquire things just *because* the price is right. Nothing hurts Foundational and Educational phases like extra stuff around the house which consistently and very silently robs energy and focus from your education and your time with the kids. With growing kids there is never a short supply of toys that are no longer played with or which cannot be used (broken, pieces missing, etc.), shoes that stink, jeans that are too "holy," tee shirts for smocks (how many smocks do you need, anyway?) dresses that are woefully out of style, suits that nobody will wear because they prefer dockers and a white shirt, etc. A good rule of thumb is to throw away, donate or store twenty-five to fifty percent of your belongings at least once a year.

Another good idea is to bake up several plates of cookies and take them around to friends once a month as you return other peoples' belongings that have been left behind at your house. Throw your library books in a bag as you head out to drop off on your way. If you make it yummy and fun, you'll get it done!

Ingredient #25: The Weekly Lesson

This ingredient does not apply to Core Phasers. Some Love of Learners and nearly all Scholars will get a great deal out of a weekly lesson—be it piano, voice, strings, martial arts, swimming, golf, dance, etc. This provides a valuable social outlet, a rest from the regular routine, and most importantly, it fosters discipline and inspires long-term follow through. Picking one or two skills and really mastering them is better for most youth than skipping around from one kind of lesson to another. Look closely at the young person's mission and help him select an area of expertise and begin to train for it.

Practice between lessons is vital, and should be part of the daily routine. Year round lessons are usually better than seasonal involvement. If you do choose a seasonal project like baseball or soccer, make it an annual project. Weekly lessons are more ideally suited to the long-term mastery of a set of skills. And be careful to avoid lessons that are held more often than weekly, at least until Scholar Phase.

The type of teacher you select for your youth's weekly lesson is very important. As you get to know them, take the time to observe which of the Seven Keys they apply. An instructor using only one or even none of the Keys is unlikely to inspire long-term excellence, and will probably foster a learning style that competes with your ideal. Look for instructors who use six or more of the Keys. We have been able to find them for each of our children in our very small town. Of course, often the teachers apply the Keys naturally or because they have learned by experience, rather than being specifically "Leadership Education trained," but if they use the Keys, they will help your youth excel.

If you simply must have lessons for the young ones, understand that you are paying your hard-earned money to have them *exposed to greatness*. This is worthy and admirable, and we believe worth every penny, if you can afford it and if you have a teacher who understands and works toward this objective. But lessons to Core and Love of Learning kids must not be results-driven in order to *justify* the expense. If this is your mindset, wait until the kids are in Scholar Phase when that type of accountability is appropriate and actually bears fruit.

A dear friend was giving lessons to another friend's daughter, Shelley, who had recently turned thirteen. The girl amazed everyone by progressing almost beyond her teacher's ability to mentor her within just a couple of months. She was considered quite the prodigy. I know the girl well, and she is indeed quite talented. Her incredible progress resulted not from being so much more gifted than her siblings or other students, but from the fact that she practiced several hours a day from the time she began. Such was her desire and temperament as a girl in Scholar Phase. Our own Emma considers Shelley her good friend. Emma has taken piano lessons for several years from a gifted mentor. She was wistful as she watched Shelley go from ground zero to far surpassing her in a matter of weeks. But as Emma entered Scholar Phase, a curious thing happened. All of a sudden, when she began to practice several hours a day, several days a week, she also made a punctuated leap in her sight reading, her coordination and her repertoire. Suddenly, she was a prodigy, too! Previously she could only long for the discipline and commitment that Shelley exhibited. At length, it came to her naturally, and shortly thereafter to her younger sister Sara, while Eliza looks on wistfully (we must remember to point out to her the organic nature of the shift and reassure her that her day is coming as well).

It is important not to use lessons as an excuse to become an SUV chauffeur. It is more important to have time and involvement with a great mother mentor than to have lots of lessons, so balance this with overall family needs and use it as best fits your unique family. Some families wait until Scholar Phase to do lessons, and even require Scholar youth to earn their own money to pay for lessons.

Finally, we started this Ingredient by saying that Core Phasers should not take lessons. We believe that this is generally true. Furthermore, most families today take this ingredient way overboard, thinking that every three year old should be in dance, voice, piano and strings or they will never get ahead in life. We disagree. What Core Phase children need are parents, good parents, and lots of quality time with them. Still, you may find a time when the best thing for a Core Phase child is to be in lessons. Our oldest three—Oliver, Emma and Sara—all waited to take lessons until they were in later Love of Learning. But their sister Eliza started piano lessons at the age of 7 while still in Core Phase because the FEC decided in one of our Sunday meetings and after much discussion that this would be best for her. We strongly believe if she were the oldest child this would not take place. It should be understood, however, that her lessons are of the "exposure to greatness" variety. Her initial commitment and zeal spent itself as she found it impossible to keep up the level of practice her sisters were doing, and could no longer convince herself she wanted to. Many things are affected by the dynamic of the family; later children should be treated in the context of the family on a case-by-case basis, rather than by rule of thumb. At age 10 she has taken a break from lessons, although she does dabble at the piano for her own enjoyment. We anticipate introducing the option to her again in late Transition to Scholar.

As the youngest of six children in a home where both parents played instruments, Rachel began playing the piano by ear at age three. She went on to become quite accomplished at an early age and devoted much of her Scholar Phase to the refinement of her talents. Music has been a life-long passion for her, and she looked forward with anxious anticipation to the time when she could see her children share in it. Even so, she never felt right about putting our oldest three children in lessons until Oliver was almost twelve, Emma was ten and Sara was nine. She probably would not have put Emma and Sara in without an older child leading out.

Rachel's sister Holly, a homeschooling mother of 10 and Rachel's primary home-school mentor, put her oldest two girls in lessons at ages fourteen and twelve. They progressed so quickly that within three years they were teaching lessons themselves and actually paid for their own college with their earnings. A rich musical education is practically vital to the development of our children in their early years, but weekly lessons *can*, and for many families, *should* wait. If you just can not handle the wait, sign yourself up. We know of several moms who discontinued their kids' lessons and took up their own. The little ones actually benefit more from their mom's show of discipline and joy than from their own frustration and guilt.

In regards to musical education, it is usually best to focus on the enjoyment of many styles. Our children love to make up stories in the back of the van while the classical station is playing. The awareness of the messages, the feelings that are evoked and the refinement of taste and repertoire of recognition are important life lessons as well as a superior introduction to music than endless hours of skill development. With this background, when a child's temperament and the family dynamic are most supportive of lessons, the child can progress at an amazing rate. Nothing is gained by teaching music to small children using the ZPD. Think outside the box! Music should be a huge part of your family life and education; music *lessons* are for those with the ability to benefit from that educational format. Isn't there some other way to give your young children a musical education than through the regimented form of weekly lessons? Isn't it best to use mentors and finances at the optimal time, both in what the student can and will achieve and in not going against the flow of the rest of your family culture and education for the Phase they are in?

Again, you are the expert on your family, and if your FEC is working it will make rules as well as the exceptions to the rules. Having said all of that, we hope this will not be used as an excuse to push Core Phasers too fast. That is a real disease in our nation, and it has caused another disease where our modern youth hardly study at all. We somehow seem to think that our children must keep up with the Jones' children and that they are behind if they do not take the same lessons at the same ages as other kids in the neighborhood. So, if you choose to be an exception to the rule and do put a Core Phaser in lessons, be sure you are doing it for the individual needs of the child, not to fit into the conveyor belt norm and be especially sure that the teacher you choose is a Seven Keys-style mentor. Anything else is not worth the money and can actually (will usually) shorten your Core child's love of musical education. Remember that a Core Phase child makes assumptions experientially. Refer to the list of lessons learned when academics are rushed and adapt them to music education with fairly consistent results.

Ingredient #26: The Safety Kids Class

We do not endorse products very often, but the Safety Kids course on Personal Safety by Janeen Brady of Brite Music is an exception. We think every parent should consider it for his children. Emma and Sara (aged 10 and 9) led a class using this program as part of their achievement of their Mother Teresa Medallion for their Young Stateswoman Society, and it was a huge success for their Love of Learning progress and the safety of the thirty-seven children who came to their class. The younger children still sing the songs and re-enact the role-plays long after the course, and we have the opportunity to talk about safety rules and teach important principles that they apply nearly every day.

We recommend that Love of Learning youth teach the class with the help of parents, and that attendees have a parent present. The whole course can be taught in a three-hour afternoon activity (although Emma and Sara stretched it into four afternoons, including skits, role plays, crafts and activities). We suggest that each family be required to pre-purchase the CDs and workbook for repeated use later on. The intent is that this not be a drop-off-your-kid fun time, but a life-changing experience that the whole family shares.

Through this course you will establish or at least revisit your family's rules of safety, and in this modern world this is sadly a real necessity. The course combines acting, singing, discussion and stories to make it a lot of fun, and it provides a set of guidelines which help in other field trips, library trips, events, etc.

Ingredient #27: The Mom School

When homeschooling was first resurrected in the 1960s, people began establishing Home School Co-ops. In some states, the lobbyists for homeschool freedom actually assumed co-ops as the norm and the laws were written accordingly. In other places, people met as co-ops in addition to other educational formats. In the late 1990s, however, we noticed a new trend in the homeschool world, something quite different than co-ops, from East to West Coasts and everywhere in between. We coined the phrase "Mom Schools" to identify this trend.

A Mom School exists where a mother or father sees specific needs in their own child(ren) and organizes to fulfill those needs. Setting up a Mom School is simple (though not easy). Watch your children closely, stay in tune with their needs, interests, hopes, dreams, fears, goals, talents, etc., and when you see something they need, help them get it. Sometimes that means a certain book, other times it means a field trip or a long talk, and sometimes it will require them interacting with other children or youth in a club or other group.

When the latter situation occurs, as it will for every parent of a Leadership Education youth, don't just wish your community had something that would fulfill that need, offer it! Set it up, get it started, get your child excitedly involved, and invite others along. Charge a small fee if you need to cover costs or enlist appropriate levels of commitment, do not charge if it will function well without, and do whatever else is needed so that your child gets the full opportunity.

When our daughter Emma told us she wanted a club, we basically ignored it at first. Our lives were very busy and it seemed like a passing fancy. But she attended her older brother's scout meetings, saw him receiving awards and honors and simply could not live without similar opportunities. A close adult friend told Emma she would help but it was so much work that it really was too much to ask. Emma was still sure she needed a club. So we looked into everything available: 4-H, Girl Scouts, church groups, etc. Finally, after about the 10th interview where Emma said she needed a club, Rachel sat down with her and outlined everything Emma wanted. Then the FEC spent hours and hours putting the details together. It took a lot of work, and it still does—but the Young Stateswomen Society has been a huge blessing to Emma and her sisters, as well as to over fifty of her friends in the community and a growing number of girls around North America.

Colesville Academy, a private school, grew out of Rachel's concern that our children would not have a peer group that respected their choices and their direction and that would inspire them to be better, study harder and accomplish more. This group has resulted in thousands of hours of research, hundreds of speeches and seminars, a dozen publications, and a life mission teaching the Leadership Education model. Perhaps your family will not get involved in the same way, but it has been a superb education for our family—parents as well as each child. The children are very actively involved and do real work that earns them money and helps the whole family.

Ingredient #28: The Computer

When used correctly, the computer is an important part of a Leadership Education. But how do you use it correctly? Put succinctly, the computer is an adult tool for adult-type activities such as communication, writing, researching, purchases and world event monitoring and involvement. This can include young adults, those who are learning to be adults, but it should be limited to adults. Those who use the computer for child entertainment just have another television in the home, and in fact the computer and television can destroy the natural love of learning period of childhood by making passive entertainment activities the most appealing. A good way to destroy Leadership Education and guarantee conveyor belt attitudes is to offer lots of computer "educational" software along with time to watch "educational" TV.

An exception to this is those with special needs like autism or brain injury. Sometimes specialized technology helps can be used to bridge processing or communication gaps in a child. But much care and prayer must be used in determining the optimal use, and these decisions should be revisited and confirmed on a regular basis.

Scholar and Depth Phase adults will use the computer frequently, showing younger people the importance of writing. Advanced Love of Learners who are starting to write might be given a typing game with time limits and a password protected user account on the computer. As they increase their writing skills, they can be given more time to write on the computer. Parent-assisted research on the internet can also take place, but never alone. Computer games are an inferior use of time and should be treated like any other addictive substance or behavior—as a treat once in a while, or not at all, depending on the content. Video games should be strictly left for play time; even having them in the house can, for some families, mean that there will be fewer youth or adult Scholars in the family.

Make sure the children and youth see you writing important things that matter to you. This establishes an expectation that adults write, that writing is important, and that someday they will be writers too. Writing is becoming a lost art in the general American populace; this is an antidote.

It is important for adults in the family to be wise and not overuse the tool that the computer can be to the detriment of their own and their family's education. Even when used for educational and uplifting purposes, computer use can be as addictive for adults as for children. This is an area which can be a major time-stealer from the most important functions of a Leadership Education home if allowed to become so. Adults must model self-discipline and restraint with the computer just as in the area of television viewing. Time spent with these two mediums must not be allowed to displace essential activities and irreplaceable investment in other more worthwhile relationships and educational pursuits.

Ingredient #29: The Kitchen Table

Meals are for oral exams. Elsewhere in our writings we have discussed the Five Environments of Mentoring. The environments that mentors need to ensure for their students are: tutorial, group discussion, lecture, testing, and coaching. Meals around the kitchen table are the ideal setting for tutorial, testing and coaching. Do not define the kitchen table too narrowly. The whole process of mealtime includes: discussion while shopping, cooking, setting the table, eating, after eating, and clean up. All provide excellent opportunities for small group tutorials— asking questions about what is being learned and then asking follow-up questions in as much depth as the student can handle. Meal time also provides a great environment for one-on-one coaching to help individual children and youth progress.

We call this the "Milo Talon Effect," taken from a character in several Louis L'Amour novels. Milo often refers to the dinner table discussions he grew up with when his father used the time to instruct, question, debate and talk about things. Family meals should occur often, and turning them into informal, pleasant instruction and learning time is a great way to guarantee that you are consistently in touch with what the children are learning.

Once in a Sixth Month Inventory, Rachel was trying to narrow down her schedule so she would have more study and teaching time. As we listed everything she does, it became clear that long six or eight-hour study blocks were not an option because she had three meals a day to prepare. By focusing on asking questions and turning the preparation, eating and clean up time into real, substantive discussions of what was being learned, she added four hours a day. For some, that will create a whole Scholar Phase!

This is really very simple. Meals are for oral exams. Meals happen several times a day, and everyone is a captive audience. Ask questions. Set a rule that everyone should stay at the table until an appropriate break in discussion, and then should be excused by permission from the head of the table. When you break, you can bring up a new subject with those cleaning up. Of course, this can become burdensome if you hammer it into them. Instead, casually talk to them about things they (and you) are interested in—and do it regularly day after day.

Ingredient #30: The Cleaning Time

Cleaning can kill an otherwise excellent Leadership Education home. It can take mom's time, dad's time, and the students' time—so they feel they are always cleaning and never learning. Or, cleaning time can be a fast, efficient chore that you get out of the way without much concern. The key is getting in touch with what makes sense for the size and makeup of your family. We have listed some special considerations for cleaning with differently aged family members and situations:

Families with young children only:

In this family situation, Mom does Scholar Phase (after re-negotiating Core and/or Love of Learning herself as necessary) and leads the children in Core Phase. Just before morning school time, do a whole house pick up; then repeat it right after school time. Repeat again when afternoon projects are finished, and again just before bedtime. Get the children to pick up all their projects immediately when they finish and before moving on to anything else—run it like a Montessori classroom where there is a spot for everything and children must put things back before getting out anything new. Note, of course, that Mom and Dad end up doing most of the other work in this situation. This can be considerable; not so much because there is too much work, but rather because unstable and shifting sleep times can leave parents wandering the house feeling like zombies. It is especially beneficial during this phase for Dad to help a lot with the house, or at least to not be too perfectionist about it.

Families with children in Core and Love of Learning Phases

A significant part of Love of Learning Phase is to learn to work like an adult, thus many responsibilities can be given to Love of Learners. Still, Love of Learners need to be trained to do jobs well, so we recommend that Mom be released from any cleaning and instead be given a training and supervisory role only—what

Cherie Logan calls "the promotion." In homes with large families (where things can deteriorate to an unbelievable extent within ten minutes), we also recommend the quick full-house clean up. This consists of an adult (Mom or Dad) going from room to room and giving errands; all the children and youth go with the adult, doing what is assigned—everyone working together on the same room. When one room is done, move to the next. This can work for deep cleaning (for example, during The Sixth Month Purge) and also just before dinner for a quick clean up. This might not work unless you have children in Love of Learning or older, and it may need to be modified if you have only two children, for example, one in Core and another in Love of Learning. In this latter case, simply do assignments in the same room with your Love of Learner as if you were another child. The damage of two kids should be commensurate with the cleanup they can do; same with five or ten kids. If you have two-year-old sextuplets—we're out of our league; you'd better find a better cleaning mentor in that case!

Certain responsibilities can be assigned as family "callings." We like this term because of the weight of moral obligation that it carries, and the attendant level of commitment and accountability. Mature Love of Learners and Scholars in our family receive callings to be responsible for specific tasks in our home. This is a decision based on individual readiness. Eliza was mature at 8 and could handle her own calling. The older girls in our family were not ready at her age. We select such callings in FEC and meet with the youth in a personal Sunday interview to "call" them to the responsibility. We make it voluntary. But they understand what FEC is and how it works, so they virtually always say "yes" and then do their best (with some inspiring and encouragement of course). They may bring up concerns for the FEC to consider, but they consider the decision of the FEC binding. Parents may readily see the importance of earning that sacred trust and being careful not to manipulate things in the name of the FEC.

Following their acceptance of the duty, the family votes their support of the family member's calling in full Family Council. So far we have never had a calling rejected or voted down. When we make a change, we vote to release them from a previous calling in Family Council so everyone always knows who is called to what.

Scholars

We recommend giving Scholars full-charge stewardships, such as breakfasts, laundry, caring for the lawns. They are young adults with young adult privileges; they need to earn them. They need to make a regular accounting of their stewardship to the FEC-assigned parent overseeing their work.

Dads

The "quick clean up" time puts the power in the hands of any adult who wants things cleaned. They can call everyone for cleaning time and go room by room getting it done; they can do it themselves if nobody else is home. And they can gently and consistently train the children as they go. Homes where fathers help, instead of just complain, tend to do much better.

Some families choose to deep clean one room per day, so the house is always on rotation. If your schedule is not very consistent, the house and therefore the study time can suffer, so use this method under advisement. Some rotate cleaning "zones" on a weekly basis, others take on an assignment for extended periods of time. If having an orderly environment is a particular challenge for you, we recommend you seek a housekeeping mentor and entrust your progress to their guidance. Two popular ones that have publications for those who are "booklearners" are Don Aslett and "Flylady." You may prefer to get a friend or family member to give you assignments or systems and hold you accountable for your application of the principles they teach you. However you go about acquiring this skill and establishing this environment, the peace of mind and freedom of time and space are worth the investment of effort, compromise and sacrifice. And your family culture and education will flourish in the wonderful nest you provide!

Applying Ingredients 13 through 30

At this point, we would like to encourage you to look at the creation of a leadership home as a process that will occur over time, not in an instant. As you have read through these ingredients, ideas have come to your mind on personalizing the information to your own home and family. Take some time to record your impressions and make some resolutions and priorities. Tackle and achieve one improvement at a time. Remember that the feelings you and your family experience with each other are as important to success and progress as the activities in which you engage.

Mothers, particularly, tend to feel overwhelmed and undercapable to complete an unending list of demands that are: partly, an inherent component of their job description; somewhat, born of their own expectations and desires; and finally, externally imposed. It is extremely challenging to be a woman nurturing home and family in today's era. We want to affirm your personal mission and unique purpose and share with you our conviction of the incomparable importance of home and family as the venue in which you have dedicated your best efforts. You have the potential and capacity to accomplish what is needed. You have chosen to dedicate your genius to the forum containing the most potential for impact. The repercussions of your efforts in this arena will be felt in society for generations to come.

Not only those you love and serve, but you, personally, will develop in ways you can not imagine as you persist in educating yourself, family members and others who will look to you as a guide and mentor. Every sacrifice and diligent effort you make will be fruitful in some way at some time and minister to your own success and happiness. Some women wonder if they are "missing their mission" as they nurture family members and "keep the home fires burning." In fact, they are fulfilling their mission and preparing themselves for future purposes through a refining crucible of greatness that has no equal.

The principles of Leadership Education call for—and, when understood and applied, will provide—a huge paradigm shift about education. That is just the start. You will find whole worlds opening up to you that are personal to your mission. Such remarkable growth takes time and trust. Ponder the growth process of a babe in arms to a wise and respected family patriarch… step by step, day by day, act by act, experience by experience and choice by choice.

Give yourself time to let the ideas for facilitating and providing an environment conducive to Leadership Education sink in. Tailor them to your individual situation. Prune dead branches of old conceptions and ways of doing out of your life and mind in order to make room for new growth and life. It may be a little painful and discomfiting, at first, but the tasty, delicious, soul satisfying fruit will be worth it. We promise.

CHAPTER FIVE

Core And Love Of Learning: Ingredients 31-55

By now, you should be getting a better idea of the ingredients that will be included in the lives of future leaders. Keep reading as we examine the final chapter of ingredients. These ingredients will enrich and facilitate the success of those previously discussed.

Ingredient #31: The Academic "No"

The first academic "no" refers to curbing your tendency to push, push, push. The second is a mental "no" to set boundaries that do not allow the voices of pushy, opinionated, well-meaning people to distract you from what you know is right for your family.

In the Oriental tradition, the great master required new applicants to wait for long periods of time to see him (a tradition purposefully copied by modern Western medicine). Similarly, in the Western world, the master charged huge amounts of money to discourage those who were not really serious (the medical profession seems to have mastered this one also). When you really need the doctor or any other type of mentor, you are willing to both wait and pay—a testament to the value of their expertise, as well as the mentee's level of submission and sacrifice. Those who push past the initial "no" and demonstrate persistence are much more likely to be really ready to benefit from the relationship.

On the conveyor belt, we do exactly the opposite: we push everyone, whether they are ready or not, and then get anxious and affix labels when someone is "behind."

If you need permission to go at a healthy child's pace, here you go: It is okay to go at the child's pace, to let them learn when they are ready and to enjoy doing things they really like instead of frantically trying to keep up with someone else's curriculum. You also have permission to take time and get yourself off the conveyor belt. Focus your energy, discipline and deep, burning desire to "stay ahead" on yourself instead of on the kids. Under FEC advisement, set up an educational plan and demand follow through from *yourself*. This way you will get the education you always deserved and they will get the example they need. Keep yourself busy enough getting your own education that you can let the children enjoy their childhood and stay in love with learning as they grow.

It is always ironic that the more deficient the education of the parent, the more frantic they are likely to be to push their toddlers. Adults with a quality education tend to relax and let their children enjoy learning. Think about that. Adults with a great education are the least likely to burden their children with the fear that they will not get one. They are most likely to expose their children to greatness and inspire them to fulfill a personal mission. We just need to remind ourselves that being highly-trained is not equivalent with having a great education. This is not to disparage training—for most peoples' mission, excellent training must be a part of the preparation. But it is not the same thing as a great liberal arts education.

This ingredient should not be used to say "no" to Core Phasers who want attention or to do projects. It is to remind you to tell yourself "no" when you want to ZPD them into quantifiable progress or you are feeling insecure and are imposing an agenda upon your child based on external judgments that emanate from conveyor belt mentality. The academic "no" is for work that compels and sends false messages that are directly opposed to core values. If your child is engaging in learning activities that he chooses and loves doing, by all means, encourage him! And by all means, make sure that your home environment is providing adequate—no—*abundant* exposure to the values of Core and Love of Learning. When all signals suggest that your child is ready to move on to Scholar Phase, tell her "no" and watch how she takes it. If she is relieved, she was not ready. If she says "fine" and nothing changes, she was not ready. But if she just keeps persisting, pleading, demanding and begging to go to Scholar Phase, she *might* be ready.

Ingredient #32: The Discipline "No"

Often at this point in seminar presentations of this material, somebody in the crowd raises their hand and asks (usually in an exasperated voice), "so you'd just let a toddler run out in front of a car?" or "so we should never make our five-year-old eat his peas?" The principle here is "Inspire, Not Require," and it is fundamental to training leaders. But it is so far from the conveyor belt that people often experience huge culture shock when we teach it and ask questions like these.

Let's answer these questions directly, just for effect. "We recommend that you run and grab the toddler and keep him out of the busy street," and "we recommend that you follow good nutritional guidelines in feeding your children." We separate discipline from academics.

If you want him to be safe, stop him from running into the street. If you want him to be healthy, provide good food, exercise and rest for him. But if you want him to get a great education, show him how to love learning and then let him make that choice. If you force him, you are likely to get a fourteen-year-old who prefers video games, malls, and hanging instead of learning; one who will only do the bare minimum you require and who seeks constant entertainment. In short, you will get a teenager instead of a young adult.

The irony here is that there are two proven ways to create a teenager: 1) force and push children academically and 2) let them do whatever they want in their personal life. In contrast, young adults are raised by parents who: 1) have firm disciplinary standards and 2) a high-quality freedom-oriented educational system. The two components of creating youth are natural and excellent complements.

Set rules and be firm in following them. Do not set too many, and be consistent. When a youth breaks a rule, tell her: "try that again." It might take a few tries, but eventually she will get it right. Start this system while they are Core Phasers and it will be natural later. If you simultaneously set a great Scholar example for them and help them love learning—you will have fourteen-year-olds who beg you to allow them to study. This really works, as thousands of parents have shown in the last fifteen years since we started promoting the Leadership Education model.

By the way, this is not hyperbole. At the time of this writing, young Oliver is almost 17, Emma is 15 and Sara is 14. They study almost all day long. They literally must be interrupted from their studies to eat or to help out when necessary. All day, they study. And lest this be construed as vanity on our part, let us here say that we personally know literally hundreds of youth with the same game plan. It would not be appropriate to name them all here; but for those who are tempted to view this as a hopeless exaggeration: rest assured it is not, and our case is by no means isolated.

Ingredient #33: The Yard

Sun and fresh outdoor air is very important to the Foundational Phases. So is a place to run, fall, jump and run some more. A place to play and a place where real work is necessary for the good of the family are vital. Good fences, lawn and dirt are also very helpful. In short, your yard matters when you are raising and educating leaders.

Fences keep them separate from the neighborhood, except when you choose to invite the neighborhood over. This is extremely important. Just as architecture can really impact the success of your Leadership Education home, so can the landscaping and set up of the yard. We are not recommending manicured landscaping maintained by a professional. This looks great but can cheat children of fabulous work opportunities with their parents. Spend time working with them on things which really upgrade the family's life, and you will increase their preparation for leadership.

Yards are wonderful for rolling in the snow, making a snowman, raking leaves, mowing lawns, cleaning the pool, weeding the flowers, planting and nurturing the garden, etc. Sun, wind and rain are necessary to Leadership Education, and yards are the best place to learn many of these lessons. The smell of rain in your yard is different than anywhere else. In fact, it is worth living and dying for. If your children do not learn important realities such as this through working, living and making family memories in your home and yard, they may not be willing to fight, die or even vote for their fundamental rights.

Trees are better than textbooks. Each limb you climb teaches a new perspective, viewpoint, and worldview with a host of corresponding lessons. Parks can teach part of this, but the allegorical life of the tree itself must be known up close; the metaphorical array of beings it hosts must be studied up close and personal. A relationship with a place, a land, and a country is necessary for true leadership and effective statesmanship.

Basketball, football, volleyball, baseball, kickball, horseshoes, camping—all are better in your own yard than anywhere else—better educationally and better in raising future leaders. They are also better attended to and engaged in when the television and computer are properly limited or in storage.

The yard is a valuable part of Leadership Education on so many levels. Consider the yards in the educational settings of *Laddie, Little Britches, Little Women, Pride and Prejudice*, etc. Do the best you can to create an outdoor environment that is ideal for your children's education.

Ingredient #34: The Evening Reading List

We strongly believe that no one should rely on somebody else's classics list; we each need to carefully develop our own. However, there are a few classics that we just could not leave off our list of ingredients for success. We call this our Evening Reading List, and it contains those classics which we have found to be particularly helpful in healing family culture and fostering healthy views of each one's role. Reading these together as a family is a priceless experience: *Little Britches, Man of the Family, Mary Emma and Company, The Fields of Home, Laddie, Where the Red Fern Grows, Pollyanna, Carry on Mr. Bowditch, Charlotte's Web, Little House in the Big Woods, Little House on the Prairie, Farmer Boy, Trumpet of the Swans* and *The Cricket in Times Square*.

Several years ago, we ran out of books to read in the evening. We tried several dozen different titles, and either did not finish them or agreed that they just were not up to the quality we wanted. We kept looking for something of the same caliber, but kept being disappointed. "I guess we've just covered the really great ones and we'll have to settle for less," Dad said one evening as we decided to quit reading another disappointing book. But then four-year-old Ammon brought Mom a copy of *Charlotte's Web* and asked her to read it. He had seen the picture on the shelf and was interested. After some initial groans from older ones who thought they were too big for that, the whole family got excited evening after evening as we read, and we realized that we had forgotten the definition of a classic: a work worth reading over and over again. In fact, the second time through was actually more fun for the older children. Even the oldest would sometimes say he would rather do such-and-so, but would inevitably end up with us every time.

Once in a while we find a book that deserves to be added to our evening reading list. But in the meantime, we love going through this list the second time—and we are looking forward to sharing these books again when our babies are ready in four to six years and later with grandchildren. Classics are great!

Ingredient #35: The Chores

As we have said several times in this article, real work is key to training leaders, and it must start at an early age. Adler pointed out that most modern students only do hard academic work after college—either in their first real job or in professional training such as law or medical school. By the latter part of the twentieth century, hard work of any kind had become something reserved for adults—a significant cause of the leadership crisis. The irony is that the end of work among children coincided with the workaholic generation of parents. Two-parent working families left latch-key kids to watch TV and play Nintendo alone, and workaholic parents put in eighty-hour weeks to "pay for play" for their suburban children from birth to young adulthood. It is normal now to walk through an upscale neighborhood and watch dozens of teenagers drive by in BMWs and SUVs without seeing a single parent—they are too busy working to provide a lazy play life for their increasingly unhappy and dysfunctional kids.

Chores must be real. That is a challenge in our modern times, but it is a necessary ingredient to Leadership Education. Chores cannot be arbitrary or they simply pit parental will against youth will. If chores are necessary to the family's well being, responsibilities that really matter, they build skills, character and leadership. If this means you need to make significant changes to your lifestyle, then do it. If the choice is between maintaining your lifestyle or raising leaders, make the right choice.

Chores are not the same as work for pay. A good model for this is the book *Little Britches*, where young Ralph has numerous home responsibilities and also works for pay wherever he can—his pay contributing to the needs of the family. There are three modern mistakes we tend to make in this area. First, we pay our kids to do work at home which they should do as part of the family. Second and worse, we just give them an allowance for doing nothing. Third, we encourage outside work but do not expect them to contribute to the family.

It has become part of our modern worldview to do things the easy way, to take short cuts wherever possible. This sickness has almost killed quality education, which can only be restored if we are willing to embrace the pain of learning as the inevitable accompaniment of attaining educational goals.

Interestingly, Love of Learning and Adler's "pain of learning" go together if we follow the phases correctly. The pain portion comes in Scholar Phase, but it is important that students in the Foundational Phases learn to look forward to the opportunity of the demands and rigors of true scholarship: studying so hard it hurts, struggling, sweating, crying themselves to sleep trying to get past a writing slump or to understand a classic and doing the hard work needed to have the kind of education Jefferson, Madison, Newton and others earned. There is a reason why mentors like Socrates and Jesus Christ were so demanding—why following them was like having air or worth selling all your possessions.

These ideas may seem extreme and they are definitely countercultural. In our hearts we believe they are right. Classic works and even some popular movies capitalize on this theme. How many movies are considered classics because of the way they illustrate this mentoring process that takes the individual through pain and struggle using sports as the medium (*Rocky, Miracle, Hoosiers*, etc.)? How about comebacks from health crises or injury (*The Other Side of the Mountain, Ice Castles*, etc.)? We find these stories inspiring but hope they never happen to us.

At the same time, in our society, we seem to be perfectly comfortable with torturing our little kids with stress and tears in the name of "what is best for their education," yet we somehow reject the notion that crying real tears in the process of getting a Scholar-level education for ourselves might be worth it. IT IS!

There are too few of us who get to the other side of that mountain, so we do not have myriad examples and testimonies of the joy that follows the pain. We fail to internalize the process as a goal that we aspire to personally. We celebrate and respect those who make that sacrifice, but somehow do not make the leap of owning that objective for our own personal struggles. Whether or not we choose the path of greatness, we will struggle nonetheless—that is just life. Unless we consciously choose to embrace that ideal and take the road less traveled, we will lack the vision or focus to give our trials real meaning and the sense of divine purpose that consecrates them for our good.

The answers are clear and simple, and have been around for centuries. Children need to play more and work more—with their parents at their side. If lifestyle changes are needed, then they are needed. Just being honest about this is a huge step toward success. And real chores that require hard work and are truly necessary to the family are a vital ingredient in a Leadership Education.

Ingredient #36: Grandparent Mentoring

Wherever possible, each living grandparent and several adopted ones should be engaged as mentors. Children need to be tied to the older generation, and nothing does this more effectively than quality mentoring. Grandparent mentoring takes on a unique focus by emphasizing the teaching of skills. As part of your six month inventory, write down each Grandparent and possible Grandparent mentor, and list at least one skill they could pass on to each child. Then build your family vacations or other times together around this opportunity.

For example, our oldest son spent hours and hours on one trip learning to weave the seats of antique chairs—taught by his Grandpa. Emma spent a whole vacation learning to crochet from her Grandmother, and she has made hats, scarves, sweaters, etc. Her hand-made crocheted gifts to people have been amazing. She now develops her own patterns her Grandmother and others copy.

Oliver learned hunting from his Grandmother and Dutch oven cooking from a Grandpa.

Grandparents can be fabulous mentors when engaged to pass on skills to a new generation. It builds relationships, binds generations and significantly increases a young person's education. Love of Learning is the time for skills focus. It is a time of fun and growth that is constantly open to new projects. Grandparents can be a wonderful part of this (more on this from the Grandparents' perspective in Part IV).

Ingredient #37: Teaching the Model

It is essential to teach the young person the entire educational model over and over. We suggest teaching each child the Seven Keys and all the phases during Core Phase, and then re-teaching them repeatedly during Love of Learning and Scholar Phases.

We suggest teaching the model at least once every six months, and reinforcing it as appropriate in weekly interviews and whenever it comes up in daily discussion. If the goal is an adult who fully accomplishes their mission in life; we need youth who love learning and will study long, hard hours of their own free will and choice. To accomplish this, we need young children who play and work with their parents and older children who gain knowledge and skills and love learning and working.

The educational model must become part of the family culture, part of life's focus for each member of the family. When people ask our children what grade they are in, they answer "Love of Learning Phase," or "Scholar Phase." Then, when questioned, they explain what that means and what they are studying. They do not see themselves as children or teenagers, but as Core Phasers, Love of Learners and Scholars.

Teaching the Seven Keys is also vital. For example, a young person who understands "Inspire, Not Require" and "You, Not Them" knows their education is their own responsibility. Such a person studies to learn, has taken on the stewardship of their own education, is not dependent on someone else to teach them and is on the path to getting a true Leadership Education.

Unlike the conveyor belt, which keeps older grades and future curriculum under a shroud of expert secrecy, leadership educators outline the whole system right from the beginning. The more the young person understands the system, the higher the opportunity for leadership, initiative, and excellence.

We have noticed that many of the people who are best applying the Leadership Education model attend the Face-to-Face seminar series themselves then come back with their Scholar Phase students and go through the whole seminar series again. This reinforces it for them, and simultaneously helps the young people really know the Leadership Education system.

Ingredient #38: The Central Classic

All classics flow from a central classic, and all great classical education centers around a National Book: a centrally accepted family or national source of truth (*The Bible, The Qur'an, Bhagavad Gita,* etc.). The central classic is the book which it takes a whole lifetime to study, the book which everyone in the family reads from each day. Central books differ by family, but having one and spending a lifetime studying and applying its precepts is a necessary ingredient of Leadership Education.

The central classic should be read together daily. Everyone should be there, even the little kids. Those who can read participate, taking turns reading a verse or paragraph or more at a time. Everyone should have his or her own copy and follow along during the reading. We like to stop and ask questions, teach details that add depth and breadth, and discuss the meaning as we read. We let the teeniest kids play most of the time, right there on the floor in the middle of the room as we sit around them and read and discuss together. Once in a while we will have non-readers take a turn "reading" a verse by prompting them in their ears and having them repeat it to the group.

Scholars and parents should do a more in-depth daily study of the same central classic. Whatever your family's national book, making it a central part of daily education is vital to Leadership Education.

Ingredient #39: The Awakening

One day not long ago, our son Ammon had his "Awakening." He had been joining us for daily scripture study for several years, mostly playing in the middle of the floor—disrupting when his cars or dinosaurs got too loud, and seeming to pay no attention. Once in a while we would say, "It's Ammon's turn" and have him repeat a whispered verse out loud, but mostly he was too engrossed in his play to take part much.

On this day he was sitting looking through his books that had been pulled off the messy bottom Core shelf of our Leadership Education bookshelf, while everyone older than him took turns reading and everyone younger played on the floor or in somebody's lap. At one point in our reading, Dad asked a question to try to bring depth to the reading. There was the slightest hesitation after he asked the question, as Oliver James, Emma, Sara and Eliza considered whether or not they knew a good answer. In this brief moment of hesitation, before anyone said anything, Ammon looked up from his book and blurted out an excellent answer.

Everyone looked at him in surprise and with respect. "That's a great answer," Dad said. "Does anyone else have anything to add?" Ammon beamed, and then he went back to his book. He had awakened. Later that very same day, when Mom said "it's time to pray," Ammon yelled out "let me say it!" This was another first. We have seen it with every child, though not always so dramatically. Younger family members are there for the family routine, but allowed to play and not required to take full part. But suddenly one day they are ready, voluntarily jump in to participate, and from the answers they give it is clear that they have been listening for some time—maybe they were aware all along.

That same week Ammon started coming to Kidschool. He had been in the same room all along, but now he actively and voluntarily started participating in all the activities, studies, readings, etc. The Awakening had come.

Ingredient #40: The Interruption "Yes"

When Core Phasers—babies, toddlers and children—interrupt during your studies and work, gladly give them real, focused attention. It is amazing how the conveyor belt has conditioned us to boss, push, structure, schedule and demand when the child has his own wants and interests, but when he comes asking questions or requesting help, to be too busy.

We have covered several "no's" so far, and this is the first of several very important times to say "yes." When the child is asking questions, even three-year-old "why" questions, it is the perfect time to answer, teach, stop and talk or read together, answer with a project, initiate a game or lesson. Whereas the conveyor belt motto seems to be "when the student is ready, the teacher is too busy maintaining the structure for all the students who aren't ready," Leadership Education optimizes the teaching moment when the student is ready.

Ingredient #41: The Stateswoman

Implementing this whole recipe in order to effectively train leaders is very demanding. Parenthood—both fathering and mothering—is the most challenging, fulfilling and rewarding "career" or mission available. It is interesting that some modern feminists have described the stay-at-home mom or homemaker as caught in a life of boredom, subjugation and sad mediocrity. But true feminine ambition focused on the training of future leaders who fully understand and can accomplish their missions is the greatest challenge and opportunity of our time or any time. It is not enough to train up one's own children. The true mother must also train and properly raise the whole community in which her children grow up, looking ahead three or four generations and acting accordingly. This is not a government village raising the child, but a mother raising her own children, her future sons- and daughters-in-law, and communities of great and good leaders who will ensure the liberty of her grandchildren. Not, "It takes a village to raise a child," but, "It takes a mother to raise a village."

The greatest educators are fathers and mothers—from Eve, Mary, the mothers of Moses, Washington, Jefferson and Lincoln, to the women who embrace and magnify their roles and responsibilities as mothers in your neighborhood and your own family. These are statesmen and stateswomen engaged in the work of building the family—the basic unit of society. A stateswoman puts her relationship with God and spouse in their proper place of preeminence, leads an inspirational life, is actively progressing through the phases herself, runs a Mom School, has her home arranged as a leadership home, says "no" and "yes" in the Leadership way, and mentors through the Phases of a Leadership Education. She is a powerful example of a woman living a life of challenging, fulfilling, exciting feminine ambition and expertise that is literally world-changing. It takes a mother to raise a nation.

Ingredient #42: The Core Reading List

A few books we recommend every home should carry, thrown in a jumbled pile on the bottom shelves of the leadership bookshelf in the Family Room, include: *Oh, The Places You'll Go, Emma's Pet, The Cat in The Hat, Horton Hatches the Egg, Even if I Did Something Awful, Blueberries for Sal, Ferdinand the Bull, Peter Rabbit, Winnie the Pooh, I'll Love You Forever, The Monster at the End of this Book, Are You My Mother?, The Little House, The Stories of Little Bear, Hop on Pop,* and *Go, Dog, Go.*

There are many others, and each family should collect its own list of favorites and read and re-read them many times with each child. In our family, all of these are favorites. We especially have had fun with *Are You My Mother*? and *Emma's Pet*. Indeed these early classics, read repeatedly, teach many of the lessons which are later covered in more depth by youth and adult classics. We stop and discuss, even with toddlers, and relate principles to those of our central classic. We hear our Love of Learning and Scholar children referring back to these stories, emphasizing their principles or utilizing their analogies during conversations about a wide variety of topics.

Classics are a powerful source of cultural literacy. We recommend that people studying a foreign language start with the central classic and children's stories in that language and from that culture, since true native fluency requires cultural as well as phonetic and grammatical knowledge. Of the three, cultural fluency is the most valuable. We certainly all benefit from such an understanding of our own culture, and one of the best ways to obtain it is through repeated readings to and with children.

Ingredient #43: The Degree Program

Yours! To truly do early Scholar Phase yourself, just start reading as many classics as possible. But at some point, in order to get the Scholar Phase you deserve and that your children need you to have, it is important to engage a high quality Liberal Arts Mentor. This can be done informally or by enrolling in a degree program.

If you already have a college degree, ask yourself whether or not you actually had a true Scholar Phase—5,000 to 8,000 hours of mentored study of the great classics. Upon such an examination, you may decide that you are ready for additional mentoring.

There are so many reasons for not pursuing your education and/or degree and getting the superb education you want. But there is such a huge difference, a world of difference, between the education you can offer your children when you have a true Liberal Arts education and when you do not. Now we are not saying a "formal," that is, "institutional" education is necessary, but we are saying that a *great* education is—one attained with the help and guidance of great mentors.

The biggest roadblocks are time, money and will. In reality, only the third is the absolute obstacle. We have seen hundreds of people pursue advanced Scholar and Depth Phase studies with great mentors who had no more time or money than the thousands who do not. Rachel started her master's degree with three children under age three—a difficult time during which she lived on very little sleep and constant interruption. When she finished, she still had a number of challenges and three little children—but in addition she had a superb education from which to mentor them, not to mention an amazing sense of accomplishment and a new avenue of service and personal depth as a teacher of Hebrew.

There is such a difference between the community book club and the same group with a great Liberal Arts mentor. There is such a difference between the homeschool with a really dedicated and conscientious mother and the same mother with a superb, mentored education. Rachel has been asked countless times for help in starting groups in other areas that mirror her own Colesville Academy. Her answer was a delicate but frank one: it cannot be done. To duplicate what she does, one would have to *be* her. By contrast, those who do have even the beginnings of a Leadership Education rarely ask her for anything but very general advice on how to run their own Mom Schools. They do not want to duplicate hers, they want to do their own thing! The have their own "mine" to draw from.

It is tempting to think "not right now." But when is better? When the kids are themselves in Scholar Phase and need your world class mentoring? Or when they have moved away and will not benefit first-hand from your educational example? Another temptation is "I just can't afford it." But we have seen hundreds of people who could not afford it find a way—because they knew that in reality they could not afford *not* to have a superb Leadership Education. Even more, they knew that their children vitally needed them to have it. There are many things vital to your children's well-being that you would not dream of foregoing in the name of finances. You would simply find a way to make it happen.

We feel so strongly about this that we challenge you to do whatever it takes to get the education you need and see what miracles you can witness in your life. As with many miracles, however, you probably will have to step out onto the water before you find out for yourself that it will hold you up.

We are spending so much time on this because after years of promoting Leadership Education or the Thomas Jefferson model, the only people we have seen do it really well are those who get mentors and do the full Scholar Phase study. Remember, it is "You, not Them." The fact that getting great mentors takes some commitment and that getting a superb education is hard should not deter you from achieving excellence.

Ingredient #44: The Formal Ball

At least once a year, attend a formal black or white tie event. If possible, get the kids dressed up for it and have them attend too. But at least let them see you dress up and go. This is powerful socialization, and very important in training leaders. Leaders need to be comfortable in every setting and with any group of people. Great educator Arthur Henry King taught that the language of the classics is like any other language—if you learn it while you are young, you speak it like a native. If not, you will probably always carry at least a slight foreign accent.

Our point is not that the future leaders you are training in your home need to fit into the formal world. Churchill, Jefferson, Lincoln, Adams—none of them fit the mold. But they were familiar with the mold, knew its language, and knew how to *effectively* not fit in. There is a great difference between 1) the bumbling hick accent which constantly communicates "treat me as an inferior," 2) the polished courtier "I want to fit in more than anything because I want to feel superior" worldview, and finally 3) the habit of "I am at ease with anyone in any setting so let's talk because you are truly important and I want to get to know you." The third one comes attached to "I stand for something, and I care about what you stand for too." The latter is the view of statesmen—calm, sure, confident, not easily swayed but always openly optimistic and interested in others more than self.

There are many types of socialization, and the first two listed above leave much to be desired. The formal event is ignored, even avoided by the first, and overly emphasized, often worshipped by the second. It is attended by the third, attended because people are there with missions to accomplish. Love of Learners and Scholar youth who are comfortable in such settings will be comfortable accomplishing missions in such settings. The self-conscious are as unlikely as the self-absorbed to look around and follow spiritual promptings that are needed in formal settings where many important decisions are made. Indeed, perhaps the most important decisions leaders make is whom to trust, and formal events are where many first impressions are made. Besides, such activities are a lot of fun, and they can inspire additional studies—before the fact as well as after.

When we give our families a smorgasbord of social experiences, it is natural and obvious that different skills, tones, and manners are effective and appropriate in different situations, and family members become agile in their social skills. By contrast, when teaching etiquette to adults in preparation for an event there are inevitable objections: "This just isn't natural for me," "I feel false when I behave this way," or "But what happens if...."

We do our children a disservice by bringing them up to believe there is only one correct way to behave. This leads them unwittingly to attitudes of bigotry, bias, isolation and segregation. We and they should become fluent in talking with, building rapport with and cooperating with homeschoolers and public schoolers, people of our own religion and those of different beliefs, people of our own political persuasion and those who passionately hold another viewpoint, etc.

Too often artificial boundaries of "us" and "them" are drawn simply because we lack the aptitude or inclination to bridge the gap with those who could be our allies and friends by building on the common ground that almost always does exist, if we know how to identify it. And in the trying times our children will undoubtedly face, an indispensable asset will be the talent of forming alliances with those who can help us accomplish our missions and with those whose worthy purposes we may advance.

Ingredient #45: The Assignment

When the student is bored, struggling with a project or book, or just seems caught in a rut and can not seem to get going, try giving an assignment. The conveyor belt builds its entire system around assignments, an open admission that it assumes all students to be in trouble and in need of outside direction at all times—to be incapable of self-direction and excellent pursuit of personal interests and talents.

In the Leadership Education model, we do not give assignments all the time—just when they are needed. We highly recommend the excellent book *The One Minute Manager Leads High Performance Teams*. It teaches that we all start new things with high energy and low direction, then move to a point of low direction and low energy called Dissatisfaction. As with the Seven Keys, this must be appropriately implemented in the context of the Phase the child is in. It is most explicitly applied in Scholar Phase, and as most parents of this generation who have children in Core and Love of Learning are in Scholar Phase themselves, a review of this principle in this context can be valuable.

With Core Phase, frustration and dissatisfaction are often just a by-product of a logistical problem: too little sleep, inadequate nutrition, lack of a meaningful routine, uncertainty regarding family and/or chore roles, etc. An Inventory will most likely reveal the issue at hand, and FEC can prescribe the solution.

When the inventory reveals that the dissatisfaction for an older student is Dissatisfaction, or, that part of the learning cycle when enthusiasm wanes and challenges loom, it is time for The Assignment. In Love of Learning and early Scholar Phase, you may need to jump right in and start doing the assignment with them. By later Scholar and Depth Phases, you can simply give the assignment with a due date and reporting time (then be absolutely sure to follow through—in fact, mentors and parents should read *The One Minute Manager* in addition to the sequel on teams mentioned above).

Your assignment immediately gets rid of Dissatisfaction, since direction is high even though energy is low. As the student gets into the assignment, both energy and direction will be high and they will begin working hard and learning. This takes a few hours in some cases, and perhaps several months in others. But by knowing this pattern you become what Aneladee Milne has called the "parent mentor." The parent mentor can immediately move a student from Dissatisfaction—where many conveyor belt students stay for years and years. We do not mean to communicate that this is easy, but it is quite routine and simple even though it takes creativity and some hard work for the parent mentor.

The real challenge is to know the perfect thing to give the student, the perfect assignment that will inspire them to do the hard work needed to get past Dissatisfaction. There are two essential parts to this. First, as we have said above, the parent mentor must personally experience Scholar Phase. A parent who has pushed past Dissatisfaction with the help of an assignment from a mentor will know how to do this better than if they have never had the experience. The second essential part of giving assignments is to help the youth make the assignment fun. It must be truly inspiring, and for Love of Learners that means really, really fun.

One easy way to do this is to jump into it with them and have fun yourself. When Love of Learning Phasers are in Dissatisfaction, the measured and inspired use of Assignments can motivate progress and learning. However, do not leer and hover, waiting for the opportunity to interject an assignment just so you feel like a mentor. In most cases the Love of Learner benefits most when they overcome the slump on their own. They need "the right kind of vacuum" to motivate them to do what they feel they should and have been avoiding, or to try something new as a last resort to avoid dying of monotony. When an Assignment is called for, it should be of the fun and horizon-expanding variety.

Note that this is most likely the wrong way to do this in Scholar Phase. Again, if you have done Scholar Phase or are doing it with a great Liberal Arts mentor, you will know this by experience. In Scholar Phase, "fun" is not nearly as inspiring as "really, really hard." And most often the called-for Scholar Assignment is not to branch out into a new area, but to delve deeper into the one we're struggling with already. We know this runs counter to the current wisdom. The conveyor belt says teenagers "just wanna have fun." The truth is that youth naturally, passionately, even desperately want much more than to have fun. When they get into Dissatisfaction, they will willingly choose fun as an escape. But it leaves them feeling empty, ever wishing there were something more. What they really want is depth, quality, meaning, opportunities to really grow up. They want a true challenge. They want an adult challenge.

It was a source of pride and joy when Emma recently announced that she was in Dissatisfaction and would therefore be tripling her reading commitment in a book she had not been particularly enjoying (it was to be discussed by the class she was participating in). She was pleased to announce two days later that Dissatisfaction was long gone. She had been taught by her mentor about Dissatisfaction and took steps on her own to overcome it. Her maturity in the way she handled the situation brought us great satisfaction; but more than that, she felt a sense of personal triumph and a defining of character to have chosen to do the hard thing against her more self-indulgent inclination. This lesson will stay with her and her ability to self-correct during hardship is expanded simply because her mentor, Dr. Henke, taught her this principle and she trusted him enough to apply it.

Many youth might tell you that "fun" is what they really want, that "hard" is nowhere on their list. They do not fully know themselves yet—many never will, especially if they do not experience a mentor who understands that they must get past Dissatisfaction through hard, demanding, stretching assignments which pull and grind. Now do not get us wrong, they want "fun" too—pretty much every evening. But having fun will not pull them out of Dissatisfaction. Only doing a really hard and challenging assignment will do that.

As a mentor, your education is hugely important here, since your depth or shallowness will directly impact what assignment you give. You cannot pass on what you do not have. But you can get what you do not have, and you can start getting it immediately—today. If you are a chapter ahead, you can assign effectively. If you are fifty books ahead, you can assign more effectively.

By the way, you may have noticed that during this discussion, we have made little mention of Core Phase. We do believe in assignments during Core, just not too many academic assignments. Learning to work, obey, treat others respectfully, make apologies when they are called for—there are many worthy Core Phase assignments for toddlers and young children.

Ingredient #46: The Mission

The basic source of inspiration for achieving a Leadership Education is mission. Those who know they have a mission desire to prepare for it—to do the hard work necessary to get the needed education. This is not to say that a person must know every detail about his mission, or have any idea what it fully is. Even Jesus Christ learned line upon line. Simply the knowledge that "I have a mission" is enough to inspire the corresponding "and so I'll prepare for it." Mission is the inspiration behind Scholar Phase, the impetus of the focused attention of Depth Phase, something parents should help students prepare for, something everyone has. We believe that a person who fulfills his mission will literally change the world. We believe this is true of every single person who is born and every single individual mission.

Core Phase is a very important time for everyone to learn the parts of their mission that are shared by everyone. There are certain things that all human beings have as a mission, and Core Phase teaches these things. In Love of Learning Phase, we continue this universal learning and simultaneously begin to explore areas of personal mission—which often come to us as interest, talent, skill, ability, intelligence, gift, etc. Most importantly, the parent mentor must clearly understand and be able to articulate what he knows about his own personal mission(s). Young people think in terms of whom they want to be like much more than what they want to accomplish. Being able to tell them what your mission is when they ask or at some other key moment is incredibly inspiring. Share this sparingly, in special moments when it feels right.

Finally, it is essential that you clarify what your mission is and align your life to be actively pursuing it. There are few things more incongruent than someone who says they have an important mission and then lives in conflict with it. This is a great way to confuse children and to leave them with only one strong conviction: that they will never amount to much. If you do not know your mission, spend the time to clarify, discover and articulate your mission. And if you are not living your mission, make the necessary changes to do so. What else could matter more to your personal satisfaction and the happiness of those around you? If you do not, your mentoring will not be inspiring no matter how many books you purchase, seminars you attend, or techniques you employ. If all you have is the conviction of what you are supposed to be doing right now that will take you toward fulfillment of your mission—just do it. Honestly, this is the way it works for most of us. The most important thing about mission is to carry out yours and invite your children to do the same with theirs.

Ingredient #47: The Friend

We need to speak for a moment directly to the mothers, though the fathers can listen in and be supportive. Great mother mentors have a few close, great friends. The great friend is someone you can trade off with when you have a bad day—who can take your children and not change the schedule at all because she is following it too. She shares your values, has children with ages close to your children's ages, and follows a similar Leadership Education pattern in the home. Such a friend becomes a mentor to your children, and what Tiffany Earl calls a "Soul Mentor" to you. You share ups and downs together, often letting her help when you are down and in turn helping her when you are up.

At least one such friend is invaluable to a Leadership home. If you do not have one, or if you do not feel there are enough such people in your community, muster your feminine ambition and go out and build such a community of support. We have been so blessed to have literally dozens of such friends in our small community. Rachel has worked very hard in helping this community to develop, broaden its scope and deepen its educational roots. Numerous others have done the same kind of hard work in our community, and the networks now intersect. One way to build a community of like-minded families and nurture friendships is to create an opportunity for an activity of interest to many that will bring families together. Some wonderful and inspirational Leadership model activities that work perfectly to build a community of families and gain Leadership Education friends include:

Spelling Bee	Theatrical Production	Science experiments
Geography Bee	Risk Tournament	Sewing Class

Math Bee	Night of Poetry	Chess Tournament
History Bee	Talent Show	Musical Group
Sewing Bee	Family Ball	Build something
Cookoff or kid potluck	Garden	Sports Day at the park
Create recipe book	Girls Clubs	Service Project

We look at it this way: if you look around at your community and see many young people being raised in the perfect way in order to marry your children a few years from now, then you have got a wonderful community and need to actively take part in improving it. If not, you have a lot of work to do, and a Mom School is just the ticket. A great friend, likely more than one, will naturally arise out of the process. The work needs to start with your own Scholar Phase education, and progress to training and organizing a community that fits the needs of your family—for the next four generations. Nothing small, just something that will change society for the benefit of your posterity. This is the essential endeavor of any good, healthy civilization.

Ingredient #48: The Core Phase Curriculum

The curriculum of Core Phase is short. It is sweet. It is ignored in most homes and schools. It is vitally important:

Right and wrong, true and false, good and bad.

This curriculum is best taught through work and play with loving parents at home. No other institution can teach it as well. Few other institutions are even trying. But worse, few homes give it full attention for the first eight years of a child's life. So many other things are allowed to enter in—good things, positive things.

But anything which distracts from teaching right and wrong, true and false and good and bad during the Core Years from birth to around age eight are just that—distractions. And they should be labeled and treated as distractions.

If you truly want your child to succeed in his mission, to be happy and fulfilled in life, be sure to give full parental focus on the Core Phase curriculum during these vital years.

Ingredient #49: The Love of Learning Curriculum

Example	Inspiring Parent	Freedom
Environment	Mentors	Fun
Opportunities	Guidance	Personal Attention
Work	The Bookshelf	Younger Siblings
Play	Mornings	Older Siblings
Study	Afternoons	Mom
Projects	Evenings	Dad
Field Trips	Summers	Grandparents
The Library	Winters	Questions
Family Room	Exploring	Discussions

Ingredient #50: Spring is for Science

Each spring the world is re-born, and science in all its varieties fills the air. Just as there are natural patterns of age, time of day, weeks and months, the year also naturally lends itself to the training of leaders. "Spring is for science" is a great motto, one which will bring numerous exciting field trips, library trips, discussions, outdoor activities, and family evenings. It will open books on your bookshelf that have collected dust much of the year, and will naturally take you to parks where Six Month "No's" and Six Month Inventories are achieved in the bright sunshine to the smell of fresh flowers. Experiments, readings, studies and other science projects flourish and grow in the spring.

Ingredient #51: Fall is for Beginnings

In our family we do The Six Month Inventory each spring and each fall. This seems to work especially well since the summer and winter months are so different from each other. In the fall, students are excited to set goals, raise the bar to a new level of study, and make plans for the months ahead. Vacations and activities are past, and a return to normal structure and routine feels wonderful to parents and children alike. Inventories in the fall naturally outline a world of learning for the months ahead, carefully considered with each individual child in mind.

Ingredient #52: The Subscription

A few carefully chosen subscriptions are a real help to the Foundational Phases and beyond. In our family we subscribe to two monthly magazines, which we read each month to the Core Phasers and Love of Learners. First, our church publishes a wonderful children's magazine, and we love the faith promoting stories, introductions to other young people, and messages from religious leaders. Second, a wise grandparent asked young Oliver if he would like a subscription to *Ranger Rick* magazine as his birthday present one year, and we encouraged him to tell her yes. She has renewed the subscription year after year at his bidding, and though now in Scholar Phase, he still pulls up a chair to listen when we read and show pictures from each monthly issue to our Core and Love of Learning children. Indeed, Mom and Dad never want to miss an issue either (Rachel's subscription to *Ranger Rick* did not lapse from early Love of Learning until she left home to go to college at age 17).

We recommend that you spend some time at a library or bigger bookstore reading through the various magazines available and pick a couple that suit your family. We have had other subscriptions, but found it best to maintain the top two and carefully read them together each month. Scholar and Depth Phasers have moved on to other subscriptions more applicable to them as they get older, but it is interesting that everyone in the family still looks forward to reading the Core Phase subscriptions together.

We also suggest letting grandparents know how much your children would love such a subscription for their birthday. Another great idea is perhaps a year's worth of lessons for Christmas (they could pay for them or better still give them personally where applicable). Of course, this requires communication so that gifts are not given that do not meet FEC approval. It is unfortunate when gifts are trivial, especially when a little communication would result in them being integrated with the family's goals and efforts.

Ingredient #53: The Dinner Meal

We already talked about the kitchen table, but the dinner meal is extra special. It can bring so many of the 55 ingredients together in one place. The dinner meal is a little like the instruction to "stir well" or "thoroughly mix until smooth" in most recipes. In our current twenty-first century paced world this vital step is often forgotten or justified away, but it is essential to the leadership home. If you truly cannot have a family meal with all family members present daily, have one as often as possible—at least a majority (four) of the days in the week.

At the dinner meal, etiquette can be taught, not from the "here's how to impress" model, but rather from the perspective of training politeness and polish which allows for unaffected graciousness now and later. World events should be discussed and important ideas shared. Children can recite, perform or share work accomplished. The future, personal missions, books just studied, and events attended are natural topics of discussion, along with so many other things which will come up naturally if we just spend regularly scheduled meal time together.

There is something about eating that is very bonding, a natural concept that seems to be hard-wired into our biology. Just as evenings bring bonding, eating together in the evening is perhaps even more powerful. Sometimes the smallest things make the difference, what a recent bestseller appropriately called "the tipping point"—the little detail that affects everything. Eating together in the evening is one such thing, a small detail which may make the difference between your family's successes and failures. Like Sunday FEC's and interviews, inspirational evenings and consistent morning routines, the dinner meal can make a huge difference in your Leadership Education.

Ingredient #54: The Discipline "Yes"

During the Sixth Month Inventory it is essential to say "Yes" to your own education, re-assessing your strengths, weaknesses, areas that need work and subjects you should be studying and making a plan to follow through. The conveyor belt has taught us to have structure, good discipline and to conform to the demand to follow through. All of these skills are wonderful if applied to the one person whose education you really control: Yours.

A few of the Seven Keys have particular aptness in personal application to your own life. "You, not Them." Structure your education and discipline yourself. "Simple, not Complex." Read the classics, get a mentor and work hard. "Structure Time, not Content." Have a set time, perhaps in the mornings, where you study, study, study. "Inspire, not Require"—others. Go ahead and require of yourself that you follow through on your plans. If your tendency is to be Sergeant Mom, give yourself some orders and get in your own face until they are accomplished. Say "yes" to disciplining yourself and getting the education you want and that your kids need you to exemplify.

Ingredient #55: The Academic "Yes"

Once you are disciplined and following through—which is to say, once you are ready for your own Scholar Phase—say "yes" to the hard areas you have been avoiding. Maybe it is math for you, or an advanced branch of science. Perhaps you just have not been able to muster up the will to wade through Euclid or Newton. Or maybe you started Einstein but did not seem to understand anything and did not want to spend time deciphering equations with the help of a physics dictionary and a lot of hard thinking. Perhaps for you the issue is non-fiction works, or all those Great Books that seem such a pain to dig into, including Shakespeare. Or maybe you love Shakespeare but Sophocles and Homer seem too remote. Maybe you need to ramp up your vocabulary or your skills with spelling or punctuation.

Whatever your areas of weakness, the Academic "Yes" says it is time to raise the bar. Of course, do not even try this unless you are doing The Discipline "Yes." Until your discipline is there, you cannot really raise the bar effectively. But once you have structured time and are following through, tackle a few of the hard things.

This does not mean you have to focus only on the hard areas. You can still keep studying all the things you love. Just push yourself by adding in some of the areas you have not dared to do yet. Venturing into the hard and challenging is truly worth the sacrifice. This is where the lifetime of learning comes in.

We still have fond memories of when Oliver realized that literature had to be a central part of the leadership curriculum that he was developing. He loved the Great Books, the Harvard Classics, the deep philosophical, political, legal, economic and historical texts. But he saw the literary works as lighter and less valuable. When he read the entire Great Books collection one year, he went slowly and took detailed notes through Plato, Aristotle, Hobbes, Plutarch, Locke and other deep non-fiction works, but he simply made it through the "lighter" literary works of Euripides, Sophocles, Aristophanes, Shakespeare, Tolstoy and others, and really chafed as he read Homer, Dante, Milton and the other poets. He had a love of the deep and philosophical but the literary seemed less engaging.

Then a mentor insisted that the most important lessons of Western Civilization were to be found in its stories, literature, poetry and art. At first Oliver resisted, even to such an important mentor, but the mentor held firm. Oliver reluctantly started re-reading all the great literary works, this time looking closely for what the mentor called the "real lessons learned by Jefferson, Madison and the other great statesmen." It did not take long to reach Dissatisfaction, and Oliver returned to the mentor sure that he had good reasons why these works were inferior (as a side note: There are undoubtedly those reading this who, having heard Oliver lecture on the importance of literature over the years, may gasp or sputter with incredulity. We nonetheless affirm that this is absolutely the unadulterated truth. This is evidence that we all go through the phases; even those we consider our mentors were once where we are now, and we can certainly progress to where they are).

The mentor was not fazed. Instead of listening to Oliver's wonderful arguments, the mentor did what all great mentors do when a Scholar or Depth student comes in Dissatisfaction: he gave him a very hard assignment. In this case he was to read a list of ten key literary classics in a very short time period and return to report. Oliver, doubting the mentor's words, but trusting the mentor, set out to accomplish the task. The first two books were valuable; he learned a great deal and wrote a few notes to supplement lectures on other non-literary works. Then he read *Les Miserables*.

Rachel drove to a Mexican restaurant (it was date night) while Oliver sat in the passenger's seat finishing the last few pages. As she turned into the parking lot, she glanced over and noticed that tears were trickling down his face. By the time she pulled the car to a stop a sob had escaped, and by the time the ignition was turned off he was hunched over, weeping. Neither of us remembers much of what we said as we talked there in the parking lot for over an hour about life, tests, trials, Christ and the atonement, real leadership, family, truth, love, honor, justice and mercy, paying the price of greatness, much more. We covered it all. But we both remember very distinctly how it felt. We never did eat Mexican food that night, but we certainly had a feast.

Yes, literature was about ideas; deep and moving and profound ideas. Yes, literature was also passionate and feeling. Yes, literature was actually better at teaching the principles than the other type of writing (the mentor had been right, as usual). Yes, both types of writing were important. Indeed they powerfully complemented each other. Yes, God must have inspired both, and on purpose. Yes, the arts, sciences, math and other fields would be studied as well and no doubt they would be equally important.

But it was much more than this. These new lessons and values, albeit very important, paled to the real lessons of this book. This was not a book about Jean Valjean, Cossette or Javert, this was a book about Oliver and Rachel, about little Oliver and Emma, about the 1990s and the coming 2000s (then just a vague image of something far away), of world challenges and healings by the 2030s, of new forms and statesmen who stood and said "no" and swayed the course of history, of documents written and liberties purchased at an incredible price and millions freed to live and love. It was a book about equations with new mathematical symbols where tithes and offerings factor in returns of ten- and hundred-fold, of math that shows why mom staying home significantly increases the bottom line, of plays on stages and oils on canvas eclipsing the masters of old, of children with children and grandchildren of their own and smiles on their faces. *Les Miserables* was about our mission, and yours—about our children, and yours. And it still is.

So is *A Tale of Two Cities, Pride and Prejudice, War and Peace, A Merchant of Venice, Principia Mathematica, Guernica, Starry Night*, the ceiling of the Sistine Chapel, *Laddie, Little Britches, The Weight of Glory, "MacDuff"* (the actual title is *Macbeth*, but this title makes more sense to Oliver), *Faust,* Smetana's *"The Moldau," "Finlandia"* by Sibelius, and so on.

Classics are about more than they are about. They are about each new reader and what God wants to communicate to him, if he will listen. As we build on the shoulders of the greats, God continues to inspire greater and greater things. We believe that the very best the world has to offer—in literature, art, science, math, government, family, in everything—is still ahead. It will come precisely as we move outside of our personal comfort zones and push ourselves into the unknown, as we "put our hands in the hand of God and step out of the light into the darkness." That experience with *Les Miserables* communicated on so many levels, but the most basic and enduring lesson is that we must trust our mentor and venture into the hard stuff. It is truly worth the sacrifice.

We are so optimistic about the future. In this time when so many people seem to be full of anxiety, we are thrilled to be part of the future that is coming. The lessons and cycles of history leave no doubt that the future will bring challenges, troubles and struggles. But of one thing we are certain: this generation and those ahead will rise to meet the challenges and build a better world, with God's guidance, than anything we have yet seen.

We believe that every person has a mission that can make all the difference. We want to see each person get an education to match their mission, and for that to happen parents must step up and create Leadership homes which mix the ingredients in the unique way best suited for that home. This will create the leaders of the future. You are the expert on your home, and as you mix these and other ingredients into your recipe, as you pay the price to inspire, not require, you will, in Gandhi's words, "be the change you wish to see in the world."

Mixing Instructions: Training a Generation of Leaders

Together, these 55 ingredients and others like them will create a mountain or move it, whichever is necessary. None of the ingredients are perfect alone. Nobody that we know does them all perfectly—least of all, us. But together they create the recipe of a fabulous leadership home, of world-class, superb leadership-level education in children, youth and adults.

"Thoroughly stir, mix, and bake" your ideal mix of ingredients to get educated parents and children, grandparents and community. The ingredients train leaders, citizens, statesmen and ultimately the parents of the future. Some are helpful, others are vital. Together they are the basis of success in educating children who will become adults and leaders who move our societies, nations, and world forward toward a better place.

CHAPTER SIX

Transition To Scholar

The transition from Love of Learning Phase to Scholar Phase is one of the most important facets of a young person's education. Those who transition well will almost invariably have an excellent Scholar Phase experience; those who do not will likely continue to struggle. Fortunately, this transition is natural and virtually any healthy child will quite automatically make many of the transitional changes on his own. The challenge is that parents who were trained on the conveyor belt may not realize what is happening, and may in fact, block, slow down or otherwise frustrate this natural process. That is why it is essential for parents to recognize and understand this vital transition in a young person's life.

Transition occurs in most girls between ages ten and twelve and in most boys between eleven and fourteen. Some psychologists and counselors speak of this age as the root source of most problems in men, who are often pushed too hard at this age to "put away childish things" and take on adult responsibility. One of the biggest pressures many boys feel at this age is pressure to perform academically. Girls are usually ahead of boys at this age, yet boys are often pushed to keep up to girl "grade levels."

The key words of this period often conflict in parent's minds: independence and protection. Children at this age need to feel both. In a healthy child, without undue parental or societal pressure, this is a positive, happy and enjoyable age. Speaking of important life transitions, Montessori observed: “The middle age crisis signals that the adult is on their way to death; in contrast, transition excitement about learning signals that the child is on their way to life.” It is important during this transitional time to remember that the child is still in Love of Learning Phase and to consider and treat Transition as such rather than as the beginning of Scholar Phase.

J. S. Ross expressed that a “being from another planet, who did not know the human race, could easily take these ten year olds to be the adults of the species; supposing they had not met the real adults.” Just as puberty signals physical readiness for Scholar Phase and getting certain permanent teeth signals the move toward Love of Learning Phase, a height spurt between the ages of nine and eleven often signals readiness for transition.

The following chart lists typical traits and behaviors of children in Transition to Scholar stage:

TRAITS AND BEHAVIORS INDICATING TRANSITION TO SCHOLAR
Physically, a growth spurt after age nine for girls and eleven for boys often signals that your child is getting ready for Transition.
Calm and Happy
Mentally and Physically Healthy
Emotionally Stable
The child hits “diversity” age, when parents and teachers notice major emerging differences between children.
Play with older children is more “peer play” than tag-along; play with younger children becomes organizing or calling the shots in the activities rather than just joining in.
Heightened concern for fitting in with peers—in dress, activities, academics, etc.

Heightened concern for appropriateness of self and family in public or social settings
Increased independence
Increased attention span
Loves focused projects of his or her own interests
Likes to learn new things
Initiates projects without supervision
Greater level of follow-through on projects
Takes some things to extremes
Starts getting very messy about room and/or grooming
Gets excited by a collection: Star Wars Cards, stamps, model horses, etc.
Likes to get away from home and be with friends
Starts to worry about life, his/ her future, and the problems the parents are facing
Tests the rules, or tries to argue for personal exemptions from the rules
Has strong likes and dislikes
Wants more personal attention
Initiates more discussions with parents
Loves praise
Loves and thrives in structure

Transition Discoveries

In addition to these specific lessons and skills, Transition to Scholar is the ideal and natural time for the child to make a number of interesting, fascinating and exciting discoveries. If we take away this time of discovery, or push it too soon, a "hate of learning" ensues rather than the healthy love of learning most children will encounter. Some of the discoveries that a child will naturally make during a healthy Transition to Scholar include the following:

- Learning never ends.
- Learning is used in adult life.
- I will someday educate children as part of the cycle of life.
- Learning combines doing with talking with practice (and later with thinking).
- Imitation speeds up the learning process.
- Unconscious creation needs to be followed by conscious work.
- There is not an answer to everything (but there is to the most important things).
- Character flaws hurt.
- I can contribute to society (or make the mistake of trying to achieve to impress).
- I have an impact on my own future.
- Mom and Dad have flaws.
- Mom and Dad also have authority, so I live in a potential tyranny that must be closely watched.
- There are other cultures, many of which are different than my own.

During this same period of great discovery, youth go through several world-shifting experiences, including:

- They enter society.
- They begin concentrating.
- They wonder how things work – a radio, a tree limb, a dandelion, etc.
- They can absorb massive amounts of information.
- They draw conclusions about what they are good at, bad at, etc.

As you can see, the discoveries of Transition to Scholar are numerous and wonderful. It is so important that parents help provide an environment where children can make these discoveries in a natural and healthy manner. As they do so, they will also learn the following Transition Skills, as outlined by Wayne Dyer in *What Do You Really Want for Your Children*?:

- Take smart risks
- Don't put yourself down
- Inner Approval: Don't emphasize external measures of success
- Don't complain or whine
- Don't be judgmental
- Never get "bored"
- Learn from mistakes
- Learn to lose and win well
- Practice smart self-reliance
- Choose to feel at peace and serene
- Realize that life is about smiling
- Never fear your own greatness

Students in Transition also learn many of the skills that will determine their learning effectiveness (or weakness) in the years ahead. In fact, during Transition to Scholar ages, students develop fully half of the nine ways necessary to human learning, as discussed in *A Mind at a Time* by Mel Levine. Study the following chart to learn the skills of each system and the Phases in which they are learned.

EIGHT SYSTEMS OF LEARNING, SKILLS AND PHASES WHEN LEARNED

SYSTEM	SKILLS	PHASE
Language	Automatic/literate, concrete/ abstract, basic/higher Receptive/expressive, understanding, interpreting	CORE

SYSTEM	SKILLS	PHASE
Motor	Large and small muscle movement/coordination	CORE
Attention Control	Alertness, mental effort, arousal, consistency Selection, depth/detail, activity, span, satisfaction Previewing, options, pace, quality, reinforcement	TRANSITION
Memory	Story acting, task accomplishment, short/long term	TRANSITION
Spatial	Perceiving, sequencing, patterns, remembering, creating, organizing—managing time and materials	TRANSITION
Sequential		
Social Thinking	Relationships, popularity, intrapersonal politics	TRANSITION
Intuitive Thinking	Downplayed in modern conveyor belt; powerful and vital skill marking readiness for Scholar Phase. EQ (emotional intelligence) has a much higher correlation to leadership, relationship, career and life success than IQ (conveyor belt measure)	TRANSITION
Higher Thinking	Conceptual, problem-solving, rule-guided, creative	SCHOLAR

The healthy child naturally learns all of these thinking skills openly or subconsciously—unless they are squashed. Unfortunately, the conveyor belt rejects Intuitive Thinking and simultaneously over-emphasizes the need for Higher Thinking skills at an early age. To compensate, many young students turn to Memorizing as a way to fake Higher Thinking skills which their brains are unprepared to utilize. If success and happiness in life, mission and relationships were not good enough reasons to safeguard the foundational phases, this alone should be compelling. Many who substitute memorization for Higher Thinking maintain this habit through adulthood resulting in a nation of highly-trained but narrow experts. In such a society, expert training passes for education, and rote expertise substitutes for independent thinking.

It is not hard to see the effects in society of the combination of these two examples of bad education: The "good" student with a high ability to memorize before the age of ten (leading to a "straight A" label which sticks) often grows into a careerist who "succeeds with renown" in his or her professional field at the expense of lasting and nurturing family relationships.

Parents can have a significant positive influence on all this simply by helping children identify and choose wisely in the Transition to Scholar age between nine and fourteen. Of course, this starts by not pushing too hard when the child is still learning Intuitive Skills, and in waiting to push higher order academic subjects until the child's natural maturity has equipped him for Higher Thinking.

Whichever life path (conveyor belt or leadership; see discussion in Chapter Two) is chosen between the tender ages of nine and fourteen will likely be maintained for a long time. A central reason for this is that the two paths teach their own set of lessons, and once we learn them it takes a long time to change the values, assumptions and life patterns which these lessons instill in our hearts, minds and souls. Thus it is vital for parents to understand and teach their children the contrasting lessons of the two paths.

LESSONS AND RESULTS OF THE
TWO PATHS DURING TRANSITION TO SCHOLAR

	CONVEYOR BELT	LEADERSHIP PATH
Lessons	to copy to count to compare	to create to value to impact
Result	dependable followers	responsible leaders

Ponder these two sets of lessons and results. What kind of education comes from focusing on the abilities to copy, to count and to compare? What kind of career does this prepare a person to pursue? How does this measure up in training future parents? Voters? Community leaders? Perhaps most importantly, what are the inherent values that are learned from this type of education?

In contrast to the sad consequences of only learning these mediocre lessons, future leaders need to know how to create, to truly value, and to effectively impact the world around them. These three lessons are essential traits of leaders. The result of training young people with these abilities is better fathers and mothers, better citizens and voters, more effective entrepreneurs and leaders, more creative artists and scientists, and a society of independent thinkers and statesmen.

The leadership path teaches the young person both sets of lessons. The most important skills and curriculum of Transition to Scholar are the habits of creating, valuing and impacting. Youth who know how to create naturally learn to copy, while those who can value and impact must be able to effectively count and compare. But the reverse is not true; the conveyor belt path does not train students for leadership. The leadership path trains students in all the knowledge of both paths with the attitude and vision of leadership.

It is a sad and unfortunate circumstance when a nation sets as its educational target the inferior skills of copying, counting and comparing. This is especially lamentable when the youth of the day are bright, inquisitive and interested in creating, valuing, impacting, and leading. To "dumb down" a nation of natural leaders, telling them that they must put their interests aside in order to qualify for a future job, is a tragedy. Twelve or more years of conditioning to spend their days doing things they do not want to do, because "that's just the way it is," readies them for the modern jobs their parents so highly prize and personally hate in such high numbers. The solution to this all-too-typical process is simple: Leadership students must learn to create, value and impact.

In summary, Transition to Scholar is an exciting and wonderful time for a child on the leadership path, and parents largely choose which path the child will take—at least at this point in her life. The right choice can make a huge difference in the education of each child, and in the life mission she will pursue. During Transition, the future is in the hands of parents, and is a product of the proverbial mix of "inspiration and perspiration."

Parenting Skills for Transition

Transition to Scholar has a huge and lasting impact on each child, and the parental role is central and extremely influential. How can parents provide the best possible Transition to Scholar for their children? In this section, we will outline, consider, apply and gain mastery in thirty-five parenting skills for parents of children in Transition. These skills were derived from the works of Mel Levine, John Holt and Wayne Dyer as well as our own experiences. We will discuss each skill in the context of mentoring a Transition to Scholar child on the path of leadership.

Of course, we reiterate what we have said many times. Parents are the experts on their own homes and families. Everything we suggest here should be applied by wisely considering what will work best in your unique situation and with your one-of-a-kind child. Many were born to be great leaders in the decades ahead and no "one size fits all" system will work for them. Personalize and incorporate skills from this list that meet the current needs of the individuals in your family along with any other skills that you know are needed. And of course, keep in mind that we are not suggesting that every parent must apply all thirty-five skills at once, but we hope that a close reading of all thirty-five will help you identify which you need and perhaps spark additional ideas that will be helpful to your family.

The first six skills come from the work of child psychologist Mel Levine.

1. Focus on Strengths and Affinities

Too often parents emphasize weaknesses, a conveyor belt lesson based on the assumption that education is about not letting children get behind in any of the "important" subjects. This lesson often travels through the person's life. Business guru Peter Drucker blames much of business failure on hiring people for their lack of weaknesses instead of for their strengths. When business leaders hire based on strengths, their organizations are much more effective.

The same is true for children. When parents and teachers emphasize the child's strengths and affinities, the child grows in ability, confidence and learning, and naturally applies these strengths to overcoming areas of weakness. So much of conveyor belt education is fear-based—worrying that the child will not measure up. In contrast, Leadership Education assumes that the child will not only meet but exceed basic levels of learning, and more importantly, totally excel in certain chosen areas of focus. During Transition, parents should pay attention to the child's affinities and interests, strengths and passions and areas of focus.

2. De-mystification

During Transition children have lots of questions. They want to understand why they are the way they are, why the world is as it is, and why you, as parents, are the way you are. Leadership parents take the time to de-mystify things, to explain, and to talk and discuss things at great length with their children.

3. Accommodating

This is of vital importance in the training of leaders. In contrast to the conveyor belt, Leadership parents do not require or push the child to fit a preconceived system, curriculum, social status, or other arbitrary label. Instead, parents treat each child as an individual, and do the hard work to build a system around them that works! When they are well into Scholar Phase they can move into a different, more demanding system (such as a program defined by a mentor) as needed to progress, but during Transition they should be treated as a unique individual.

In fact, even in Scholar Phase they only enter a program at their own choosing, and for a relatively short time period. Overall, their entire education is personalized. This can be a challenge for parents whose educational experience was conveyor belt, but as we have stated many times before: unless parents get off the conveyor belt, they will struggle to train leaders.

4. Interventions at the Breakdown Points

When things do not work, when the child has discipline problems or a learning meltdown, parents should intervene and help the child through this difficult period. Interventions should be used very sparingly, and the wise leadership parent realizes that a certain level of getting bored, frustrated, or wanting to push the limits of the rules is only natural. Instead of reacting with anger, punishments, inappropriate structure or "rescue," a relaxed and understanding parent who laughs it off and inspires the child to do better in the future will have the best results.

In fact, if the child trusts the way you handle problems, she will often *ask* for your intervention when help is needed. Interventions should be short, direct, matter-of-fact, fair, and limited. When the student's life breaks down for whatever reason, the intervention helps them get back on track. Often the parent can simply let the child know what the various options and consequences of each choice are and allow the child to choose. Where more drastic interventions are appropriate, parents should still remember that the goal is to help the child return to the natural leadership path.

5. Protection from Humiliation

The main role of the parent during Transition Phase, at least in terms of the needs of the child, is protection from humiliation. Since it is during this period of life that the child is learning how to nurture relationships and how to deal with other people, this role is very important with lasting implications. It should go without saying that it is a real tragedy if the parent is the instigator of a loss of dignity. Core issues of confidence, esteem, faith and self-worth are reinforced or threatened during this period, and parental trust is crucial.

6. Supporting Expertise

If the child "develops a love," as Mel Levine puts it, do whatever it takes to support it. Transition is a period of exploration and discovery, and is part of the Love of Learning Phase. Providing children freedom and encouragement to pursue their loves and interests is essential. One of the best ways to do this is for parents to find out what their children are interested in and begin to study it.

On the conveyor belt, students are expected to study the topics assigned by teachers. On the leadership path, parents and mentors get their assignments from the students, studying their interests and loves in order to help guide them. If the child changes "loves" several times a year, or even several times a month or week, this just means that he is healthy and loving learning. Parents should seek inspiration to prioritize and invest themselves in the study of these loves as much as possible in order to be prepared when the child asks questions or needs help or validation.

Skills 7 through 11 were taught by John Holt, considered by many to be the father of modern home schooling and many non-traditional private schools.

7. Sports

Children learn better academically when they are developing the whole person, including their physical side. Beyond fitness and nutrition, being involved in athletics during Transition helps children develop confidence and work on social relationships. Oliver James, Emma, Sara and Eliza are all actively involved with their Karate, and Ammon looks forward to the day when he will join. There are many ways to fill this need, including organized sports teams or dedicated family or community sports days.

For example, one excellent practitioner of Leadership Education, Angie Baker, established a sports clinic for community youth as a Mom School designed to help her own family. When she reported about this at a seminar, Rachel felt inspired to do something similar in our community. She instigated "Sports Day," where during one fall whole families came together each Friday afternoon at our neighborhood park for a pot-luck lunch and then "recess." She remembered how much fun she had with four-square, jacks, jump rope, kickball, wargames, monkey bars, and so forth as a child. She wanted to share these things with her children and friends. Sports equipment of many types was brought, and children chose their own activities, from jump rope or kickball, to foursquare, jacks, hopscotch, capture the flag, ultimate frisbee, playground equipment or even sword play. There were even adults to mentor such things as tumbling, jump rope tricks and songs, baseball, chess, and so forth.

A visitor observed during Sports Day, "I noticed, and mentioned to my husband, that there was no fighting or problems with the kids. Then I wondered if I just wasn't catching it, so I made a specific endeavor to watch for contention or other anti-social behavior. After a couple of hours of cooperation and fun, with little and big ones playing right together without any problems, I told my husband, 'this is what we want for our son!' "

Another way to integrate sports into the equation is to invite the children to participate in a parent's hobbies. Oliver loves mountain biking and tennis. When Oliver James got old enough to participate, he enjoyed going on mountain biking trips with Dad and learning to play tennis. As they reached Transition age, Emma, Sara and now Eliza all joined in these activities and the younger children all beg to take part. Of course, during summers, our family plays a lot of sports. Several nights a week, Oliver James practices running football routes while dad plays quarterback, and often the whole family joins in for a game of touch football or basketball. Even the Core Phasers participate where they can, or just run around getting in everybody's way. Maintaining the sports equipment and playing area provides opportunity for family work to be accomplished as an accent to play.

8. Lessons

Children who enroll in lessons learn structure, practice and how to work with mentors other than their parents. We discussed lessons at some length in the Core and Love of Learning section, and will not repeat all of that here. Suffice it to say that Transition is the signal that the time to start lessons for most children is here, or fast approaching. It is also a reminder that parents should avoid the conveyor belt temptation to enroll the child in every lesson available. Most children get more out of mastering one or two areas of focus rather than a shotgun approach which turns mom into a mini-van chauffeur.

9. Do-ing

Children in Transition learn so much more by doing things than just reading. While books are a very important part of Transition, projects take a center place in the curriculum. Projects can and should vary: one day doing science experiments and another day working on artistic creations. We followed up a project on geology with a visit to a rock shop and a field trip to Zion's National Park. Oliver James and Ammon fell in love with the subject and started a rock collection. Another time, we followed an art project with a field trip to a museum after which Sara spent hours and hours working on her drawing talent. Children need to do, not just see or hear.

10. Show-ing

Over the years, as we have spoken at numerous seminars and events to parents about Leadership Education, we have had so many mothers ask about how to get their children to study math. We always respond by asking them what math classics they have read in the past few months. The typical response is for them to look at us like we are crazy. "Why on Earth would I read math classics?" they seem to be thinking. If we want our children to value something, just telling them to do it will not work. We have to show them. In short: don't just tell them to study math, do it. Love numbers, shapes, diagrams, and read the biographies of Newton, Pythagoras, Nichomachus, Archimedes and Hawking around the house. Show them what you want them to do by doing it yourself, and they will value it. The fact that Rachel plays the piano and that Oliver takes martial arts lessons has drastically impacted our children's desire to keep taking these lessons even when they are hard. Without example, children tend to lose interest.

11. The Arts

Artistic learning is valuable for everyone, but it is especially important during Transition to Scholar where the child's brain development is going through significant growth and patterning. Art can be done as lessons, projects, field trips, performance, or just for fun. For example, we know that if we ever want to motivate Emma, we need to tie the project to a performance. Once when we were reading Shakespeare as a family, Oliver paused every few lines and asked the children to translate Shakespeare's phrases into modern English. We immediately noticed that Emma had a real gift for this. She naturally understood the meanings and nuances that the rest of the family struggled to interpret, or missed entirely. We felt that she should develop this strength, yet she showed no desire to pick up Shakespeare and read. When she auditioned for a youth play, however, she got very much involved in Shakespeare.

On another occasion, when we were memorizing poems and writing poetry, Emma got excited about the project when Dad suggested that she write a poem about our disabled son, Hyrum, to send out to extended family members. The performance opportunity inspired her to work long hours on writing, polishing and improving her poetic gifts. Sara, on the other hand, prefers to do artistic projects for her own gratification. She often reworks something to make it excellent and then just files it away in her journal without showing anyone. In both cases, including the arts during Transition to Scholar helped our children develop their unique talents and interests and inspired them toward further learning. Whatever the needs of your child, many experts affirm that artistic projects help with brain development and build all areas of learning, not just artistic talent.

Best-selling philosopher and family expert Wayne Dyer taught skills 12 through 27, and we highly recommend you familiarize yourself with his other excellent writings for all ages and family situations.

12. Listen to them

Transition age children have a lot to say, and they need to be heard. Parents who listen, who really take the time to talk and discuss, are training leaders. If they cannot get you to listen your children will search elsewhere. Indeed one of the sad stereotypes of pre-teen and teenagers is the "generation gap" myth, where youth simply have nothing to say to parents. In many cases, this is more the parents' fault than they realize. Certainly they have more power than they realize. The so-called generation gap is actually just a communication gap that started in Transition, or even before.

Unfortunately, the conveyor belt teaches that this gap is normal and even healthy. This is reinforced by modern lifestyle wherein we flip on the radio instead of talking while we travel. We used to talk while preparing meals or washing dishes; we now grab fast food and load the dishwasher with the television on. Dad used to work long hours with his children, but he is now away at work somewhere—and so is Mom.

Ironically, this faster pace actually slows down our education. Our thirteen-year-olds are more sophisticated than past generations, more cosmopolitan in their language, tastes and morals, but they are far less educated. Refinement and wisdom are seldom the goal of modern education during the Transition years. A powerful antidote could be a healthy dose of listening from parents.

Be aware that for some, listening means just being silent and doing something physical together, like watching a sunset or going bowling. The volumes that are spoken non-verbally just might lead to the three words you are longing to hear.

13. Hold, hug, and kiss them

Children in Transition need to be treated like children: held on your lap, kissed on the cheek and forehead and hugged several times a day. Referring back to child psychologist Erik Erikson, children at this age are choosing whether to feel inferior or competent, and the determining factors are how much they feel loved and how industrious they feel. Transitioners need to be actively engaged in doing important things, and to feel secure and loved by their parents. Industry in this context means meaningful play, work and service. Parents who treat ten year olds like they are still children (which they are!) in the physical relationship, such as sitting them on your lap and giving them a big hug, while simultaneously talking to them and treating them with dignity and respect as an adult, will see the best results. And it may be that this formula does not expire even as the child grows older.

14. Treat them like adults

When you talk to Transitioners, treat them like the adults you want them to be. Interacting with them on the adult level shows respect for them as individuals and confidence in them as they begin to take on responsibility for their own lives. Sadly, many parents treat children this age like adults in the physical sense, seldom hugging them, tickling them or making them treats, but speak to them with condescension or even contempt. It is little surprise that they turn to their peers for the emotional support that should come from their parents.

Of course, we are not down-playing or criticizing the positive and natural relationships that all youth want to have with friends near their own age. We are simply saying that parents should be the best friends of Transition and Scholar Phase children. In fact, really true friends act a lot like good parents. The conveyor belt definition of a friend as someone who accepts whatever you do without judgment has prompted some experts to suggest that parents must not be friends but firm parental figures of authority. While it is true that parents do have a vital authority that few if any other friends ever should, great parents are also great friends.

Few things have brought Rachel more joy than to share with her youth her love of classic rock and roll, or to have them rave about a book that she recommended (having read it at their age), or to have her jaw drop to hear a clever witticism come out of one of their mouths.

As much fun as babies are, having those lovable critters stand tall and look you in the eye, and knowing that they will be your life-long friends and eventual peers, is one of the greatest rewards of having a family.

15. Encourage their friends to "hang out" at your home

This is so important. Several years ago our lifelong friends and Leadership Education partners moved away and new neighbors moved into the house next door. The new neighbors had children the same ages as ours, but they had different perspectives on life, the "teenage" years, and education. Our daughter Emma quickly became a "bosom friend" with a wonderful girl her age (she was reading *Anne of Green Gables* that year and used this phrase to describe her new friendship), and we worried that the new relationship would decrease her interest in studying and increase her focus on boys, clothes and make-up. It turns out that we had a lot to learn about being good parents.

Over the course of the next two years, we learned so much from this great family—the parents and the children—and they became dear friends. We invited their children into our home, and they did the same with our children. During the summer, their children, who were out of public school for the summer, joined ours in daily school studies and projects. Rachel tutored Emma's new friend right along with Emma, and we even established various Mom School activities to benefit the neighbor kids specifically. The family also taught our children a number of skills, and when discipline was needed, we found that our new friends were a lot more like us than we had first thought. If anything, they were much more consistent and strict than we! It was amusing for our children to come home from their friends' house in shock because of the amount of chores they had to complete before they could play, or how long they were on restriction for sassing. We loved it! They helped our children learn important lessons every bit as much as we helped them.

A community is a wonderful thing, and inviting our children's friends to hang out at our home created a lot of fun and boosted rather than detracted from the learning environment. We had good mentors in this, taking as our examples Neil and Cherie Logan—great Leadership Parents who seem to always have the "whole neighborhood" in their home involved in some positive activity. In short, bringing your children's friends into your home and educational environment is an important Transition and Scholar Phase parenting skill.

16. Keep reading aloud with them

As we mentioned in the Core and Love of Learning discussion, families should adopt a core of great books that they read together as a family. Ours include Scriptures, *Laddie*, and *Little Britches*, among others. We have found that re-reading these books is not a negative at all for the older children. They love being re-acquainted with these old friends multiple times. The story is a different experience for them each time, and they learn more than they did in past readings. In fact, it now takes us longer to get through these books, since Oliver, Emma and Sara have comments to add where it used to be only Mom and Dad.

Adding new books to the list helps also. Remember what Andrew Pudewa, one of the foremost authorities on reading and writing instruction, teaches: what you hear read out loud has the most impact on your ability to write well later in life. Beyond the educational benefits, reading out loud may be the most bonding of all possible family activities. Families which learn together also think together and feel together, thus creating powerful lasting bonds and improving life-long relationships.

17. Be involved in their age-related activities

This would seem obvious to any generation but ours, but the conveyor belt has conditioned many of us to applaud our children's activities from a distance instead of getting actively involved. As valuable as it is to include the children in our interests and activities, it is also important to put aside our own hobbies sometimes and get deeply involved in theirs.

Doing this in Transition to Scholar, and even before, communicates to them that their interests are important, that they are competent to choose good interests which others also value and that you are fully committed to them and their lives. Do not just send them off to basketball practice; spend a lot of time working on the fundamentals with them one-on-one, or one-on-four if several of your children share interests. Instead of just driving them to piano lessons, take the lessons with them; and where you would otherwise tell them, "It's time for you to practice the piano" say, "Do you want to practice first or shall I?" Volunteer to help with scout activities or to assist the director of the play. Learn to surf or collect coins because they are interested.

A word about territory might be wise. Some parents overdo, or have a child who does not value the *shared* interest. Be sensitive to let the kid have "his thing" without co-opting every new opportunity as a "bonding experience." In such a case you can accomplish much by letting her be the expert and being appropriately impressed by her depth of knowledge and skill. You can experience solidarity with this type of child simply by having your own passions that help you resonate with theirs.

18. Avoid political labels for you and them

Young people need to learn to think and lead before they start dividing themselves into camps of allies and enemies. Unless you are actively running for office, where a party affiliation is vital to your message and effectiveness, a specific label will tend to limit your leadership options.

Religious labels should be taught in an inclusive and respectful sense rather than as disdainful of others on the one hand or elitist on the other. A deep respect for all good ideas, people and organizations, and the ability to identify both the good and the error in all things is an important part of Transition. This is an age where the child notices differences and draws conclusions that will either lead to a life of bias or respect. Parental example in this is very important. The real lesson that is passed on will not be any political view (which the adult child will eventually re-evaluate anyway), but rather the choice between an attitude of wisdom and careful thinking and an attitude of closed and blind partisanship.

19. Encourage them to try new foods, especially ones you do not like

At first blush this seems out of place in a list of parenting or education skills. But in truth, it is a really powerful parenting technique that teaches independence, confidence, and that you value your children's unique personality, tastes, choices and individuality. Because taste is so personal, and so very tactile as well as emotional, the lessons taught by parents about food are often translated to other arenas of the child's life.

20. Positively reinforce their dreams and goals, even if they sound impossible

Transition and Scholar Phases are not the times to shut down dreams, and parents should never be the ones to kill dreams anyway. The world will exert enough pressure to frustrate and block the child's dreams. Particularly during Transition and early Scholar Phase, parents should ask children about their fondest dreams and hopes for their lives and future, and parents should reinforce the possibility of great things. Not only should parents avoid attacking youthful dreams or goals, they should also not attach too much active focus on them. Chances are that the dreams will evolve or just flat out change and parents pushing an eighteen-year-old toward a dream he mentioned at age thirteen but gave up at fifteen is sad, wasteful, and all too common.

Transition and Scholar Phasers will "float" a lot of ideas, and parents do best to calmly and positively support these dreams and not get attached to them. When students ask for specific help toward a goal, parents can provide support and active guidance and then enthusiastically shift to a new dream when it comes up. Remember that Transition and Scholar are designed as simulations for adulthood. Youth are allowed to play at maturity without lasting repercussions. This should extend to their passions and goals. Parents can affirm that this is appropriate for this age, and that a different level of focus is appropriate for another phase to come later. Most importantly, parents should share their own dreams with their Transition and older children, and they should model the *adult* level of vision and commitment that brings dreams to fruition as they actively set an example of pursuing those dreams.

21. Live your life through your own contributions, not through your children's accomplishments

Few things are more sad than a child spending his or her life unhappily trying to achieve the dreams of a parent. If the child shares the dream, of course, then this is a wonderful generational project, but far too often a child gives up his own mission to seek the approval of or carry out the directions of a parent.

Leadership parents set the example of living their life in pursuit of their own dreams, and by helping their children pursue *their* own dreams. In most cases, questions and discussions about life and goals start in Transition. When children ask about discovering and achieving their own life mission, dreams and interests, parents can help most by setting an example, giving positive guidance and reinforcing the importance of a high-quality Scholar Phase in preparation for whatever mission the child eventually chooses.

22. Stop using blame

If your own personal Transition years were less than ideal, this may be a challenge for you. But this skill is vital: Stop using blame. If you want to raise leaders, stop using blame. If you want your children to develop and learn effectively and happily, stop using blame. To stop blaming them, it helps to stop blaming everyone—including your own parents. One sure sign of maturity is lack of blaming. If you want to immediately improve your parenting, stop using blame. Focus instead on what needs to be done to move forward, take positive action and solve problems.

23. Be type A with yourself, type B with the children

We have taught this before, but it is worth repeating. Take all your educational angst and pushiness toward the children and their learning and apply it to your own Scholar Phase. Structure your own education, make demands on yourself, and push yourself to sit down each day to learn all those subjects in the curriculum. Let your Transition Phasers have their own life and gain their own education.

24. Don't get them "ahead" in life; relax

Help your children get a superb education by setting the example and teaching them about the Phases of Learning, Seven Keys of Teaching, Five Environments of Mentoring and other principles of a Leadership Education. Keep in mind the old fable of the tortoise and the hare, with a small modification. On the conveyor belt, the hare does not finish the race at all. If you have a clear vision of you (and your child) making an impact in the world in your waning years, trust the process.

Apply the old Zulu proverb taught to tourist-climbers of Mount Kilamanjaro: "Po-le po-le," meaning: *slow and steady gets it done*. In the lower elevation, the novice climbers tend to rush ahead. Those who attempt the climb without a guide can be clearly seen passing up the groups with a guide. He shakes his head and assures his wards that they will later be helping these foolish, hurried ones, who think they need no guide, to make it home. When the trail grows steep and the air thin, the climbers' reserves that seemed plentiful down in the foothills will be all but exhausted before the climb is through.

Always trying to get ahead can lead to burnout, where the whole process of education is virtually abandoned. Besides, the drive to "get ahead" is extrinsically motivated, and thus has no long-term power to stand up to the trials, tests and traps that inevitably appear on the path. Again: trust the process, proceed diligently and an amazing education, an amazing individual, and an amazing mission will unfold before your eyes.

25. Don't compare them with anyone, especially their siblings

Each child is her own person; treat her like it. The conveyor belt promotes many comparisons in order to teach the central lesson of "compare." Leadership Education teaches each individual instead to "value," which means to look at things for what they really are instead of just comparing them. The leadership path also teaches the student to impact, which includes individualizing and focusing. The one exception to this rule is when you use a positive comparison to inspire greatness followed immediately by personal differences, such as: "I can see you having a mission like Newton or Hawking, except that your focus is in chemistry and your contribution will of course be unique to you. What do you think about your future?" Using "comparison" as a sub-point of valuing and impacting is more in keeping with the leadership path than "why can't you be like Johnny?" or even "you're just as good as Johnny."

26. Live in the present more often

Transitioners are children, and so they nearly always live in the present. Many parents, in contrast, either live in the "glory days" of past achievement or in a planning state for future events. When counseling those in Transition to Scholar, parents need to put themselves in a present state where they can be happy, at peace, and enjoy the projects, play and other activities along with their children. Not only does this help the children, but it helps parents improve their leadership abilities and happiness.

27. Discipline yourself to have long talks with them where they do most of the talking

This skill is a lot like #12. It is important in many of your discussions to simply be quiet and let your children talk. Listen, make comments as appropriate, but learn the discipline of holding yourself back and allowing them to express themselves while paying close attention and focusing on what they are telling you.

Rachel recently had the opportunity to take young Ammon (Core) to the Emergency Room for stitches. Due to some other complications in our lives at the time (it was during a period of Hyrum's needs required most of her attention), it had been quite some time since the two of them had talked at length alone. She was amazed at the vocabulary he used while engaged in a conversation when he did not have to compete with older siblings to take part. He had so much to say and share!

The same experience has been true with Eliza and Sara. It was a reminder that all of our children benefit from our individual attention, and there is no substitute for listening intently to understand. Transition to Scholar is a hugely important time to revisit this skill, as the child is becoming more set in his patterns of trust and communication. If he shuts down now, it is only under stress or great duress that he opens up later, and then the expressions are often highly emotional and even destructive.

We have included skills 28 through 35 from our own experience and research.

28. Use the library

Your children's interests may well outrun your knowledge, but should never exceed your own enthusiasm. When your child says she is interested in a new subject, one you know little about, say: "It's time for a library trip! Get your backpack." One of the best skills you can teach during Transition is how to find things in the library, in your home bookshelves, and on the computer. Just go with them and keep looking until you have found everything you, and they, need. Note that both of you will be studying the new subject, so a combined search will help you both find what you want to use to study. Just remember not to take over or to soak the fun out of it by making every expression of interest into "school." Gauge your response to show support and enable you to be a resource and safety net.

29. Be the authority

Many times people hear our philosophy of "inspire, not require," and assume that we do not think parents should use discipline or exert authority. Nothing could be further from the truth. In family relations, the classic equation of "Low Authority = High Insecurity" is still true. Children need to know their boundaries, they need to know the rules, and they need to be held accountable for their adherence to appropriate standards. This is especially true in Transition to Scholar, where the natural tendency of the child is to "push the envelope" and experiment with what might happen when rules are set aside.

But the other equation of parenting is equally true: "High Authority = Low Creativity." Children who are constantly pushed and forced, from verbal or emotional abuse to simply lots of nagging, shut down their intuition, creativity and leadership, and they feel insecure, inferior and incapable at best; and often they compound these hang-ups with anger and disengagement from the parental bond. Leadership parents understand that neither Low Authority or High Authority are effective, but rather that parents must exert high levels of inspiration along with effective and consistent authority.

Where needed, discipline and consequences must be used. We struggled with this for years, because our disciplinary styles were so different. Finally we learned to wisely follow our own systems, and consult with each other as a check and balance on mistakes. We are learning to avoid consulting in front of the children and try to uphold each other in the moment of conflict or crisis. We make a point of speaking to each other in private about the effectiveness and/or appropriateness of the discipline and its outcome. Then we make changes as we decide together in committee.

There is a time and place to require, and children need to know the boundaries and be held to them. But even at that, the principle is not devoid of inspiration. They are not required by threats of pain; there is simply a consequence following both obedience and disobedience. Consequences, in questions of good/bad, right/wrong, can actually be inspiring. However, parents should be careful to clarify that discipline is discipline, and is not designed to require children or youth to excel in academics.

30. Nutrition matters

It really does. For example, after an upsetting dental bill, we offered a special reward for anyone who cared for their teeth and did not have cavities at the next check up. Oliver James and Emma decided that they would not eat sugar for the next year and that they would do extra flossing along with their regular daily dental care. Oliver's resolve lasted until his next scout meeting, when the soon-to-be-world-famous Kaczmar Chocolate Chip Cookies ended his new plan. Emma, however, stuck to her plan for over two years. An interesting side effect was that we all noticed a significant increase in her education. Her attention span increased, she needed less sleep and was less moody, and her mind just seemed to grasp things more quickly and in a deeper way. We all wondered if these changes came from her maturation; but after she reached the two year goal and went back on sugar, some of the same weaknesses and tendencies that had been exhibited two years previously by Emma returned.

Every time our Six Month "No" comes around, we find ourselves restructuring the family dietary plan. When it is high quality, we all learn better; when it deteriorates, we learn at a lower rate. We are not here to advocate a particular regimen; but many, if not most people, are aware of certain food sensitivities in their family, or predisposition to this or that. To neglect this information when considering our family culture and education is to lay aside a valuable tool. And the transition toward puberty is a time to be particularly vigilant of elements that might lead to emotional distress. Heaven knows it's difficult enough without introducing a food or substance that the specific child's body doesn't metabolize well. That's like administering a psycho-active drug, or even a poison!

Perhaps even more significant is the impact we have noticed diet has on children's ability to cope with stress, their patience, compassion, initiative, sense of moral obligation, etc. This can be especially true for children with disabilities or other special needs. We have wondered for a long time if the incredibly high rate of Ritalin prescription in America may be correlated to the high sugar or high-allergenic diet Americans generally consume. British children, for example, consume lower amounts of sugar and are given similar drugs at a much lower rate. In any case, improving nutrition will impact your children's education and the quality of life in your home.

We know of many good books and mentors that can assist a family who feels like they need to emphasize improved health habits and principles as a part of their family culture and education plan. If this applies to you, seek one out and use the FEC to apply the advice you receive.

31. Sleep matters

Dr. Michael Platt called modern America "The Teenage Society," and one of the evidences for this is that many parents today subject their children, even little children, to adult schedules and bed times. It is not uncommon for two year olds to be put to bed as late as eleven or twelve p.m., in order to accommodate parents' entertainment habits. This model of teenagers raising teenagers, in both sleeping and dietary habits, causes untold distress to education. Again, the same stress is put on the child's ability to function and mature in an emotionally healthy manner.

Relationships are strained for no greater reason than sleep deprivation, and the ability of the child to make good choices is impaired in exact proportion to their getting insufficient rest. Children do not learn, interact, or choose well when they are tired, and nearly all of today's children are tired if compared to, say, children in the 1950s. The greatest concern may be that the child makes assumptions about their learning style, their will to do what is right, and their attitudes toward others based on skewed data. They do not actually know what they are like, and how good they can be, when they are not over-tired and under-nourished. These negative and incorrect assumptions can be carried into later years and solidified by the complications of hormonal and other changes to routine and environment that further stress them. Adequate sleep and good nutrition should be considered an essential basic for a healthy Transition to Scholar.

32. Schedule matters

A daily schedule is the difference between chaos and a high quality leadership home. In other words, "Structure time, not content." When we take our children with us to seminars or conventions, the question they get asked the most by people is what our family schedule looks like. Sara usually answers: "We start with devotional at nine a.m. and then we study whatever we want. I study math, I work on art projects, and I read a lot."

Emma, on the other hand, says: "We get up at six a.m. and get Hyrum ready to take the bus to school as well as get groomed and ready for the day. Then we clean our rooms and have breakfast by around eight, then clean up from breakfast and clean the house by nine. At nine, we have devotional, then Mom reads and works with the little kids while I read and study. At noon, we break for lunch and clean up, then I study more until dinner. After dinner we have family activities, or youth activities like Karate or church events, and then we go to bed about nine p.m. Actually, we put the little kids down by eight p.m. and then read some more. Saturdays are sometimes different, and Sundays are always a different schedule. And some days we drop the whole thing and go on a field trip or to the library for the afternoon."

If you asked Meri, age four, what the family schedule is, she would likely cock his head to one side and wonder what you were talking about. Eliza, age eleven, would report a schedule similar to the one Sara outlined: school from nine a.m. to five p.m. with projects through the afternoon. There are many schedules that could work, and as the expert on your home you will want to choose one that works best for your family. The key is to have a schedule and follow it. Routine helps the children learn much more effectively than chaos. Note that Hyrum, who has cerebral palsy, functions best with even more structure. The schedule is very important for him, as it is in many ways the language he understands best. When he gets on the bus, he knows exactly where he is going. When we sit down for family study, he immediately folds his arms for prayer even though he does not yet communicate verbally. And Abigail, just two years old, is beginning to understand the language of schedule and is able to join in. A family routine matters, and learning improves with a better schedule. Of course, this should not be used as an excuse to over-schedule or over-program. Children need flexibility within structure in order to flourish.

33. The environment matters

Another seemingly small detail which actually makes all the difference is the feeling in the home. The artwork in the home, the music that gets played, the tone of parental dialogues, the entertainment that is on, and the general feeling all play a direct and highly significant role in whether or not students of Transition age receive the benefits of the Love of Learning Phase they are still in. This can be extended to the external environment in which a home is physically situated. A friend recently asked for our opinion about a troubled youth which they were trying to "take back to Core Phase."

After a lengthy explanation of the youth's escapades in just about every form of undisciplined behavior, complete with the scenes of remorse and renewed commitment, we commented that having a living room that was friendly to Core Phase might not be sufficient for healing in this case; the youth was sneaking out a window and abandoning the Core at will. There were easy and compelling choices near the neighborhood that competed too strongly for the youth's fragile resolve to withstand. The environment was not wholly dedicated to success, simply by virtue of the location of the subdivision and its proximity to the trouble that the youth tended toward. It is true in any Phase, and perhaps especially true in Transition to Scholar, that the environment we choose both inside and outside of the home contributes to or detracts from our family culture and educational success.

34. Discipline wisely

We do not consider ourselves experts in this. The more children we have and the longer we live with them, the more deficient we seem to be! We can witness that different things work for different children and at different ages. In fact, just when we think we have it figured out, our children grow up another year and we have to re-evaluate everything. But as with any endeavor, there are guiding principles that underpin success.

Specific discipline tips for children in Transition: Be willing to spend a lot of time listening to them and discussing the reasons for things. Be patient and answer their questions as if they really are trying to understand rather than assuming that they are just trying to talk you out of things. In truth, they are doing both; you need to be okay with this and not turn it into an emotionally charged situation.

Know that they are at the time of life where they are beginning to think abstractly. One of the hypotheticals they will test is whether or not you and your pronouncements of policy are reasonable, or perhaps more simply, whether or not their logic can sway you in their favor. Do not assume they do this with malice or to challenge your authority, even if they seem to relish being at odds with you. This is a natural and constructive part of their maturation process.

The best way to reinforce your position is to show you are not threatened by their newly found powers of reasoning and discussion, and to teach them through this experience how to discuss questions of divergent interest with civility and respect. Be at ease with the process and be open and calm when the circumstances permit discussion. When this is not possible, state simply and with finality that this is not an appropriate situation in which to discuss your decision. Then if you feel it appropriate at a later time, instigate the discussion yourself and see if he wants to dialog further about the decision.

35. Get Dad involved

Because Dad is centrally important in Scholar Phase, Transition is a good place to increase his involvement. Of course, ideally Dad is involved in education through all the phases, but during Transition it is even more vital that he have a cool head and take an active role in listening, talking, doing activities, reading aloud, and taking part in all thirty-five keys to Transition parenting. Because Mom is often absorbed in the tasks of homemaking and the care of younger ones who need her especially, Transition is a time when, too often, young people might find themselves being left to their own devices. Do not let this happen!

We have already addressed how important their bond of security and affection is at this stage, and their educational progress is no less important to their well-being. When Dad steps in to reinforce and cultivate his particular brand of closeness, the Transitioner quite naturally assumes the role of helping Mom as a caregiver and provider of services, and at the same time begins to look toward Dad as a mentor. This sets up a perfect Transition to Scholar where the youth has stewardship over given home responsibilities and is accountable for his study and work to his mentor.

Final Thoughts for Fathers and Mothers of Children in Transition to Scholar

For Fathers:

1. Salman Rushdie said, "The reality of a father is a weight few sons can bear." Please ponder this truism, and consider how it applies in your home. It may help to take a minute and picture the weight of your own father when you were a child. Then picture the weight your sons feel. Later, envision the ideal of how you would like it to be. And finally, identify what you would need to do to make the ideal a reality. Few things are more impactful in a young life than a father who comes close to an ideal that you have in you and can choose to become.

2. Maria Montessori said that "Play is the child's work." In short, the child needs to put as much effort into playing as you do into your work. Think about that for a minute. How are you helping them with this, or hurting their progress in this important endeavor?

For Mothers:

1. As James Dobson taught, every twelve-year-old boy is a wounded soul, desperate for healing. If and how he heals literally makes the man who will marry your daughters and become the father of your grandchildren. How can you help?

2. John Taylor Gatto, the renowned former New York State Teacher of the Year, wrote: "When I see kids daydreaming in school, I am careful never to shock them out of their reverie. What I have to say can wait." Wow! How does this apply in your home?

3. And finally, children in Love of Learning and Transition to Scholar age are energetically interested in many things (distracted), able at moving between one activity and the next (disorganized), and willing to consider almost any possibility (disoriented). Smart mothers join in and have fun with them, or at least give them the space to explore without negativity!

As with the 55 ingredients of Core and Love of Learning, wisely use these 35 Transition to Scholar parenting skills as needed and in whatever combinations best suit your family. This will help you parent more effectively as you guide your Love of Learning children in the Transition to Scholar Phase.

The Three Indispensable Choices

There are Three Indispensable Choices parents should make during each child's Transition Phase. If any one of the three is forgotten or ignored, Transition is slowed down or impacted negatively. And while it may be hard to do all three as well as you would like, understand that good parenting is hard and that doing all three will be worth it.

First, parents must remember that the child is still in Love of Learning! This is incredibly important. All the Ingredients and other principles of Love of Learning Phase still apply; few, if any, of the Scholar Phase methods should be used until later.

Second, you must be effectively progressing in the Phases! Some parents may be in the process of renegotiating their Foundational Phases. For most adults in today's society this means: time for Scholar Phase. There is a growing number of families whose parents have gotten ahead of the game (actually, who did things in a more convenient time and season) and are ready for Depth Phase when the children come. In any case, a child in Transition needs to see her parents setting the example. Your children need to see you actively progressing in *your* current phase during their Transitions.

Third, as you apply correct principles you must truly relax and trust that your youth will do a Scholar Phase and do it well. Like riding a bike, driving a car, being physically fit (in a home where physical activity is the norm) or going to college (with parents who are college graduates), Leadership Education comes naturally in homes where the parents are on the Leadership Path. Pushing them too soon will only slow down the process, and may actually push them off the Path of Leadership. Remember that you are the expert on your home and your children; trust your feelings and impressions more than the views of the so-called experts, neighbors or extended family members. Trusting does not mean giving in to your pride or paranoia at the expense of compromising tried-and-true principles. It means applying principles according to the vision and counsel of the FEC and not allowing other voices to incite you to second guess your hard won inspiration.

Be cautious when you become aware that your feelings can be characterized as "fear," "guilt," "pride," or some other self-centered, basically negative emotion or motivation. If these elements enter in, your feelings and impressions need to be double checked with

FEC so that you do not subconsciously apply your past experience in place of your new vision.

We know that parenting is an incredibly challenging endeavor; certainly, it's the most difficult and demanding task we have ever undertaken. Yet by applying true principles, just as in any other life challenge, we know that we can find success and have a lot of fun along the way.

In short, there are few things in life as enjoyable, as rewarding or as downright fun as living through a great Transition to Scholar with your child during Love of Learning Phase. Enjoy it, slow down and savor it for as long as it lasts, and smile, hug and laugh a lot more.

Questions about Transition

Q: How do you know your child is ready to Transition?

A: Use the descriptions provided at the beginning of this chapter to measure whether your child seems to show the behaviors described. Of course, it is important that the child always has a say on which Phase he or she is in. A healthy child will usually be quite reliable in assessing himself in the right Phase. Parents should teach the Phases well at a very young age and then re-teach them often, letting the child know that he has a voice on which Phase he is in.

Be aware that most parents' conveyor belt training impels them to push (even with subtle non-verbal cues) toward Scholar Phase. A good mentor will not allow her mentee to accept commitments he is not prepared for, and will do all in her power to help him get the most out of the phase he is in before taking on the new. Also be aware that in most cases when the Scholar struggles or abandons Scholar Phase, it is because of obstacles placed by the very parents who were so anxious that this time should arrive. Again, refer to the next chapter on Scholar Phase for the bigger picture of how it all fits together and how to successfully mentor the whole process.

Q: What should parents do with a child that is "out of sync" or way behind in the phases?

A: There are so many ways to answer this question, probably as many as there are children who are "behind." The first thing is to be sure that the child is actually behind, not by comparing her to other children in the Conveyor Belt model, but by looking at each individual child and the descriptions of the Phases of Learning and clarifying if she is where she should be. Another way to phrase the question is: are the Core and Love of Learning intact?

If the answer is "yes," then consider if the child is merely a late bloomer. Another possibility is that the child has already successfully transitioned and you aren't recognizing the behaviors because you were expecting something different.

For example, one mother expressed concern for her fifteen-year-old daughter whom she thought had done all the rights things up to that point, but wasn't a book worm. Why wasn't she in Scholar Phase? What should the mother do? In this girl's case, she was spending hours each day in choral groups and with an excellent mentor. Mom simply did not see that as "scholarly." Over time, this young lady progressed from there to attending college as an excellent student.

If the answer is, "no," then you already have an agenda, and it is not Scholar Phase. Go back to the beginning and help the child renegotiate the choices that need to be rescripted. With many children, the process may begin with a simple conversation with her about it to find out where she sees herself in the Phases, and where she wants to go. If the child wants nothing to do with it, or is obstinate or a discipline problem, chances are you need to go back to Core Phase. If she really wants to progress, brainstorm together and try to understand what is blocking her. In order to follow the leadership path, every child needs a solid Core Phase, to be taught the specifics of all the Phases, to understand the consequences of both life paths, and to witness someone close to him setting an example of a great Scholar Phase. Spend time studying the additional insights and personal accounts about the Phases contained throughout this book and seeking personal inspiration in your stewardship as a parent.

Q: How does a parent coordinate several children in different Phases?

A: First, remember "You, not Them." If you are clear on what you are supposed to be doing for your own education right now, today, and order your life and structure so that family life flows effectively, there is almost nothing more that needs to be said on this point. An inspired plan for personal growth and intellectual progress for the mother will almost certainly include the routines, examples, and activities that will facilitate the others in her care. Rachel comments that she cannot count the number of mothers of large families who have expressed disbelief that smaller families can make it work. Having all the Phases active in the home is in many ways the ideal.

In cases where it does not just "fit together," there is almost always a compelling issue that has nothing to do with coordinating the education of all the individuals. In these cases, it is not the coordination that deserves special consideration, but the resolution of the other issue(s), which might include: spouses with a differing vision of what the family's ideal should be, a child with emotional problems stemming from abuse or other problematic relationships, a home with too much clutter; etc., etc.... When the complicating detail is resolved and the mother is following an inspired outline for routine and personal education, it is amazingly simple how the various children's needs and interests are highlighted in a rotation that meets everyone's needs.

It is also noteworthy that it is not just individuals who go through phases and transitions; families do it too! When a young couple in scholar phase has a couple of core phasers and a love of learner, their life has a very different pace and dynamic than a couple in mission/impact phase with a youth in scholar, pre-adolescents in transition, and other children ranging between love of learning and core phases. In the former case, the routine is very simple and the time demands are relatively low. As the large family ages, the educational culture will tend to be defined by the oldest children's phase.

The parents that used to sit for hours reading literature to their young brood are now finding that their time is spent rather in addressing the needs of the older children. Mentoring writing projects, facilitating transportation to lessons, organizing peer-oriented learning, etc., can virtually monopolize the time of the parents of older children, and the family read takes far less time than it used to.

It is tempting to try to turn back the clock and duplicate the idyllic circumstances that marked the more simple early years of the family. Many lament that they are not giving their young children what their older ones got at their age. If it is true that the Core is being neglected, it is a worthy concern. But the conventions and methods of nurturing the Foundational Phases not only differ from one family to the next and from one child to the next, they will of necessity be different when older children become young adults in the home.

Consider what the young ones are getting that the older ones *did not* get at their age: sixteen-year-old Oliver doesn't sing to eight-year-old Ammon every night as Rachel did to him when he was small; he talks of religion and history and the novels he reads; he talks of the power of faith and the power of virtue being greater than any science fiction, fantasy or superhero.

Eleven-year-old Eliza doesn't have Mom by her side teaching every chore, as did Emma at her age; but she does have Emma roping her into helping her study her Latin vocabulary and Sara asking her to help her memorize lines for Shakespeare.

We don't have the same type of time or life that we did when our family was small. But in a large family, the development and security of each child is not as hinged on the parent/child relationship. The inter-sibling dynamic has an extremely powerful role. It is like a Virginia Reel of relationships, with each one having a unique value in the individual's progress. In our family there are at least forty separate relationships; this does not account for the dynamic of threesomes, etc. As parents of a large family our burden may be heavier in some ways. But it is also lighter.

Q: What should parents do in Core and Love of Learning to prepare for Scholar?

A: First, they should solidify the vision the spouses have of the home environment and family culture. Reading and discussing this book together is an excellent way to arouse the questions that every couple should address in order to come to a shared vision. Reading other literature that is strong on illustrating family culture (Laddie, the Little Britches series, Farmer Boy and others from the Little House series, etc.) can help develop shared vision of an ideal and provide a medium for discussing differences in approach, experience and expectation.

Second, they should begin a routine that will support communication and effective family rituals, such as Family Executive Committee, family prayer and scripture study (or study of the family's central classic).

Third, parents need to consider their own early Phases, including the lessons learned during childhood, to determine if any need to be re-negotiated to start as a family at the earliest common ground. Finally, as you begin to progress through the Phases (and progress after re-negotiating faulty lessons is really quite rapid and fluent), continue to build a family culture and home environment that supports all the Phases.

In particular, as parents you need to do a solid Scholar Phase and have a clear vision that Depth Phase is around the corner. One of the common questions parents ask at seminars is: "But I only have small children, so why should I worry about Scholar Phase right now?" It is a common conveyor belt misconception that the teacher's focus should be on the education of the child. Your children will learn to value education by watching you learn.

While the children are in Core and Love of Learning, set the example of progression through the Phases.

Q: What are the major predictable mistakes parents make during Transition?

A: Parents in the Leadership Education model often look at arrival in Scholar Phase as "The Promised Land" and are hypersensitive to cues that it is time to make that move. They may tend to focus on certain signs of maturity (attention to detail, longer attention span, interest in adult conversation, a desire to spend a lot of time reading without interruptions) and at the same time neglect to acknowledge signs of unreadiness (defensiveness when ideas are challenged, unwillingness to make or keep commitments, stress or sullenness when demands are placed on them).

Sometimes parents are even tempted and attempt to push the child to get ahead, try to ensure that he keeps up with the neighbors or a pre-set "grade level," and resort to force, manipulation or inappropriate rewards to make this happen.

Another common mistake is to over program the time of the Transitioner. Now that they are ready for lessons, we too often see parents putting them in several types of lessons, or classes, clubs, teams, etc. It takes a great deal of restraint to trust that we need not jump on every opportunity. Time will work its wonders, and one day at a time the young person's character, experience and education will round itself out. The next biggest challenge (probably a combination of some of the foregoing) is to focus on the child's education while ignoring your own: simultaneously pushing him too hard and not setting a positive example.

Finally, we can tend be so enthralled with the new, more grown-up Johnny or Linda that we might communicate to them in subtle ways that we prefer them so, and not so much a child. They may begin to feel that they are not allowed to be vulnerable, needy, or dependent on you for affection or positive reinforcement.

This is a time to make a conscious plan to invite your Transitioner to sit on your lap and just watch a movie for a while, to come embrace you "'cause I need a hug," to hold your hand while you are riding in the car, even as you acknowledge and make mention of how fun it is to see her getting so tall, or how you love the way that she is turning into such a fun conversationalist, or how much you respect this or that quality that she exhibits in such mature proportions, etc.

Remember to reassure your budding youth that her growing independence as an individual does not necessitate her detachment from you. It means a continually evolving, deepening relationship with you as her parent-for-life. Also remember to be explicit in your communication that you are comfortable with her being grown up on some days or in some settings, and just a kid in others and that this is natural, healthy and desirable at this time in her progress. (Most families can point out Dad as an example of this duality with marvelous results.)

Q: What should parents do when things go wrong, when you have a teenager instead of a young adult?

A: We are not experts on child psychology, but we highly recommend the writings of Dr. James Dobson, especially his book *On Parenting*. In a nutshell (and we agree with every point) he suggests the following eight ways of working with a youth who has gone wrong:

1. Fix yourself. Fix your selfishness, anger, pride, ambition, manipulation, controlling, ignoring, neglecting, etc.
2. Show the youth respect and dignity.
3. Verbalize conflicts and re-establish boundaries. Be firm in this. Revisit #1 above as a part of this.
4. Plan rationally, but act toward bonding.
5. Link behavior with desirable and undesirable consequences. Again, revisit #1 as a central part of this.

6. Help the youth search for identity—personality, mission, vision, lots of talking, etc.

7. Turn to spiritual, religious and community sources for help.

8. Spend some more time on #1.

Of course, there are many other questions which could be asked about Transition to Scholar. Remember that nobody is the expert on your children except you, and also that nobody does this perfectly. We certainly struggle to parent effectively in Transition and all the other phases. We find ourselves making mistakes at every stage and with every child and we learn a great deal from our mistakes. Nobody has to be perfect in parenting; and one of the most important things our children learn from us is how we function in spite of our frailties and foibles, how we respond to problems of our own making, how we repair relationships that we have helped to injure or neglect, and how we address our own weaknesses. The fact of our imperfection is unavoidable (as is their growing awareness of it), and it is not an excuse for anyone opting out of parenting in a principled fashion.

Also remember that your children can help too, by coaching and giving suggestions about ways to improve. If they have had a solid Core Phase, they will surprise you with the wisdom they will share. For example, once we were having an intense discussion about a gap in our communication, and eleven-year-old Sara overheard and made a truly insightful and helpful comment. Oliver was so touched by it, and how much it helped, that he called in Oliver (age fourteen) and Emma (age thirteen) and asked for their help. Both of them provided very wise and relevant counsel. While we are not recommending that children be involved in every decision—they benefit neither from the burden of adult issues nor the confusion of roles—there are times when we have much to learn from them and we do well to listen.

Some children are downright obnoxious starting with Transition and into Scholar years. Many factors can exacerbate the challenges of adolescence:

- a neighborhood environment with distractions or personalities that are toxic to healthy home relationships
- poor nutrition
- lack of sleep
- too many commitments (either on the part of the parent, the youth, or both)
- too little responsibility
- undiscovered/unremedied trauma, such as sexual abuse in the recent or distant past
- marital strife, past or current
- addiction (many forms: emotional, sexual, substance, etc.)
- too little government in the home
- too much government in the home

The remedies are even more varied than the causes, but there is almost nothing that prayer, principles and patience can't improve. Through Inventories, Purges, FEC, the Dobson list above and other ingredients well-applied, you will have done all you can do and can safely entrust your youth to Providence.

The Transition to Scholar Phase is a powerful, pivotal time in the life of a person. Your valiance, serenity, affection, acceptance, patience and vision will help to establish from this time a relationship that will endure whatever else comes along; and the growing independence, character and competence of your youth will bring you satisfaction and joy for the rest of your life.

Part III

....

A Blueprint For Leadership: The Educational Phases

CHAPTER SEVEN

Scholar Phase

Hardly anybody completes Scholar Phase in the United States. Scholar Phase is done by a few students in the nation's public schools. A slightly higher percentage of private, homeschool and preparatory school students do it, but still a very small minority. Military and boarding schools do even better than private schools, but again only a small group of American students get a Scholar Phase as part of their education. Standards are low across the board. In many cases this is because the concept and vision of Scholar Phase for youth is virtually lost. Even the best and brightest students do not aspire to Scholar Phase because *they do not conceive of it*. They have no peers or mentors to recommend it to them (whether explicitly or by example) and it does not occur to them on their own.

In fact, most American students only study really hard in medical, law and other graduate schools where the focus is on specialized depth and the time for an excellent broad liberal arts education is past. Jacques Barzun noted this over fifty years ago, Mortimer Adler brought it up again several times since, but Scholar Phase is still ignored by most students. Only a few of our liberal arts college and university students complete Scholar Phase effectively.

The result is that we live in a democracy of highly trained and under-educated people—an environment in which freedom has never endured in history and is unlikely to flourish in the twenty-first century. Of course, a quick look at the news tells you that the world has never enjoyed more freedom. But a deeper study of history shows that such quick looks are deceiving. History does repeat itself—or at least its patterns repeat—and nothing is more certain in history than that highly trained but poorly educated people do not keep their freedoms for more than a generation or two. Even if they do, the lesser-educated classes do not know how to or do not have the prerogative to benefit from or maintain these freedoms.

But you can change this. You can change it by getting a Leadership Education yourself, and by helping your children do the same. In a nutshell, you get such an education by reading, studying and incorporating into your life the principles contained in the great classics of humanity.

In our day, knowledge is more readily available and accessible than at any time in history. We must avail ourselves of the wisdom of the ages if we desire to lead and fulfill the mission that is ours alone. It does not take much study to recognize that though times have changed, some things have always remained constant. We have much to learn. All that separates us from the wisdom available from the past that will solve the problems of today is our choice to engage ourselves in significant study from the best minds and records society has to offer. These important classics are not only books but elevating works and individuals from every field, land and walk of life. Our minds will be expanded to comprehend the greatest ideas throughout the history of mankind as we study the lives and think the thoughts of leaders of the past and present. As we incorporate into our lives timeless principles that bring success, we will find ourselves living with increased capacity and impact. We will not only come Face-to-Face with Greatness, we will become great ourselves.

Desire and commitment to learn and do are the only traits needed to be able to make this happen. There is nothing to lose and everything to gain. The growth you will personally experience and the friendships and contacts you will create will accelerate your personal growth and your family's education.

Facilitating Your Child's Scholar Phase

Helping your children get a Scholar Phase Education is challenging. The first step, vital and unavoidable, is that you or your spouse (usually both) must show them how. You must set the example. Your family educational culture will almost inevitably become the educational culture of your children—one that they will embrace and seek to emulate, or that they will labor to put behind them. The first step to creating leaders is providing an environment that is conducive to and inspires Leadership Education. The next step is to help your children have an effective Core Phase followed by a wonderful Love of Learning Phase.

The Scholar Phase is the crux of the whole Leadership Education model. It consists of four distinct levels. If you want your youth to get a superb Leadership Education, they need to do Scholar Phase. Specifically, there are four levels of Scholar Phase, as first outlined by Aneladee Milne.

Note that the ages we suggest for each level are simply a median, not the rule. In this chapter and with all the phases, ages are not to be rigidly followed or even idealized, but rather considered simple examples based on successful Scholars from history who progressed naturally from Phase to Phase. Phases will unfold according to each individual child's timetable as we raise our children according to true principles. We want to clearly state that children and youth should not be expected or forced into meeting a pre-set age guideline. Trust the process and endeavor to meet the focus and guidelines of each level rather than conform to specified age ranges.

It is also important to acknowledge that the approximate ages we have listed for youth progressing through each scholar level overlap. Children are different. They develop at different rates and have unique interests, goals, talents, and missions. But the Phases and Levels do build upon previous ones.

Each of the four scholar levels covered below has its own focus. The most common reason they are not done effectively is a simple lack of awareness of the specific characteristics and goals of each scholar level. In reality, mentoring scholar levels with the guidelines given in this chapter will take less teacher/mentor time than most parents are currently giving, and with better results.

This chapter is designed as a guide to parents—the most important mentors of students in the Scholar ages twelve through eighteen. Parents with children in public or private schools should consider sharing applicable concepts of Scholar Phase and its various levels with teachers—and the children themselves—and work out agreements that incorporate them. If one parent is chiefly responsible for a student's education, he would do well to discuss this chapter with his spouse and reach parental agreement on how the phases and levels will be implemented in their home with their children. In other words, the FEC (Family Executive Council) should consider these issues and set policy for them.

For many families it may be the ideal for Dad to become the mentor at this point. In most homes, Mom is the primary facilitator of education in childhood, and with the emotional and biological shift in the scholar's life, the transition to Dad as the mentor may be called for. In many, if not most, homes, Dad has a different approach than Mom, and the change might be just the right thing. Dad will often demand an upgraded structure and also serve as a buffer between the student and Mom's household demands. However, in these transitional times where two generations are playing cultural catch-up to restore a civilization of freedom and family, Mom's level of scholarship and mission often include community outreach that facilitate an excellent scholar phase. Pay the price to know what is optimal in your family, and for each child.

Equally important to successful Scholar Phase is a Mom who really does the legwork of the Core and Love of Learning Phases.

The family structure as described in the previous chapters of this book works! In fact, your personalized application of it as best fits your home is ideal for the great education of your family.

Historical Roots

For thousands of years before the Industrial Age, indeed, virtually all of human history prior to about the 1920s, young children were primarily educated by Mother in Core and Love of Learning until about age twelve, when their education then became divided among several other mentors. Uncles were primarily responsible for the teaching of the skills of war, hunting and trades; aunts taught the social mores of the tribe or culture. Unmarried or widowed family members were invited into young families as appreciated members who provided inestimable support and assistance with the day-to-day nurturing and responsibilities of living, feeding, clothing and sheltering families. Fathers were responsible for spiritual growth and for helping the individual know her place in the community. Grandparents taught the old ways—the history of the people. They supplied unconditional love to the young ones and held the adults accountable for the exercise of their roles in the clan. A deeper study of tribal culture (there are remarkable similarities, whether we are speaking of Polynesian tribes, Germanic, Native American, African, Aboriginal, etc.) will yield fascinating insights into human nature and culture.

It is difficult in our day and age, with the extended family now splintered into individual units, for the parents to absorb the roles of all the tribal adults. Over several generations, certain jobs became the role of the father or of the mother; some were shared; some became the function of public schools, while for others, society turned to churches. It is commonly believed that young men became Dad's work and that young women stayed under Mom's tutelage—but this is not true academically. Where families could afford it, both male and female young adults received a superb scholar education.

In our current society, when the father owns and fulfils this responsibility with commitment, youth flourish academically. Of course, Mom and Dad are ideally both active and very involved partners, both before the Transition to Scholar Phase and after. All of this having been said, for some families, Mom will still be the best choice for primary mentor during Scholar Phase, or at least at some levels. There may even be a "tiered" approach, where Mom does most of the facilitating and Dad oversees the accountability. Employ the FEC to choose what is right for your family.

Simply by correctly understanding the material presented in this chapter, you should be able to facilitate an effective world class Scholar Phase for your children and students. This information is a gold mine taken from the educational experiences of great men and women of history and modern educational programs which are effectively accomplishing Scholar Phase.

Tiffany Earl explained the goal of mentoring youth in Scholar Phase this way: "I know what this looks like, but I want them to taste it, to feel it, see it, breathe it, smell it. I want them to be with Reuben in the library studying Freud, I want them to be with Newton in the loft of his barn building and calculating. I want the youth to be with Lincoln and a book by a fireplace. They need to feel it!" The best way to communicate this feeling is to set the example, and share these feelings with your children and youth. Additionally, we highly recommend the "Youth For Freedom" conferences held each summer.

The Practice Scholar (approximately ages eleven to thirteen)

Somewhere between ages eleven and thirteen (give or take 99 years), your student will become a Practice Scholar. You have already taught him the Four Phases of Learning, so he knows that Scholar Phase is coming. He has lived Core Phase, so he knows he is loved and valued; his Love of Learning Phase helped him internalize that you have an important mission, and that one awaits him, too. He began to understand that Scholar Phase would allow him to focus his efforts on laying a foundation for that mission. He knows that he does not need to know his whole mission right now—he just needs to know what the next step is. He knows that how valiantly he takes the next step will impact his future mission, and might even have some strong feelings about what his mission might be.

He knows that for now his non-academic mission is to learn to be a leader during work, play and study with brothers and sisters and friends, to be a peacemaker and problem solver, and also to learn to work and accomplish by being a significant help to adult family members. In fact, he has taken on some real responsibilities in family chores and helps Dad and Mom quite a bit—to the extent that they may even wonder how they can do all they are doing if he trades in his errand running and household managing for mission preparation in the form of scholarly study.

He knows that right now his academic mission is Love of Learning, and he pursues learning in all he does. He has a structured time each day, four to six days a week, ten to eleven months a year, during which he actively studies things he loves to learn about. He knows that when he goes into Scholar Phase, studying will be his major contribution to the family, and others will take up the bulk of his chores and non-academic duties—just as if he were working outside of the home. In Scholar Phase, he will be a Young Adult with responsibilities and privileges distinct from those he had as a child in the home.

He has watched you (and maybe older siblings and your spouse) study math, science, history, literature, government, writing or whatever else you think *everyone* should learn, and so he makes these part of his Love of Learning study. He anticipates that in Scholar Phase he will gain further knowledge in most, if not all, of these areas.

Of course, this is more a feeling or general impression than a specific plan. And because of the way you have studied and shared and involved him, he is familiar with, or at least aware of, the subjects you are sure he will need—though you or he may be expert or accomplished in relatively few. He may already be way above the average conveyor belt grade level in some of these—the ones that interest him. If this is your student, he will soon become a Practice Scholar.

If this does not describe your child, more time in Core or Love of Learning is probably needed. Relax; it is still "You, not Them." Or, more accurately, stop relaxing and get to work—on you, *not them*. Utilize the inventory in the Transition to Scholar chapter to consider how you might have a positive influence on your student's *optimal*, not rushed, progress. Then quit worrying about a timeline that is not inspired and FEC-endorsed and go in search of one that is. In many, if not most, cases, this will mean to stop concerning yourself with any timeline and pay the price to become truly inspirational. Apply the Five Environments of Mentoring and help him fall more deeply in love with learning and his future mission (remember that Love of Learning is more about the *love* than the *learning*). While he is doing this, you get the education you will soon need.

If the description of Practice Scholar does describe your student, it is time to teach him about the levels of Scholar Phase. Make this exciting: a picnic, a retreat, a lunch date, a camping trip, etc. Plan it ahead of time and tell him you have got something really important to tell him. Give him some time to anticipate it, remind him about it and build it up so he looks forward to it. Make it fun.

When the meeting time arrives, tell him that soon he will be moving into Scholar Phase. Reassure him that he will get to choose when and that he will not be forced to do it until he wants to, but that you can see he is getting close and you want to teach him what it will mean and what it will be like.

For the child who is not ready this will be exciting on the one hand, and a relief on the other. He will feel from this communication that the entrance to Scholar Phase, and indeed his education from here forward, is his responsibility. He will likely feel the gravity of the choice and take stock of his own readiness. You may sense his trepidation; merely reassure him that when the time is right, everything will fall into place and it will feel natural and fun for him. Reinforce that it is not advantageous to rush into the change. It will come almost unbidden when the circumstances are ideal.

For the child who *is* ready to progress into Scholar, your restraint and reassurances will serve only to light the fire under her and challenge her to take on the commitments that await her. In either case, you have put her firmly in the driver's seat, where she needs to be.

Tell her how exciting, fun and wonderful it will be. Then teach her the Four Levels of Scholar Phase. Of course, she already learned the Four Phases of Learning back in Core and Love of Learning, so she looks forward to this exciting new information. Give her an overview of all four levels, and then teach her the Practice Scholar and Project Scholar levels in depth. Tell her she can move into Practice Scholar Level whenever she wants.

Clarify that she will be choosing the levels, and that she should do so prayerfully. Help her understand that God has a plan for her, and express confidence that she will know when the time is right if she will seek it. Talk to her about how she will know. This is a powerful time to reaffirm and expand what you have taught her about communication with the eternal, pondering and meditation, prayer and inspiration, intuition and revelation. If her Core Phase was done effectively, this will probably be simple. Use these techniques yourself to know when to have this meeting with her. You know how to get answers; employ the FEC to get them and trust the decisions you make.

After the meeting, go back to Love of Learning as normal. Answer any questions she has. A few days or a week later, in an appropriate one-on-one moment, ask her if she has any questions about the Scholar Phase meeting you had as you continue your typical Love of Learning structure and lifestyle.

When she comes to you and says she thinks she is ready for Practice Scholar Level, have her try it once to see if she likes it. If your impression is that you should invite her to try it even though she has not asked: check to make sure you are right, and then follow your inspiration without pushing. It is just a practice, after all. And it is okay for your child to decide she does not like it and stay in Love of Learning for another six months or two years. Keep the Love of Learning structured time going, and help her fall deeper in love with learning.

If he does like it, ask if he wants to do another Practice Scholar day. If he does—great.... If not—fine, go back to Love of Learning. Give him all the benefits of Scholar including reduced chores and other duties for the hours and days he is doing Practice Scholar, and regular Love of Learning requirements whenever he is off. Clearly vocalize and plan this together so you both know exactly what to expect.

Even now, with our three oldest in higher levels of Scholar Phase, we will have one of them from time to time announce that they are going to have a Love of Learning day. This has happened to coincide with large snowfalls (when all the little kids were doing science by sliding down hills in sleds) or when a family of friends was visiting from out of town and a great game of mutants (some pretend thing with everybody declaring their powers and how they interact with everyone else's) ensued.

A true Scholar will not be pulled from their pattern with every whim. If you find yourself being bobbed on a string by an adolescent who is calling the shots of what kind of day he will be having, you need to restructure the plan. *You* dispense the Practice Scholar privileges in a reasonable fashion. Once they take on the commitment of Project Scholar, they should be much more stable and not moved by every childish game that entices. You will be shocked at the things they pass on in order to meet their personal goals when they are truly committed to their path.

Be matter-of-fact but precise with this: in Project Scholar, get benefits; out of Project Scholar, no benefits. This cannot be a punishment, or even held out as a bribe, or he will quickly dislike Scholar Phase. It must be a natural result—that is all. If he is in

Scholar, he is too busy for the normal schedule. If not, he has plenty of time to help. When he likes that arrangement he will know it, and so will you.

Because our first three children are so close in age, we had three dabbling with Practice Scholar at the same time. Oliver proceeded on to Project Scholar like a duck into water. After all his struggles with reading, now nothing pleased him so much as to have license to read all day long. Whew! We were thrilled, and not a little relieved. When we met with Emma and Sara (separately, of course) the next fall to make plans for their coming school year, the question of their placement in Scholar Phase was high on the list. Emma was 13½ and Sara was barely twelve. Emma enthusiastically plunged in to Scholar Phase. Sara was thoughtful, and asked for time to consider the question. She ultimately came back to us with the decision to remain in Love of Learning for a few more months. She actually set the date, several months in advance, when she would enter Scholar Phase in earnest. It turned out to be an accurate prediction, and she was then anxious to get on with it!

Rachel was grateful to have our next child, Eliza, in the less demanding schedule of Love of Learning and available to help with family work (remember the Scholars are no longer errand-runners and can not be interrupted during Scholar hours—basically 9-5—unless it is an emergency). The younger ones were still in Core, learning valuable lessons through work and play and gaining competence in their relationships, social skills and chores.

Practice Scholar Level Guidelines

The definition of Practice Scholar Level is that the student moves in and out of Scholar Phase for a few hours, and eventually a day at a time. Here are a few important guidelines to this level:

- As the parent you should support but not push the Practice Scholar.

- Whenever your student is in Scholar Phase, meaning she is doing Scholar studies, free her from non-academic responsibilities for those hours or that day. For example, if your Love of Learning study time is five hours and she has two hours of chores, have her Practice Scholar day be seven hours long and have someone else do some of her chores.
- Do not plan Practice Scholar Level studies for a week or even two days. Take it day by day and let her live a Scholar schedule or go back to Love of Learning on any given day.
- The Practice Scholar moves back and forth between Love of Learning Phase and "trying out" Scholar Phase. The key is to reward her with study time as she wants it. The natural consequence of studying is that she spends time on studying rather than other things.
- If your children are in public or private school, you may be thinking that most of this applies mainly to homeschoolers and that your children are getting all they need away at school. This is not true. Most public and private school students actually spend very little time *studying* at school. The classroom setting is powerful for lecture and for group discussion (both important environments of mentoring), but personal study time is almost non-existent. The truth is that homeschoolers typically get more study time than their peers; so, if your student is in a traditional classroom school, it is even more important that special arrangements be made (simplifying other outside time commitments, lightening family workload) in order to get enough study time. In her six hours away at school, she will typically study far less than two hours—so she will need six to ten home hours of study daily to get Scholar Phase. As mentioned earlier, hardly anybody in America does Scholar Phase anymore, but it is still the foundation of any great education. If a traditional classroom model is right for your student, try to work out long library study blocks, or better still, no-class study days

with his teachers. Go back and re-read *The Chosen* and note the class time versus study time. Remember, Scholar Phase is lots of study time, not lots of seat time.

- Where applicable, promote younger siblings to more responsibility to take up the slack of extra chores to be done. This is a powerful chance for your younger children to develop the skills of responsibility and follow-through that oldest children typically experience, and for your oldest children to experience the security and nurture of middle and youngest children. Where needed, take up the slack yourself. Families really are ideal to great education; use this "natural order of things" rather than fighting it like the conveyor belt does.
- Do not make any formal scholar agreement with your student yet; just give her a daily option of doing Scholar studies that are more demanding than her normal Love of Learning schedule. It is not going backwards if she is on for a while, then off. For most kids this is normal and healthier than just going into Scholar and never backtracking into Love of Learning. Expect her to back out numerous times in the first one to two years. Support her when she does.
- Never, ever gloat, manipulate or use extra chores against her. Try to keep the academic relationship, the home management relationship and the unconditional acceptance relationship separate. There are times for accountability in both the academic and home management arenas, and reprimands and praisings will follow. But the one should not be confused with the other (either by the parent or the scholar). Praise for scholarly achievement must not be withheld based on low performance around the house; excellence in family duties should not translate to release from study time as a "reward." This is extremely important! Adolescents, with their hormonal mood swings, tend to bring the emotional volatility of a Core level child and

couple it with the self-analysis of an adult. They will judge themselves in absolute terms (either thinking they've got all their ducks in a row because they study so long and hard or thinking they're worthless because ---- well, because their hair is too straight, or whatever....). As a parent and mentor you need to help them find clarity in self-evaluation by being cool-headed and helping them to separate the various roles they are fulfilling so that they can approach each one with vision and resolve and enjoy the successes and learn from the failures based on real issues. And even as we keep separate the relationships of mentor/scholar and home manager/worker, no performance or failure in either of these should affect the unconditional love, support and acceptance that a child feels from a parent.

- When she goes back into Love of Learning, revert to the old time structure. This does require the family to be flexible and can be a logistical challenge for a time, but it is a critical element of choosing to do the hard work required as a scholar and should not be shortchanged.
- In all of this, allow her to study whatever she wants (within the bounds of morality and decency, of course; the goal here is academic freedom and inspiration, not an absence of common sense or parental wisdom). If the FEC determines that she really needs to study a certain topic, be prayerful and inspirational in getting her to voluntarily choose to study it (even if in a few cases it is only out of trust for *your* insight and not for personal passion).
- Use the testing environment: ask questions about what is being learned, have her give reports to family and friends, perform, showcase, etc.
- Tell her she can go on to the Project Scholar Level whenever she wants, after she has shown that she can do multiple Practice Scholar days in a row. Both the student and the parents should seek direction about this change. Do not

push her to it. She may spend as much as one to two years in Practice Scholar Level.

The Project Scholar (approximate ages thirteen to fifteen)

The Project Level will likely last about two years. Students who do a long Practice Level may choose a shorter Project Level, and vice versa. The student must choose to move to Project Level, and will likely do so naturally as he seeks more and more Practice Days over Love of Learning. Re-teach him the Scholar Levels periodically during Practice Level, and let him know without any pressure that the next step he will make someday is Project Level. Some will make a relatively abrupt transition; others will dove-tail into it with more and more Scholar days and progressively fewer Love of Learning days over time.

During Project Level, your student will be permanently removed from children's chores and be able to do Scholar studies almost every day. If a student moves quickly into this phase, with a very short Practice Level, that is okay; as long as he has chosen it on his own without pressure. When he decides to go into Project Level, sit down with him and write out a formal agreement. The agreement should be very short—probably less than half a page. The agreement should include the following:

- Two columns: Left column labeled "Responsibilities"/Right column labeled "Benefits"
- Under "Responsibilities" list items such as the following:
  - The family responsibility(ies) that he will own (remember to keep it simple and reasonable)
  - His daily/weekly/annual study time structure
  - Daily written summary and time it is due
  - "Act like a Young Adult in morality and righteousness"
  - "Act like a Young Adult in continual nurturing of relationships in the family"

- Under "Benefits" list the following:
  - Ownership of responsibilities, not errands
  - Only one or two responsibilities, on his own time and schedule, with standards clearly outlined (e.g. laundry once a month might be sufficient for the Scholar, but the rest of the family would run in to problems)
  - Time to get a great education of his choosing
  - Time to pursue the preparation for his mission in life
  - Mentoring as he needs it
  - "To be treated as a Young Adult in the home instead of a Child"
  - "To be included as a Young Adult by parents in settings outside of the home, instead of a Child"
  - All of the above, as long as he satisfactorily fulfills all of the Responsibilities listed.

Note that to be treated as a Young Adult in the home might be to include the youth in certain discussions, or when other adults are visiting; outside of the home includes finding opportunities to give the perks, like—do an adults-only activity (a certain movie, or going to dinner with Mom, Dad and Scholars).

Project Scholar Level Guidelines

Teach your Scholar about Project Level during Practice Level. You may decide to tell him he can qualify for the Project Level when he has done at least three consecutive Practice Scholar Days on three separate occasions. Here are some specific guidelines for this level:

- Create a Written Contract that both the student and parents agree upon.
- Keep it brief, and follow the Responsibilities & Benefits format.

- Hold a meeting with the student and parents to formally agree upon the Written Contract, and clearly talk through expectations. Agree upon which parent will be the mentor, and what time the daily reports will be due.
- If the agreed-upon mentor is not a parent, parents still need to be part of the meetings and party to the final agreement. In fact, in such cases the parents must be very actively and closely involved in the whole process.
- Hold a family meeting, announce that the student is now in Scholar Phase, clearly show what responsibilities he will have, and discuss the new structure of who will get chores done and how the family will work under this new arrangement. Clarify what the Scholar will be doing and not be doing, and begin the planning for how to rearrange family structure.
- These points apply to all Scholar Phase students, whether they attend private, home or public school.
- Post the written agreement in a high traffic family area where the Scholar can refer to it if the parent is tempted to violate it.
- Honor it. If you want to change it, call for a meeting with the Scholar (and parents if someone else is serving as mentor) and ask to arrange a new agreement. But strictly honor whatever agreement is written and posted.
- The Scholar turns in a daily summary of what was learned. It should be brief, but the student needs to do one every day.
- The mentor looks at each daily summary and spends a few minutes asking questions—this is the Testing Environment. This can be done daily or weekly as best fits the mentor's schedule and the Scholar's needs. But it must be done consistently.
- The student studies what he chooses following structured time, not content. The mentor gives suggestions and guidelines about what should be studied, but supports

the student's final decision. However, the mentor can recommend that the student find a different mentor if there is a serious difference of vision. And, of course, parents always have veto power on issues of morality and decency.

- The student accomplishes the agreement, and any other specific commitments that he makes.
- The mentor holds the student accountable for completing the agreement and the commitments.
- If the student breaks the agreement or commitments, he accepts the mentor's response including consequences. It is highly recommended that mentors study and apply *The One Minute Manager*.
- The Project Scholar is ready to move to the next level when the mentor feels that the student is self-directed to the point that the daily report is unnecessary and that a monthly meeting will do.

The Self-Directed Scholar (approximate ages fourteen through seventeen)

The Self-Directed Scholar studies eight to twelve hours a day, five to six days a week, ten to twelve months a year for three to four years. This 5,000 to 8,000 hours of intense study builds a huge base of knowledge and skill which can be applied to whatever mission the later adult embarks upon.

This model is based solidly on the experience of great leaders of history and how they were educated—the great statesmen, thinkers, artists, businessmen, generals, historians, philosophers, mathematicians, prophets, sages, composers, and entrepreneurs. "Success" may be possible without a superb Leadership Education, but lasting freedom is not. And a great education enhances anybody's abilities, talents, opportunities, skills and options. The foundation of this education comes in the Self-Directed Level and is expanded in the Mentored Level.

One of the most valuable ways for a Self-Directed Scholar to learn both knowledge and skills is to have teaching opportunities. This can be accomplished by having him teach what he is learning in regular tutorials with Core and Love of Learning or early Scholar students. Again, the family structure will provide ample opportunities for this to occur and is ideal to learning. Other opportunities can be found in community groups, in discussion groups, with extended family where the Young Adult finds his peer group with aunts, uncles, grandparents, close family friends and other Young Adults rather than the "teenager" crowd. Community involvement in martial arts, piano recitals, singing groups, scouts, sports and other activities started as early as Love of Learning also provide valuable opportunities for skill, intellectual, leadership and spiritual development.

Self-Directed Scholar Level Guidelines

The Self-Directed Level begins when the Project Level Mentor feels that the student is progressing well enough that daily reports are no longer needed. Guidelines for this level include the following:

- The mentor meets with the student and recommends that he move into the Self-Directed Level. Together the student, both parents, and outside mentor if applicable, meet and create a new Agreement which moves to 8-12 hour study days at least 5 days a week for the next 10 months. The Agreement allows time for the student to do up to 12 hours if he chooses.
- Daily reports are discontinued.
- Reports are now turned in as they are completed, including papers, articles, poems, art projects, recitals, art shows, book reports, seminars, events, performances, etc. The mentor puts some real time and effort into giving feedback to these submissions, applying the "Quality not Conformity" principle. Anything less than high quality is not graded.

Instead, the student is coached on how to improve and sent back to work—over and over until excellence is attained.

- The mentor meets each month with the student in a formal meeting. The student brings a list of everything read and copies of work done to this meeting. Together the mentor and student outline the plan for the next month, structuring time and some general content plans. The content may be changed by the student at any time, but the discussion will help outline areas of student interest and spark mentor input and teaching. The student and mentor should be disciplined in holding the meetings, coming prepared and spending enough time to make them valuable.
- The mentor's main job during this phase—next to inspiring—is to schedule and hold good monthly mentor meetings, where the main focus is the Coaching Environment.
- The student and mentor should make sure the Five Environments of Mentoring are all healthy. As Tiffany Earl put it: "Some of these environments take place in the home, but often they are supplemented with outside experiences—great lectures by inspiring men and women, classes where classics are read and discussed among peers who are seeking the same demanding education and where teachers expect written and oral tests. The key here is to look at the ratio of study time to class time. If a student studies eight to twelve hours a day, how much time is left for colloquia, lecture, testing, coaching and tutorial outside of the home? Enough to take advantage of peers and outside teachers but not so much as to distract the youth and tempt him to put the responsibility to educate himself on others. Do not underestimate the power that other youth can have on your student, for good or otherwise. Use that power for good—for high standards, for nobility, for greatness, for statesmanship."

In addition, mission phase parents can band together to create an optimal peer experience coupled with the high-quality instruction and tutoring by engaged mentors.

The Mentored Scholar Level (approximately ages fifteen to twenty)

At some point, the student has a good, broad, quality education with some depth in a few areas of interest. The student eventually reaches a point where he wants or needs to move out from under the wings of parents and take on the world. The increased maturity of youth who have been engaged in a Leadership Education to this point puts them in an interesting position. Some may be ready for the educational intensity that a mentored scholar experience such as college provides but are too young to live away from home on their own. We would like to direct a few remarks to this group of mentored scholars in particular and then will proceed to discuss mentored scholars who are ready for a college experience away from home.

The Mentored Scholar At Home

The need and commitment of the mentored scholar to take on the challenge of more intense scholarly preparation will coincide with the age of life during which contemporary society will be asking them about their professional and college plans, and expecting their highest excitement to be centered on driving, dating, getting a job and engaging in entertainment. The mentored scholar will hunger for increased depth, breadth and mentoring in scholarly studies combined with a need to reach out to ever-expanding circles and relationships. Parents and mentors must be especially vigilant and play an active role in helping their youth find or create an environment in which their needs can be met in a way that furthers their Leadership Education and personal mission. If this is not done, all of the powerful drives the youth will feel at this point are in danger of being met in less ideal ways; this can lead to disillusionment and failure.

Consider implementing one or more of the options that have proven highly successful with youth in this situation. One option is the creation of an academy led by a high quality liberal arts mentor that focuses primarily upon scholarly studies and discussions. It may be time for individual studies with a carefully chosen scholar mentor well-versed in the methods of Leadership Education or the mentored scholar may wish to do college courses through a distance learning program. Some students take courses from local schools or mentors that are tailored to their life mission while they have the time at home to dedicate themselves to improving their skills in these areas. Some start a business or find an apprenticeship arrangement.

Many parents have had great success creating organizations of like-minded youth and families that provide experiences which provide refinement and growth for the scholar as well as friendships with friends and families who share similar goals. These groups take the Mom School one step further by allowing the youth to take on and grow in leadership capacity, being an influential and responsible part of creating and running the group with parents and other inspirational adults as mentors. Some activities that have been successful in groups such as these are: mentored book discussions, projects such as play-writing and acting, creative publications, leadership and character development, public speaking, simulations such as mock trial and constitutional conventions, field experiences such as community involvement and cultural events, writing, Shakespeare, social dance and sports, inspirational guest speakers, service and performing opportunities and on and on.

In our case, we have created a "College Prep Finishing Course," which is designed to "fill in the gaps." Youth at this stage of development are ripe and anxious to address any deficits in their preparation, and have far less difficultly overcoming the personal opposition to working on their weak points than they did even six months earlier.

Our College Prep class addresses advanced survey knowledge of cultural literacy, history, geography, the scientific method, basic and advanced math, spelling, grammar, punctuation, public speaking, research, computer skills, writing, logic, debate, negotiation and diplomacy, social dance, vocabulary from Latin and Greek roots, and colloquia. It is an ambitious project, and the fifteen- and sixteen-year-old youth who attend are thrilled to add refinement to their depth and ambition. Most have an amazing education and social skills reflecting the years they have followed their own interests. They are now primed to accept the guidance of a mentor in addressing the things they did not focus on previously, and their learning curve is sharp as they pick right up on the things they didn't concern themselves with before. They are growing in confidence and competence, and feel like they have a real plan on how to be college-ready when the time comes for that step.

This time is far too valuable in the life of a scholar to be wasted or misdirected due to lack of filling some important needs of the scholar. Take care to maximize the potential of these few years.

The Mentored Scholar at College

When the mentored scholar is ready for college away from home, parental mentoring is not yet completed. First, the student needs help in choosing the right place to go. College students need to be mentored, not just run through another conveyor belt.

Starting over away from home is like a new birth, an intellectual and social birth, and the choice between a conveyor belt or leadership college experience is every bit as important as the same choice at age six or twelve. In some ways, it is more important, because this time you will not be there daily to pick them up, dust them off and re-assemble dropped pieces. Ideally, your Scholar has been well prepared to make such decisions. And with your help and counsel as you continue to trust yourself and tell her what you feel inspired to share, she will know how to get the right answers and make the right decisions.

The first year away from home and attending college is crucial. Once she is there, the weekly (or even more frequent) phone call is vital. She will want to talk about social things, and you should. But she may not want to talk about academic things and that could be a problem. She needs to tie what she is learning to what you have always taught her. And you need to learn what she is learning. Some of your most tightly held pet ideas could probably use some challenging.

Families work, and this is one of the most important phases in a family—yours and hers. Keep the discussions going, social as well as academic. When she hates a class, it is time for you to hit the library and bookstore. You know how to inspire, so start studying and get on the phone.

When she just does not feel right and wants to come home, it is time for some heartfelt prayer and diplomatic coaching (of course she wants to come home, who would not? But if she comes home, she will have to face the same test again soon—maybe after marriage when the stakes are increased at least tenfold).

We will examine college in more depth in the next chapter. But before that, it is important to consider some mistakes that must be avoided in order to guide your youth through Scholar Phase.

The Top Eight Mistakes Parents Make with Scholar Phase

There are at least eight mistakes which parents make in Scholar Phase. Most of them (you guessed it!) are just left-overs from the conveyor belt. Some of them are also a result of the loss of the multi-generational family in the beginning of the twentieth century and of the fragmentation of the nuclear family at the end of the century.

The separation of religion from education at the same time that education was removed from our families just accelerated the downward trend, and the Industrial Age migration of the family into the workplace sped it up. Whatever the cause, our generation desperately needs to clearly identify these mistakes. Then we need to learn to apply strategies to correct, and better still, avoid, these mistakes in our own homes and families. On a purely practical level, it is almost impossible to effectively implement Scholar Phase without knowing and overcoming these mistakes.

Here are the top 8 mistakes parents make with Scholar Phase children, and how to avoid each:

Mistake #1: Treat Them like Teenagers, Instead of Young Adults

To make this clear, we need to define some terms. Teenagers are basically adolescent youth who act like children. Often, the adults around them expect them to act like children. Examples are everywhere in popular culture: just visit any local high school or watch the TV adolescent norm exhibited in a host of shows and movies.

Young Adults are children, adolescents or early twenty-somethings who act like adults, regardless of and often in spite of the environment and expectations around them. Examples of young adults are plentiful in the classics. Observe the adult behavior of the amazing children in *Little Britches, Man of the Family, Pollyanna, Where the Red Fern Grows, Down the Long Hills*, and a host of other child stories. Young adults are also exemplified in the adolescent and early adult heroes in scripture, mythology, and books like *Laddie, Jane Eyre, Sense and Sensibility, The Fields of Home, The Red Badge of Courage, The Lonesome Gods, The Walking Drum, The Chosen, Great Expectations, Farmer Boy* and others.

The classics also teach us about teenagers, such as Lydia, Kitty and Mary in *Pride and Prejudice.* Indeed, the most challenging question of this book may be how the same parents managed to raise such childish teenagers and also such mature young adults (Elizabeth and Jane) in the same home. When Lydia gloats that her sisters will be jealous of her because of what she has done and Mrs. Bennett exults in seeing her young daughter "married" (she says it with great pride and accomplishment), we see the seeds of the Anglo-American teenager. Current American culture has degenerated a step further—now we eschew the marriage altogether, promote the one night "hook up," and wonder if married thirty-somethings with children will ever start acting like adults rather than teenagers.

Even many families who do not condone this extreme "norm" still worry about a young adult who likes to study long hours, would rather sit and talk with the adults than the teenagers at social events and does not really want to go out a lot with friends. Indeed, teenagers never become adults by acting like teenagers; they become adults by acting the part.

The only way to help a young person become an adult is to give him responsibility—real responsibility. The difference between childhood and adulthood is in emotional maturity, trustworthiness and responsibility. Those in between must either be caught in the past or moving to the future. A young person with real responsibilities who fulfils them is a Young Adult. Anyone else is a teenager.

In the modern family, it takes both parents and youth to make a young adult. Only the parent can truly pass on responsibility, and only the youth can choose to fulfill it. Amazingly, in some of the most committed families, we have the strange situation of young people trying to be young adults who are forced by their parents to be teenagers. Their parents will not give them real responsibility. Historically, the poor and often middle classes got whatever education they could by age ten to twelve and then took on full adult responsibility for feeding, clothing and supporting themselves and family members. The wealthy youth also had a responsibility, to get a superb education for the future of the family. In modern America—what a blessing—even the poor classes get to educate their youth. But unless they see their education as a real responsibility, as part of their mission in life, as something expected and needed of them by God, their country, and their family, they are just teenagers playing at child's education.

Mistake #2: Start Them Too Early

This is a huge mistake, and it is committed the most frequently of all the mistakes. Each child needs a real Core Phase. Even the prodigy who reads and plays the piano at age three needs a full and wonderful Core Phase. Part of Core is discovery and play, so your brilliant son can discover and play at calculus or physics or literary analysis at age five if he wants, but do not put him in Scholar until the Core Lessons are fully and clearly learned. Right and wrong, good and bad, true and false are lessons that exceptionally intelligent and gifted people often struggle with, so if your child is a prodigy he likely needs a longer, fuller Core Phase than anyone else. In play time he can study whatever he wants.

Ditto with Love of Learning. Again, he can freely choose whatever advanced level work he wants, but he needs to absolutely love learning, and freely and enthusiastically choose it. The same is true with Practice Scholar Level.

Some students may choose Scholar Phase at twelve, others at fifteen, but they need to have solid Core and Love of Learning as a foundation. During Core, Love of Learning, and Practice Scholar Level, teach them the Scholar levels and where they are headed. Have structured time so they do study and learn, help them with their studies, set the example and make sure they meet mandatory testing or other state requirements.

Moving into Scholar Phase should be seen as an exciting and beneficial benchmark they will look forward to and seek. But do not push them into it early, or they will have a "hate of learning" experience and really get slowed down.

Mistake #3: Give Them Too Much Non-Academic Work

We have trained numerous charter, private and other non-traditional schools in how to implement Scholar Phase. One teacher after another comes back with the same story:

It took them a while to get the hang of it, but after a couple of seminar trainings and readings it finally clicked. They turned their class into a Jefferson Classroom. They threw out the "require" and tried to inspire. This took a little time, and then one day after a lot of hard work it clicked! They were on. They were inspiring.

Students sit up, then move to the edge of their seats. Even the sleepy kid in the back notices something going on and gets enthused. An electricity fills the room. The words mission, quality, depth and study seem to just download directly into the student's minds. No data error. They love it.

Students crowd around the teacher after class, eyes wide and excited. "I really can do it, can't I?" the sleepy back row kid asks. "Yes. You just have to put in the time." "Why not," the kid thinks, "everything else is pretty boring anyway."

"Everything will be different now!" the teacher punches the air in victory when the door closes behind the last student, "I can't wait for tomorrow!" The next day is fabulous, and the day after. The whole week is amazing. Students study, the teacher rewrites the syllabus, other teachers notice an amazing change and start changing their class plans.

On the ninth or tenth day of class the students shuffle in quietly and do not make eye contact. "What's wrong?" the teacher asks. Most of the students did not finish their studies. "No problem," the teacher informs them, "just get back to it tonight." But it gets worse the next day, and the next.

"I must need to inspire them," the teacher decides. So in class he launches into an even more inspiring discussion than last time. But nobody responds. The teacher ups the energy. No result. This is frustrating. What is wrong with these kids? His voice takes on an edge. "Education is so important. You have a mission. You will not fulfill it if you do not get a great education. You will not get a great education if you do not study. You have done it already. You loved it. You do not want to be mediocre. Come on ..." His voice trails off. The bell rings. The students shuffle out.

The kid from the back waits until everyone is gone. He stands up in belligerent body language and tone of voice. "Look," he says, "my dad won't let me study all that time, okay! Just back off. I'm doing the best I can. I have to mow the lawn, help with the dishes. My dad said he's sick of me just sitting around reading all the time. He says I'm old enough to help, to get my lazy butt off the couch and do something constructive. He wonders what's gotten into me anyway, just sitting around reading, not even hanging with my friends anymore. He's sick of it. So, if you gotta problem, you talk to my dad. Not me. Okay?!" He stalks out.

The teacher asks a few of his best students over the next few days. Same story. "I'm really sorry," they say, one after the other. "I really like your class," they say. "I'll still do the best I can. My mom really needs me. You're not mad at me, are you?" they ask, with big, round eyes.

The story speaks for itself. We have taken license with the details, but we have heard the story repeated over and over. When we ask homeschooled youth, they tell the same story. It might be true in your home. They cannot get a Scholar Phase education if you will not let them.

Make an agreement as outlined above, and discipline yourself to stick to it. Getting an education takes work, it is a powerful part of mission and is a real responsibility—a worthwhile one. It is a valuable use of youth; it is the best use of the young adult period in life. Young people who read all day are not lazy. They are students. And it is tempting to want to help them to "balance" their lives. But compared to the non-scholar generation they are living in, and the level of leadership that will be required to face upcoming generational challenges, these few youth *are* the "balance." And we need thousands more to achieve a good balance. There are only a few of them in America, it is true, but there should be more. And if you happen to have one in your home, or three or four, you have done something right. But do not shut them down. Let them do it!

Mistake #4: Give Them Too Little Non-Academic Work

They do need responsibilities, but real responsibilities. Adults, and young adults, have responsibilities. Children, on the other hand, help parents with the parents' responsibilities. The parents own the responsibilities, they are the adults, and the children are just helpers. They get sent on errands, or they do a job for a week because the parents say so.

When you really want the student to go into Scholar Phase, not Practice Level but full-fledged Project Level and beyond, they must graduate from child to Young Adult, and the most powerful signal that they are now a Young Adult is to leave errands behind and be given ownership over some important household duty. Dad has such things, even if he works full time. For example, in our home Dad oversees the yard, lawns and trees. They are his responsibility; if he does not see to it that they are watered, they die. Dad also has part of the house that is his responsibility; if he does not clean it, it gets pretty dirty. Mom has things that are hers. We are adults. If you want Young Adults instead of teenagers, they must be given real responsibility. This is one reason why a farm is so powerful for raising young people. If your twelve-year-old does not feed his rabbit, it dies.

But it works in any home. If your fifteen-year-old owns breakfast every day and he does not fix it well, everyone complains and the little kids cry and you do not have to punish him at all. The natural consequences take care of it and he either shapes up fast or cannot do Scholar Phase and is given a list of daily chores to report back on in addition to his daily Love of Learning structured time. If he goes back, make it matter of fact—a natural consequence, not a punishment. It is only negative if you do it negatively. If you treat him as an adult as long as he acts like one, he will mostly act like one.

Part of a young person's education should be training to be an effective, contributing adult. When you treat him like a teenager you just delay this vitally important experience. A good guideline for what responsibilities to give is: How much would he have to do if he were a roommate away at college? He would still have responsibilities, but they would be responsibilities instead of errands and they would be relatively minimal. Your younger children need to step up and learn to work; or, if the Scholar student is your youngest, or only, child, you will have a lot less to pick up than when you had three and six year olds running around the house. Families work. It is almost as if whoever created families really thought through the details and put it together perfectly!

Mistake #5: Promote a Typical Modern Teenager Social Life

It never ceases to amaze us how ingrained this conveyor belt mistake is in parents—ourselves included. Maybe it is because the best part of our conveyor belt education was the social part. Athletics, debate, theater, music, our best teachers, clubs, dances, assemblies and activities all used mentorial instead of professorial methods, inspired instead of required, used classics (in football, we never read a textbook but talked about the great players, great games, great plays; same in theater), structured time instead of content (we hardly ever knew what we would cover in practice, just when it started and ended), set the example, and so on.

But just as much as the activity side of conveyor belt schooling tends to use principles of great education, it seems that most classrooms are dedicated to doing the opposite—professors, textbooks, structured content, requirements, complex curriculum, etc. It is probably natural that we tend to see the social activity side of the conveyor belt as a good model to follow.

Since adolescents are very social by nature, we want them to have social activity outlets. And since most of what we know about social activity we learned from the conveyor belt (especially if you were one who really liked that part of your school experience), we just copy it. "What else is there?" we wonder. And when we are involved in community, church or other social activities, we model it after what we know—conveyor belt schools.

If your child spent a lot of time on the conveyor belt, you may need to rethink this together. But if he did not, if he was leadership educated all the way, you may need to sit back and learn from him. Ask him what kind of social events and activities he wants to get into and help support his interests. Contrary to modern opinion, hanging at malls and movie theaters with other kids your own age away from parents is not a staple of growing up, but lots of social interaction is. Our point is not that Young Adults should be less social. A healthy Young Adult wants more social interaction outside of the family than he will seek during any other part of his life. It is a great part of life. Young Adults need lots of social interaction, sometimes several times a week, and you can help.

Our point is that we probably should not promote the type of social interaction we had on the conveyor belt just because it was our experience. You may have loved the prom, but a real-world gala will likely be more fun for your leadership-educated daughter. Chances are the local teenager prom will not be very fun at all for a Young Adult.

Fifteen-year-old Emma recently attended a debate tournament held at a high school in Las Vegas. The Homecoming dance was to be held that night in the same auditorium, and volunteers were busily decorating for the event. She reflected on the streamers and balloons and the probably top-40 music to be played, and the mind-numbing sameness of the dances, the social mores of whom you could or could not dance with (heaven forbid that a group of girls would simply move to the music together with no partners!), the politics and heartbreaks, etc. It surprised Rachel to know that such an event held no appeal. But then again, it didn't.

Robert Kiyosaki mentions in his *Rich Dad, Poor Dad* series how the poor teach their kids to join football or basketball teams; the wealthy, golf or tennis. It is conveyor belt versus leadership all over again—employee training sports versus individualized, mentored leadership athletics. Of course teamwork is also valuable, but you can learn teamwork just as well in swimming, tennis, golf, and martial arts. The same lessons apply to other facets of our social life and activities.

Baseball was Oliver's love from ages eight to sixteen. His coaches and teammates were among his best friends and most influential mentors. He would not change that experience for anything. When our children came of baseball age, we took them to a baseball park to watch a game, and also to a martial arts studio to watch a practice. They enjoyed both, but we noticed the tension of parents arguing at the baseball game versus the order and safety of the dojo. It was ironic, but more importantly, it was a powerful lesson in leadership.

Our children who are old enough have all elected to take martial arts rather than baseball. Their younger siblings may choose baseball, and we will support that choice, but we will not make the mistake of just flat out promoting baseball even though that was an important part of Oliver's youth and education.

Mistake #6: Ignore the Written Agreement

The best way to make this mistake is to go through all the motions of an agreement and then just pretend it did not happen. Require your Young Adults to do whatever you are in the mood to assign them—dishes, diapers, tending, errands—whenever it is most convenient to you.

If they bring up the agreement, inform them that you are the parent and that as long as they live in your home they will live by your rules. Do not check daily to see if they have turned in their daily report. Do not ask them for it if it is not in on time. Do not send them back to Practice Level when they do not do the Responsibilities listed on the agreement. Just live as you did before.

You can easily predict what your results will be. If you want great educational results, be a great mentor. Check their daily work as you agreed upon, and follow the agreement exactly. Make it brief and simple instead of complex, then follow it exactly. Put real effort, energy, time and prayer into making really good agreements and then follow them exactly.

Mistake #7: Don't Have Them Mentor Younger Siblings

To make this mistake effectively and repeatedly, all you have to do is believe the following conveyor belt myths:

- Youth are teenagers, meaning you cannot give them real responsibility.

- You especially cannot give them responsibility over teaching, which must be done by experts.
- They cannot do it as well as you can because you are older and more experienced.
- They will not teach well because they are not certified, they do not even have a degree or a diploma.
- In order to do a good job, they will need to be supplied with a well-structured, technical curriculum.
- If they are teaching younger students, they will not be working on their own studies.

Of course, all of these are conveyor belt myths. The truth is you want young adults rather than teenagers in your home, and you want your children to become young adults. Your advanced youth will bring a passion, excitement and a learning curve to teaching that no expert can ever hope to duplicate.

The teacher always learns more than the student. If they are teaching, they are learning. When you start a new concept, it pays to be the student for a while because you will be soaking in information like a sponge in this new arena of learning. But after a while, you need to teach it to really understand it. So we do not recommend having students in the early part of any phase do a lot of mentoring of younger students. Late Core and late Love of Learning will teach and discuss as they choose. Just let them. Early Scholar Phase students need to just study and soak it in, during Practice and especially Project Level. Students should really do a lot of mentoring of younger students when they are in the Self-Directed Scholar Level. The more they can teach tutorials, group discussions, informal testing, lectures and coaching, the better. In the Mentored Level of Scholar Phase and in the beginning of Depth Phase they will be soaking in new information again. In late Depth Phase, they need to teach extensively.

You do not need to memorize this or outline it in a complex system. Just follow this simple guideline: when older students want to teach, mentor, or do a report for younger students and the younger students want to be involved—that is great. Support it. And follow this pattern yourself. Study, learn, share, repeat.

Mistake #8: Do Not Clearly Outline Ownership

Doctors Jim Jenkins and Terry Warner both give examples of couples who used to get upset with each other every year at Christmas. They had very different perspectives about the holidays and what constituted a "good Christmas." In fact, both of them thought they owned Christmas. This example hit home for us because we had the same struggle for years. In Oliver's words:

I thought I owned Christmas and got to decide what we were going to do, what Christmas tree we would use, how it would be decorated, what the gifts would be, etc. As you can see, this was very selfish.

I did not originally care, in fact I had not really thought about who owned Christmas. But then, one year when I was young, my mom took me and my brother to buy a Christmas tree. We took it home and spent the afternoon decorating it. We were all very excited to surprise Dad.

But Dad got really upset. He had already purchased a tree, had it hidden, and had spent hours personally hand-making dozens of beautiful paper Santa Claus ornaments to put all over it. My parents never argued in front of me, so I do not know how the discussion went. But what came out of it was that from then on Dad clearly owned Christmas. Mom could make suggestions, but Dad owned Christmas.

Now that may or may not have been the best arrangement—like I said, I do not know what went into making the decision. Maybe it was the perfect decision for them, and maybe they worked it out wonderfully. None of this was ever vocalized to me. I am sure they worked it out with each other, made a decision and went forward. But their decision seemed binding on *me*. When I got married, I just assumed that Dad owned Christmas, and since I was now Dad, I obviously owned Christmas.

Rachel came with a different view. The point is that we had a misunderstanding in this area until we clearly sat down and asked about the ownership of Christmas in our family. We did this several years ago, after a seminar where Doctor Jenkins brought up the concept, and it has made all the difference. Here are the options we considered:

- Dad owns Christmas
- Mom owns Christmas
- The children own Christmas
- Dad and Mom jointly own Christmas
- The whole family jointly owns Christmas

You can go into a lot more detail if one of these is not clearly the answer. We do not believe that there is one right answer for each of the following questions such as: the whole family should own Christmas, Dad should own the yard work and taking out the trash, Mom should own changing diapers and washing the dishes, and the oldest son should be in charge of meals. These are the kind of patronizing generalizations that the best kind of feminism fights against. But we do believe that in families we can sit down and work these issues out to the agreement of everyone. One family decides that Mom owns the meals and dishes, while another decides Dad owns it, another that the third daughter owns it, and still another that it is owned jointly. And all four families are right—depending on how they reached their decision.

This principle of ownership is powerful in many arenas of family life, but our focus here is the education of children and specifically Scholar Phase. Here is how our family defines Scholar Phase ownership:

Who owns the responsibility for feeding the children and young adults in our family?

The parents.

Who owns the responsibility for housing the children and young adults in our family?

The parents.

Who owns the responsibility for the young adult obeying God's commandments?

The individual young adult.

Who owns the responsibility for the consequence if a young adult disobeys family rules?

The parents.

Who owns the responsibility for establishing the family rules?

The parents.

Who owns the responsibility for the young adult obeying the family rules?

The individual young adult.

Who owns the responsibility for providing a consequence if a young adult disobeys?

The parents.

Who owns the responsibility for a young adult's education?

The individual young adult.

Who owns the responsibility for a young adult's educational agreement?

The young adult and parents jointly.

Who owns the responsibility for submitting a daily study summary?

The individual young adult.

Who owns the responsibility for reading and responding to the daily study summary?

Dad.

Who owns the responsibility for deciding what the consequence will be if a young adult does not follow his/her educational agreement?

The parents.

Obviously there are a lot more than these, but these are the clear ownership guidelines for Scholar Phase in our family. Your family may be very different, and that is great as long as you take the time to clearly outline ownership/stewardship. This can be done over time, but it is worth getting started. Just discuss who owns what, using whatever process you use for getting clarity on such matters, and begin putting your structure together.

Avoiding these eight common mistakes will help put the family back at the center of education, and of society. Separating family members to benefit the market may have been a success for the industrial age, but the impact on society as a whole has been tragic. If it is time for your family to get back to family basics, implementing Scholar Phase with your Young Adults is essential. Indeed, without Scholar Phase you likely will not have Young Adults at all.

Scholar Phase is not impossible, but it is hard. Families who do it well have a lot of fun, get a superb education, and inevitably impact the family, community, society and posterity for good. A great education makes a real difference in each person's future, happiness, and success. And parents make all the difference in how effective Scholar Phase is in any family.

America is desperately in need of families and schools that do Scholar Phase. Young Adults are in short supply, and they virtually cannot exist without the support of parents and the home. Whether your children are educated in public school, private school, homeschool or at a preparatory or boarding school, your whole family will benefit from a quality Scholar Phase educational culture.

Of course, as we have said many times above, you must set the example. With that done, you must give the Scholar permission to do the full-time work necessary for Scholar Phase. The rest of your family will benefit. And as your family gets it right, the whole society and nation will benefit. Scholar Phase is certainly a personal choice, but the consequences are literally global.

If you have young people in Scholar Phase, invite them to read and study this information and hold a tutorial or group discussion about what you and they learn. They can likely teach you as much about how to apply this as you can teach them. This chapter is designed to be used as a reference guide. Read it through, come back to the parts which apply to your students right now, and come back to it again and again as they progress through Scholar Phase.

Note that what is outlined is the ideal. It will work if followed. Mentoring is powerful when this system is applied; the student studies and the mentor really leverages the student's efforts. But if the mentor does not follow the system, the same power inherent in mentoring can significantly hurt the educational success. We did not *invent* Leadership Education; we codified it. There are many wonderful mentors and teachers out there who have internalized these principles from their own study or experience. They are natural treasures, and if you have the chance to employ one as a mentor do not miss the opportunity. But for most of us, these things do not come so naturally. With the education of our own children at stake, we want our learning curve to be as efficient and as effective as possible. For us, time and effort invested in learning and understanding Leadership Education and getting off the conveyor belt is essential.

Finally, we feel it is essential to repeat once again: You are the expert on your family. These principles are powerful and they work. This is all the more reason that it is worth your time and serious reflection to learn how to personalize and apply them to get the education worthy of the great missions you and your children are meant to accomplish. Base your decisions and actions on true principles and long-term life goals using your spiritual or inner eye, not social fear of what others might think or a conveyor belt hangover. When you know deep down inside something is right, regardless of whether or not you like it, go for it. You can do it!

CHAPTER EIGHT

Depth Phase

Depth Phase should ideally occur during the prime years of young adulthood, between eighteen and twenty-four. The student who has acquired a scholar education is ready to personalize and submit his instruction to a mentor who will provide increased opportunities for study and refinement of skills and knowledge that will allow the student to begin to implement his personal mission.

Students who truly desire to become leaders in their lives must find mentors who can guide their education during these years. Mentors are crucial to helping students in Depth Phase gain what they will need to move forward in their life missions.

Students who live away from home have the opportunity while on their own to live the life and education habits they learned during Core, Love of Learning and Scholar Phases. The Foundational Phases mix with the Educational Phases and character, habits and each student's life path are established. The learning environment and opportunities a student chooses during Depth Phase will have a great impact on whether or not the student will maximize the opportunities and learn the critical lessons of Depth Phase. In fact, the quality of education during this phase will determine whether or not the student will have the ability to accomplish the mission he has been preparing for throughout his life.

Novelist Dorothy Sayers wrote: "Is it not the great defect of our education today...that although we often succeed in teaching our pupils 'subjects,' we fail lamentably on the whole in teaching them how to think: They learn everything, except the art of learning." She also said, "Do you ever find that young people, when they have left school, not only forget most of what they learnt...but forget also or betray that they have ever really known how to tackle a subject for themselves?"

In short, the first question you should ask of any potential college is "do its graduates know how to think?" Here are other key questions to ask:

- Do they write well?
- Can they speak effectively in public?
- Do they know how to present themselves effectively in private and public settings where the stakes are high?
- Do they have a solid knowledge of history?
- Do they know the great works of literature and art?
- Do they know the great mathematical concepts and scientific discoveries and systems?
- Are they able to speak and/or do advanced research in at least one foreign language?
- Can they write business plans that fund?
- Can they build and lead organizations that last?
- Are they prepared to lead in family and community?

Of course, a student with poor people skills probably will not miraculously turn into a charismatic dynamo at college, so it is important to look at a body of graduates rather than just one or two. And it is often very difficult to meet with graduates and conduct interviews. The easiest way to answer these questions is to ask the college representative what skills you (or your son or daughter) will learn in the next four years. If they do not mention writing, history, entrepreneurship, business planning, or thinking, ask them directly where these teachings are found in the curriculum. If they are not, or if the answers are vague, then you know that if your student attends school here she will need to seek out special mentors (virtually all schools have some) and do outside work to get a great Leadership Education.

We hope that you will attend the college or university that is best for you, for your goals, your interests and your life mission. That is the Leadership Education path. In finding the right school, be sure to find one that teaches the items listed above. And many people find that the best way to get a true Depth education is outside of college.

In addition, there are certain lessons that are central to Depth Phase, and you should pursue them in your higher education studies. Indeed, these lessons are even more important in many ways than the actual topics you'll study. The lessons of Depth Phase include the following:

1. Initiative. The first test of any educational model is initiative. Great leaders have it; those who have it naturally lead. The purpose of Leadership Education is to encourage and empower initiative. Any student who fails to learn this vital lesson has not actually obtained an education. Their studies will probably be beneficial and they may be marketable. But a great education includes mastering the skill of initiative.

   This is what makes a man a great man, a woman a great woman: the ability to create, to add value, to increase what was given. Initiative is a primary purpose and goal of education.

2. Ingenuity. Ingenuity is the ability, skill and habit of doing things well. Those who are well educated have ingenuity, get things done, and "get them done right." Often in life, new methods or ideas are needed, and those with ingenuity improvise, adapt, and overcome. This is the second test of education.

   People with ingenuity have the ability to make a living and also make a difference. As the nineteenth-century Polish poet Cyprian Norwid put it, "To be what is called happy, one should have (a) something to live on, (b) something to live for, and (c) something to die for. The lack of one of these results in drama. The lack of two results in tragedy."

3. Integrity. Integrity goes a step further—in addition to doing things right, those with integrity do the right things. It is not enough to start, or even to finish. The leader, the statesman, starts and finishes the right things, at the right times, in the right way and for the right reasons. Of course, nobody is perfect; integrity does not mean perfection, but it does mean that you consistently try to do right.

4. Allegiance to God and/or Good. Allegiance can be given to God and/or Good, to self, or to any combination or group of "other" people. A person who doesn't believe in God can still dedicate their life to Good. We have a number of friends who are agnostic or atheist, and many of them apply Leadership Education in their homes and schools. As we have discussed the differences between our application of Leadership Education and theirs, we find few differences at all. In fact, they want to achieve Good every bit as much as we want to serve God. We are inspired by their examples. We still believe what we believe, and we are uplifted by their dedication to pursue excellence and greatness. The same is true of the many friends and colleagues we have who follow their allegiance to God and are of different denominations and religions than we are. Great Depth Phase education builds on committed allegiance to Good or God, whatever your belief system.

   When the right allegiance is chosen, when the person is truly consecrated to that allegiance, the beginning stages of education are fulfilled. In pursuing your higher education, be sure to build upon and expand your attachment to the right allegiance; too many people change allegiance or turn to doubt when the allegiances of their youth are challenged or rejected by others. Depth Phase should build upon and deepen your core beliefs, not reject them. Of course, as you are faced with new truths, be open and learn.

5. Commitment to Mission. Depth Phase should further prepare you to pursue a life of Mission. Always question if your studies and mentors actively seek to help you clarify your purpose in life; and then, passionately dedicate your time to that purpose. If not, add these vital things to your studies and seek out mentors to help. The very essence of education is to learn of one's mission and pursue it. Buddha reportedly said: "Your purpose in life is to find your purpose in life, and then to give your whole heart and soul to it."

   Mission is the reason we need education, the goal for which we learn, and the place where we apply what we have learned. A vision, a direction, a mission, a purpose—these are education. Everything else is a footnote. Mission is why we live, how we love. Each of us has a mission and purpose. When we tap into the power of our unique mission and purpose, we will discover "wind beneath our wings" that propels, sustains and directs us through our life. Choosing anything less will result in perpetual dissatisfaction.

6. Passion. Passion occurs when we engage with energy in accomplishing great things, though they may seem small or simple at the time. While most people seek peace, comfort and security, those with a Leadership Education understand that the place of leaders is in the middle of change and even crisis. Living and working with passion means that you thrive in times of challenge as well as peace. An education that creates life-long passion is worth every bit of effort and study; anything less falls short. Indeed, if you find yourself sitting through classes of a college or university with mostly feelings of dullness and glazed-over eyes, make a change! How can passion possibly be the lesson of such an environment? Of course, this should not be used as an excuse to never push yourself or work hard in subjects or assignments that are outside your comfort zone. Teach yourself to bring passion to the things you should do—whether they are initially fun or otherwise.

An education which combines initiative, ingenuity, integrity, allegiance, mission, and passion is truly something to strive for, sacrifice for, and give your all to obtain.

7. Impact. People with such an education have impact; they make a difference. The greatest men and women of history learned these traits and made them part of their character. People like George Washington and Benjamin Franklin actually wrote out such traits as life-long goals and worked hard to achieve them. Their success did not come because of their genetics, but because they lost themselves in something greater than themselves. We call this "sub-mission." The success of your life depends on your cause, and how fully you give yourself to it. A student who learns and applies these lessons has been educated.

8. Breadth. A great education covers the breadth of learning. Of course, it is not expected that you read every book in the library, but you must pursue areas of passion as well as get passionate about many areas outside of your initial interest. Study in many fields is necessary to a great education.

9. Depth. It would not be a Depth Phase unless you studied a couple or a few topics in real depth—gaining mastery, expertise and real understanding of the field. While many students do this in the field of their career, leadership students should do a minimum of two areas of real depth and ideally several. This, along with Breadth above, means that during your Depth Phase you'll do a lot of reading, writing, calculating, thinking, and so on. A quality education is a lot of work—and you are up to it. In fact, you want it. That is why you are pursuing a Depth Phase education. Perhaps no one in the American consciousness better typifies breadth and depth than Thomas Jefferson. Of him President John F. Kennedy said, while addressing a gathering of Nobel Prize winners: "I think this is the most extraordinary collection of talent, of human knowledge, that has ever been gathered at the White House—

with the possible exception of when Thomas Jefferson dined alone."

10. Nuance. This means the ability to analyze, discern, see contrasts and simultaneously understand similarities, and think. Those who have mastered nuance can see the difference between many shades and tints of things, in all areas and arenas of life. This is a valuable skill, vital to the well-educated.

No school can guarantee education; that is the job of the student. Yet a school must deliver teaching—*great* teaching, and the learning of important knowledge and key skills. It must also encourage the development in its students of character traits including initiative, ingenuity, integrity, true allegiance, passionate commitment to mission, and the power to think, lead and impact in the midst of change and crisis. It is above all the responsibility of the student to ensure that he is learning these lessons. If he is struggling with these essential lessons, he should seek out mentors to help.

These are the lessons of Depth Phase, and they are essential to Leadership Education. Since most people get Depth Phase in college, it is important to know about modern higher education—its current challenges, trends, and emerging future.

Higher Education Today

The first question of any college or university is "what is our mission?" The second is, "how well do we accomplish it?" Unfortunately, in our modern times a third question is needed: "what is the de facto mission of the university—the mission that the school is actually pursuing?"

Former Harvard President Derek Bok noted with concern that our universities are chasing the market above all else. Another former Ivy League President, Frank H. Rhodes of Cornell, wrote that given the new market realities our universities must change or become dinosaurs. James J. Duderstadt, former president of the University of Michigan (which many people consider the premier public university in America) argued that American universities and colleges must change to match the new market or decline along with the rest of our industrial age institutions. In short, modern academia knows that significant improvements are needed. But where exactly are we in the historical evolution and progress of higher education?

Roger Gieger's book, *The Ten Generations of American Higher Education,* provides an excellent overview of where American education began, where it has been, and where it is heading. The first generation of American education began in 1636 and ran until the early 1740's. During this period, America's first colleges were founded, including Harvard, William and Mary, and Yale. Harvard and Yale were established by churches in order to train ministers, while William and Mary was designed to help train political leaders for the new world. All three were four-year programs, with the first two years covering classical languages in order to prepare students to read the various classics in their original form. In the last two years of college, students read the great classics of world thought, guided by young faculty known as tutors. Schools typically had less than 100 students and about ten tutors, and the school was run by the head teacher or president who was chosen by a lay board of trustees.

The second generation of American higher education, from 1745-1775, saw the establishment of numerous "colonial colleges," including King's College, the College of Philadelphia, the College of Rhode Island, Dartmouth, Queen's College, and the College of New Jersey (Princeton). Again, nearly all of these schools emphasized study for the ministry, and many were established specifically to improve and safeguard the doctrinal purity of religious instruction. During this period schools began using Enlightenment works as part of the curriculum—many of them in modern languages.

The Republican era, from 1776 to 1800, significantly increased the influence of the Enlightenment in American higher education as the college curriculum followed the breaking away of the new nation from the Old World. Schools during this third generation were still small. For example, Harvard had three professors and ten tutors while Yale had one professor supported by a just a handful of tutors. And yet the quality of education their graduates exhibited was incredible. Is it possible that it was not in spite of their system—but rather, because of it?

From 1800 until the 1820's colleges put a lot of effort into fundraising to find the finances needed to operate. As part of this, schools began offering professional degree programs in medicine and law. Still, the central focus of these small schools remained the preparing of ministers.

The fifth generation of American higher education from 1828 to 1860 could be called the Sectional Divide. During this period, the national split between the cultures of North and South impacted higher education. In the South, denominational colleges focused on training ministers continued to grow and flourish, while the influence of Enlightenment thinkers Hume, Locke, Turnbull and others led to a new type of Northern classical college which emphasized preparatory training for citizenship and the professions—law, medicine, teaching and the clergy. The Northern professional programs grew more rapidly than Southern colleges. For example, the average number of students in Southern colleges was fifty-six, compared to the average of one-hundred-seventy-four students in the Northern classical colleges.

The focus on religious learning in higher education ended with the South's loss in the Civil War, and from 1860 to 1890 the Northern schools turned from the British and Scottish Enlightenment to the German University as the model of higher education. For three decades the American system systematically adopted the structures and traditions of the German Academy, including the following:

- a centralized university
- academic departments
- graduate studies

- the bachelor degree
- professional preparation as the focus of bachelor-level studies

Three other trends during the sixth generation included the establishment and proliferation of: 1) women's colleges, 2) agricultural colleges and 3) colleges in the American West; the latter applied elements from Northern, Southern and European colleges.

The seventh generation marked a distinct shift from the earlier two centuries. The Industrial Age brought big changes to business, transportation, government, the military, lifestyle, and of course, the university. The quarter century from 1890 to 1915 changed nearly everything about American higher education. Most of all, the university system standardized and then grew. The average American college or university in 1870 had ten faculty and ninety-eight students. By 1910, the average was thirty-eight faculty and three hundred seventy-four students. Schools already had programs in ministry, law, medicine, teaching and agriculture; they now added engineering, business, dentistry, art, architecture, music and various other specialties. Administrations grew large, sometimes larger than the faculty. Universities broke into numerous colleges, and colleges divided into departments. The four-year curriculum offered a classical education for the first two years followed by two years of job or career training.

This trend continued during the "nationalization" generation from 1915 to 1945. Accrediting agencies enforced the standardization of the curriculum, and many schools became almost interchangeable. Enrollments doubled. The number of colleges continued to grow. Junior colleges, teacher colleges, and urban universities for the middle class were added to colleges. As demand grew, the older and more prestigious schools adopted a selective admissions system.

The stage was set for the huge growth of the 1950's that was spurred on by the return of thousands of young men from war, along with the GI Bill that funded college education for returning soldiers. In this ninth generation of American higher education, from 1945 to 1985, college became a possibility for almost everyone. The first two years of classical education were dropped in favor of a full four years of job training with only shallow general education courses. Graduate degrees proliferated. With the widespread system of American colleges and network of degrees, faculties and accrediting agencies, college became a norm of American life and job preparation.

The tenth generation completed the Industrial Age expansion. Many colleges and universities had long since stopped being a check on business and government, instead choosing to become extensions of the government/industrial/corporate complex. Indeed, during this period many schools decided that they were businesses above all, simply responding to market needs in order to survive and grow. The new mission of a number of American colleges and universities, regardless of their published mission statement, was "to effectively deliver whatever the market demands." While perhaps viable as a mission statement, this left much to be desired for the institutions that once considered themselves "hallowed halls of learning."

Current Trends

We are now in an eleventh generation of higher learning in America. Excoriated by Allan Bloom's *The Closing of the American Mind* and a host of other polemics outlining the decline of higher education, the universities continue to flourish in the market. The leading current trends in higher education include:

- A central focus on market branding (selling the name of the university in order to attract clients)
- Hiring of academic superstars
- Research contracts over teaching (during the 1980's and 1990's, the priority was publishing over teaching)
- The shrinking of academic quality, humanities and liberal arts

- Running departments as profit centers (e.g. running the English Department or Art Department like the Athletic Department)
- Using technology as a replacement for increasing areas of direct student-teacher interaction
- School leaders as businessmen, not educators
- Teachers and professors on par with factory workers in terms of institutional control at many schools
- "Can" has replaced "should" as the governing value of many schools
- Accreditation agencies often follow these trends themselves; all of higher education seems to see the market as the ultimate touchstone
- The new goals of schools are to have the highest cash flow and the highest average graduate income rate
- The rise of for-profit schools (with some positive results, but also accelerating the negative trends)

From a market perspective, all of these trends may be positive. In terms of education, learning and national freedom, however, this is a potential disaster. It is ironic that many, if not most, professors are well-qualified and excellent teachers who are restricted from their potential impact by a struggling system. Still, Leadership Education students must seek out such mentors and engage their help. It is tragic that more students do not know this option is available to them.

There is so much that is good about higher education in America, and it is still the envy of the educational world. We must find ways to preserve the good and simultaneously reform or revolutionize new directions and methods for the Information Age. The Industrial Age is ending, and universities will change along with it. Throughout history governments, business, churches, media, the university and the family stood as six separate but equal institutions that checked and balanced each other when needed, and stopped the excesses of the others if they got out of line.

In contrast, many departments are now philosophical extensions of business and government, dependent on research grants to survive and taking orders from those who provide funding. Freedom cannot survive unless the university regains its independence, and that means it must adopt higher values than government controls or the market. Many modern educators and administrators have spoken out for needed changes in higher education. A few have suggested possible solutions to restore the university to its proper role as a leader of society: an institution on the same level as government, church, corporation, media and family. Indeed, to restate this for emphasis: In a democracy, these entities form natural checks and balances upon each other—whereas in a monarchy, the government dominates them all. In an aristocracy, they are all subservient to the business elite class and the market. In the twenty-first century, the rise of a global corporate-government aristocracy is nearly a *fait accomplis*, and the university is needed to combat this trend.

Many leading educators agree that the university needs reform, as summarized rather strongly by one of the leading thinkers of the twentieth century, Peter Drucker: "Thirty years from now the big university campuses will be relics. It is as large a change as when we got the first printed books." William Wulf concurs: "If you believe that an institution that has survived for a millennium cannot disappear in just a few decades, just ask yourself what has happened to the family farm." If this is true of the university, it will be a sad day for America.

Some of academia's most credible leaders have spoken out on the need for changes in higher education. Derek Bok, the former president of Harvard quoted above, says the university must set clear standards that it will not compromise, such as not accepting students because their parents make donations to the school or simply because they are good athletes.

Richard S. Ruch, a former dean at DeVry, believes that the university must go where the market directs and be as responsive as a successful business must. David Kirp, a professor at Berkeley, says we must convince the public to subsidize higher education, to fund it through government so it does not have to bow to the market.

George Marsden, a professor at Notre Dame, proposes that each university have a religious studies department.

Johnson, Kavanagh and Mattson write that the answer is to formally organize academic labor unions where professors keep corporations from controlling the university. James J. Duderstadt, former president of the University of Michigan, says that the Industrial Age is over, and with it, the Industrial Age university. To survive, the university will have to reinvent itself. His suggestions for doing this include new corporate boards instead of lay boards, increased high-tech learning options, alliances among institutions with differing specialties, and a rebirth of the college level of learning, among other things. Eric Gould, a professor at the University of Denver, suggests that every department, not just the humanities, should adopt a quality general education program rooted in the classics—with emphasis on our civic responsibilities.

Dinesh D'Souza writes that colleges have declined due to policies of affirmative action and programs of extreme political correctness and spends chapter after chapter arguing that getting rid of such policies and philosophies will fix American higher education. Frank H. Rhodes, former President of Cornell, says the university must change or become a dinosaur. It must change both by maintaining its good points: residence studies, strong faculties, quality research, etc. and by increasing its focus on these things instead of others. It must also deliver learning the way the market wants.

If we go back one generation, additional suggestions should cause us to consider and think. For example, Mortimer Adler, the editor of the Great Books, suggests that fixing modern American education is attained by *not* teaching anything of practical, applicational value. That is, education can be improved by ignoring job training and doing what schools were meant to do in the first place: educate through the classics. Ironically, the result of schools actually providing superb education is that graduates are more equipped to think, innovate and lead in the corporate and career world. By emphasizing job training in the schools, we have chosen to graduate non-educated workers who must be trained on the job anyway and only rise to leadership through personal gifts and "networking" with "influential superiors." The training of leaders, the fundamental role of college, is ignored.

Jacques Barzun, leader of the Great Books program at Columbia a generation ago, suggests 68 changes that are needed in the university system, including:

- "The faculty, which is the university, must convey at every turn what education is; therefore must reduce and disdain the opportunities for professional cant."
- Be "...choosy about new projects."
- Focus on teaching over research.
- The university must maintain its role as the "guardian of learning," not sell out to the highest bidder.
- Teach the 3Rs better and more often.
- Put learning ahead of credentials, or better still, end credentials.
- Get out of the housing business.
- Recover academic independence from the government, corporations, and other funders.
- Stop taking grant money for non-education purposes. "Education is a full-time task. University endowment or state subsidy is for education; it is a misuse of funds and talent to embark on other than educational efforts."
- Make it clear to society that education is public service.
- Create "cluster colleges": colleges which do their own thing, but work in proximity with others.
- Focus on the university's role as the keeper of learning, and drop everything else.

Allan Bloom, bestselling author of *The Closing of the American Mind,* suggested twenty years ago that we need to re-emphasize the classics in all parts of the undergraduate curriculum. He had little hope that this would occur, and his book has so far been prophetically accurate: this idea was widely discussed and narrowly implemented.

Robert Hutchins, former President of the University of Chicago, wrote in 1936 in *Higher Learning in America* that each university has four goals:

1. Liberal Education—to train citizens and leaders for the nation.
2. Academic Education—to train researchers and professors for the university.
3. Professional Training—to train students in specific work skills for the market.
4. Political Education—to train government and quasi-government workers for the state.

According to Hutchins, every college impacts all four, but every college also chooses one master—to the detriment or neglect of the other three. The history of America higher education, Hutchins said, could be summed up as focusing on Education for Liberty [from 1780-1860], then Education for Learning [1860-1932], Education for the Market [1932-?], and Education for Government Bureaucracy as the legacy of the future.

His solution to this trend was that in every generation, regardless of the outside trends, a few schools must choose to emphasize Education for Liberty. If this happens, he suggested, we will retain our freedoms. *If not, we will lose them.*

Josiah Bunting, former President of the Virginia Military Institute, wrote in *An Education for Our Time* that old schools will not make the necessary changes to train citizens and statesmen for liberty and so the founding of new colleges is necessary. This excellent book outlines how an ideal college, focused on the classics and training leaders, can significantly impact the future of a nation and the world. He wasn't calling for all schools to change, but simply for a few to adopt the Hutchin's emphasis on Liberal Education.

We are convinced that the university system must survive and thrive if America's future is to be bright, and that a number of things will be necessary to accomplish this new level of American higher education. It is our belief that one of the solutions will be the establishment of a new group of colleges and universities dedicated to what Hutchins called Education for Liberty, the training of leaders for all walks of life, community, business, government and society. For Depth Phase to flourish, there must be a number of "Ideal Colleges." Of course, this should come by the work of unaffiliated educational pioneers—so that true excellence and diversity abounds. Here we share several others views as well as our view of an ideal college model.

Recommendations for an Ideal College

If America is to create ideal colleges that emphasize Education for Liberty to a new generation of leaders, new reforms and foundings are needed. But what is the ideal, and how should it be implemented? Perhaps the three leading modern American educators of the twentieth century who spoke out concerning higher education were Mortimer Adler, Jacques Barzun, and Russell Kirk. Each had something to say about the ideal college.

Adler suggests that there are many ways to provide high quality education, but that there are five things that an ideal college should not do:

1. "First, a liberal arts college should not allow any form of special training for specific jobs, vocations, or even learned professions to intrude itself into the curriculum. This is not to say that liberal schooling has no relation to earning a living.... Liberal schooling will, in fact, prepare [students] to earn a living in the one way that it should. A person well trained in the liberal arts is able to learn anything more readily than a person not so trained. Hence he is better prepared for whatever specialized

learning may be a necessary condition of earning a living, whether that further learning takes place on the job or in the course of further schooling.

2. Second, a liberal arts college should not provide any elective courses in its curriculum, nor should it afford any opportunities for specialization in particular subject matters....

3. Third, the faculty of a liberal arts college should not be divided into departmental groups, each representing special competence in some particular subject matter, and narrow interest in some limited field of learning. This does not mean that the members of a college faculty must eschew all special scholarly interests, or that they should be chosen for their general competence and lack of all scholarly attainments. It means only that as college teachers, engaged in administering a program of liberal schooling, they should be willing to submit themselves to the whole course of study which the college is prescribing for its students....

4. Fourth, no textbooks should be used in a liberal arts college; there should be no lectures in courses; and formal lectures should be kept to the minimum and should, wherever possible, be of such generality that they can be given to the whole student body....

5. Fifth, written examinations, especially of the objective or true-false type, should be eliminated in favor of oral examinations....

These five negative recommendations, if adopted, would still allow for a variety of different positive programs, differently organized and differently administered. The negatives, if enforced, merely create the right sort of vacuum, so that whatever positive content then rushes in to fill the void has some chance of being right."

Jacques Barzun suggests numerous ideas for the ideal university, chief among them that we must as a nation take the emphasis off "educating," and focus on teaching and learning. The key to this, argues Barzun, is the faculty. Teachers *are* the university, not the buildings, library, endowment, administration or anything else. No ideal college can or will exist unless the trustees, administrators and faculty understand that the college is its teachers—and that superb education occurs by putting great teachers in a room with students and letting them alone to "do their thing."

Barzun insists that great teaching is "the transfer of personality," the core sharing of the deepest and best the teacher has to give with students who are closely associated over a period of time adequate to truly mentor them. This only happens when the administration administrates and leaves the classroom to the teacher. Indeed, when great teachers are allowed to practice their craft, students are inured with a deep and lasting passion for learning—and they study hard and learn. The ideal college puts great teachers in the classroom and allows miracles to occur day after day. The rest of the college is organized to facilitate and ensure the delivery of great teaching.

Russell Kirk rightly argues that an ideal college would have to start in the right place, by clarifying its purpose:

> "What then is the chief end of a college of arts and sciences? Why, to enable a body of senior scholars (the professors) and a body of junior scholars (the undergraduates) to seek after Wisdom—and through Wisdom, for Truth. The end is not success, pleasure, or sociability, but wisdom. Wisdom is not the same as facts, utility, training, or even knowledge....Success, increasingly, has been substituted for virtue in our curricula; facts, for wisdom; social adjustment, for strength of soul.... The aim of the old-fangled college education was ethical, the development of moral understanding and humane leadership; but the method was intellectual, the training of the mind and conscience through well-defined literary disciplines. A college was an establishment for the study of important literature. It was nearly that simple. Through the apprehension of great literature, young men were expected to fit themselves for

leadership in the churches, in the law, in politics, in principal positions of public responsibility."

The ideal college needs to emphasize liberal education and the training of leaders. This, above all, is the great need of society and the role of the college. To achieve these ends, Kirk argues, the school must do things in the right order as he describes in the following story:

> "Canon Bernard Iddings Bell once was showing an English visitor about the environs of Chicago. They drove past a handsome Gothic building of stone. 'Is that a school?' inquired the visitor.
>
> 'Yes—a new one, distressed to appear old,' Canon Bell replied.
>
> 'Indeed! Who is the headmaster?'
>
> 'There is no headmaster.'
>
> 'Curious! A kind of soviet of teachers, I suppose.'
>
> 'There are no masters at all.'
>
> 'Really? Then where are the boys?'
>
> 'As yet, there are no students. Here in the United States, we proceed educationally in a way to which you are unaccustomed,' Canon Bell told his friend. 'First we erect a building; then we obtain students; next we recruit teachers; then we find a headmaster; and at last we determine what is to be taught.'"

After telling this story, Kirk recommends: "Let it be otherwise with our model college. The first matter is to determine the program of study.... After that, let us turn to the staff, then to the students, and finally to the 'plant.'"

Our Ideal

Building on the shoulders of past greats and focused on the needs of our twenty-first and twenty-second centuries, here is our proposal for ideal colleges:

1. The mission and purpose of the college will be to prepare leaders to influence for good the families, communities, businesses, governments, media, society and nations of the world.
2. It will be a college first, then several self-contained colleges, and finally a university. There are two types of universities: those which start as a centralized unit that divides itself up into colleges and departments to allow specialization, and those where a cluster of separate, focused colleges share administration and community. Our ideal university will be the latter.
3. The most important people in our employ will be teachers. We will recruit, train and hire truly great teachers and empower them to inspire their students. The whole university will exist to support and help teachers in this endeavor. When great teachers inspire, students are filled with the lasting desire to work very hard, to study long and often painful hours, and to earn their own superb education. This is our educational model.
4. Teachers will serve as mentors rather than just expert lecturers and graders. Mentors will sometimes coach, sometimes lecture, but predominantly lead discussions. For most discussions, students will come prepared having read or written something important. The old saying that "a great education is a student on one end of a log and John Hopkins on the other" will not be the guide, but rather C.S. Lewis' sentiment that great education is a mentor and a dozen or fewer students arguing about a very important idea around a table late into the night.
5. The study of religion and God will not be focused on any one denomination or creed, but as Jefferson suggested for the University of Virginia, all religions will be welcome on campus and the sharing of personal conviction from people of all faiths will be encouraged.

6. The role of the board, president and other administrators will always be to support mentors in delivering superb education through these ideals. Adequate funds must be raised for this purpose.

7. The leader in the school must always be a superb teacher who is daily involved in teaching and mentoring. Organizations take on the personality of their chief. To the extent that a school is insulated from the vision of its chief, it is a behemoth without a cohesive vision. Schools that are run by businessmen soon become businesses—the school dies. Likewise, schools that are run by fundraisers soon turn into projects for hire, spelling the end of schooling. The chief must of course appoint and empower the highest quality of business leaders to run the administration and raise the needed funds. As former University of Michigan thinker Stephen J. Tonsor put it: "If the university is to retain its lost authority in American society, it must find university administrators who see their mission in providing something more than… 'football for the alumni, parking for the faculty, and sex for the students.' The university and college president must once more play the role of educational statesman."

8. A large number of the faculty will always consist of graduates of the school, or of schools with a similar mentoring methodology. This point, like the others, is very important, but it will be tempting to ignore it at times. As Dr. Tonsor said: "Any college or university president who at the present moment determines to make his institution unique in mission, curriculum, instructional method, student body, or educational philosophy will discover very quickly that his great enemy is not the alumni or the board of trustees or even the student body, but his own faculty." This lesson was learned by the greatest educational leaders, including Robert Hutchins at the University of Chicago, Grayson Kirk at Columbia University, Chester Finn, Jr. and William Bennett in the U.S. Department of Education,

and John Witherspoon at Princeton over two centuries ago. The way to achieve faculty unity in accomplishing the school's ultimate mission is to simultaneously train our own mentors and supplement them with great teachers from other schools who are expected to learn of and become passionate about the existing culture and mission of the college. This does not preclude diversity. Quite the contrary—where the vision and methodology are to personalize the approach for each individual student, and where students and faculty alike are encouraged to think independently rather than regurgitate approved answers for a recyclable final exam, creativity and innovation abound. Intellectual and ultimately societal freedom germinate in such an environment and the embracing of foundational principles that apply differently for each person ensures the ultimate relevance and utility of the education. What better preparation could there be for career, family, community service and statesmanship?

There are so many details that would also go into the establishment of an ideal college, yet we hesitate to go much further than outlining the basic philosophy. Different schools will ideally take different paths, all built on the core principles of great education. With these eight general guidelines, and with others that educational entrepreneurs will add, many people could help build a network of new colleges and universities, or reform existing schools, that would significantly improve the higher education of America without hurting all that is so good in the current university system. In the decades ahead there is a need for many such institutions. Students desiring Leadership Education should consider seeking a superb Depth Phase college environment in such schools.

Wherever a student goes to pursue Depth Phase, she needs to seek out great mentors, study great classics, learn the basics of a great liberal arts education, and master the ten Depth Phase lessons listed above, and others like them; this is training for life, career, and preparation to raise a family and lead in the community. One way to make this less daunting is to find and work closely with great college mentors.

Mentors in Depth Phase

The central figure in Leadership Education is the mentor. There are many kinds of mentors, some formal and others informal. For example, a friend is a mentor; indeed peer groups are some of the most influential mentors, and they most often interact informally. There are many other types of informal mentors, and there are several types of formal mentors that each person should know about. Parent Mentors, as taught by Aneladee Milne, raise us, teach us and ideally provide guidance and support through life. Liberal Arts Mentors, Tiffany Earl's phrase, help us get a superb education and prepare for leadership in life, and Mission Mentors, also Tiffany Earl's phrase, guide us as we actually achieve our missions in life.

During college studies, there are at least four types of Liberal Arts Mentors, and knowing how to work with each significantly increases the quality of your learning experience. The first rule of working with a mentor of any kind is to change *yourself* to work with the mentor's style. You have chosen her as a mentor, and trying to get her to meet your style will downgrade the quality of what she can give you. It is important to find out your mentor's style and stretch yourself to benefit from it.

One mentor style could be called the *Scholar.* This mentor focuses mostly on depth and accuracy, values consistency and thrives in the world of the expert. He spends a majority of his time on personal research, and writes and publishes to scholarly and other audiences.

Another mentoring style is the *Professor.* This mentor is interested in breadth and accuracy, values authority and rules, and focuses on teaching more than personal scholarship. She wants her students to excel, and puts most of her time into improving classroom quality, outside study, and the overall student experience.

Coaches have yet another style of mentoring. Coaches are the most purely individual mentors of the four types. They usually emphasize breadth and creativity, prefer to mentor during long talks or long walks, and love to bond and build relationships. They measure themselves according to the quality of their relationships and love to discuss deep, and often abstract, concepts and ideals.

TABLE I: FOUR TYPES OF MENTORS

MENTOR STYLE	CHARACTERISTICS
The Scholar	Depth and Accuracy Expertise Consistency Personal research, writing, publishing
The Professor	Breadth and Accuracy Authority and Rules Teaching Students Improving the Classroom
The Coach	Breadth and Creativity Long Walks, Long Talks, Bonding Building Relationships Discussion and Talking
The Philosopher	Depth and Creativity Ideas, Concepts, Models New Twists on Old Ideas Motivational Communication

Another major style of mentor is the *Philosopher,* who above all loves ideas, concepts, models and new perspectives. This mentor seeks depth and creativity, values new views of things and a diversity of presentations that add nuance to old models. He often speaks or writes like a motivational speaker because of his passion and excitement for learning.

Of course, every mentor is her own mix of styles, views, strengths, weaknesses, interests, passions, areas of expertise, etc. There are truly as many types of mentoring as there are mentors, and the key is to find out how your mentor works best and change to meet her style. Still, knowing which of the four major types of mentors you are working with is very helpful.

Unfortunately, in modern academia the scholar is sometimes considered the only credible type of mentor, with the professor as a tolerated but lesser type. This is both false and damaging. As a result of this myth, sometimes mentors argue about which type is best. For example, Woodrow Wilson (probably a Philosopher) was responding to this when he wrote his famous article on "Why I am not a Scholar." He wanted the academic community to know that there was a place for his type of teaching. In fact, learning increases when all four types flourish. Each student will obtain a better education if he is mentored by all four types—hopefully with more than one teacher from each type. Students should resist the temptation to limit themselves and their learning by keying in on one type of mentor and only taking classes from that type.

As you work with various mentors, from all four types and even other types that you run into, how do you best interact with each mentor? There is a key action to look for, but this key action differs with different mentors. Table II outlines the key action for working with each major style of mentor.

TABLE II: KEY ACTIONS	
MENTOR STYLE	KEY ACTION
The Scholar	learn facts, details, precision, consistency and accuracy, along with the tools and techniques of the profession
The Professor	learn discipline, quality, and the love of learning a field in depth
The Coach	learn submission and trust (because he understands you better than *you* do), along with personalized studies for your life mission
The Philosopher	learn how to think, how to see nuance, a passion for ideas, and the interconnection of all knowledge

All of these lessons are vital to a great education, so students should seek several mentors over time and learn these lessons and others from each. As you work with various mentors, don't waste time trying to make your current mentor be like your last one, or wishing that all mentors were the same. A key part of leadership education is learning to work with other people of diverse and even opposing views, and this is true as you work with your mentors.

There are other mentors for you during your Depth studies: the authors, artists, mathematicians, composers, entrepreneurs, statesmen and others whose work we study are mentors—some of the most important ones. Be sure to really take the time to be mentored by Tocqueville, Newton, Austen, Hugo, Euclid, Picasso, Toynbee, Cervantes and all the other great mentors you spend time with in your studies.

Your classmates are also mentors—teaching and instructing, challenging and listening, sometimes passionately debating and other times showing little interest. As you learn their views on a variety of topics and studies, you will gain much new information and ideas that you didn't already know. You should learn to learn from others, especially those who aren't your allies and confidantes. Having the ability to truly resonate with their point of view and to inspire trust and cooperation when your interests coincide is an invaluable skill and will benefit you in all of your relationships.

Finally, another great lesson of the Depth Phases is that everyone you meet is a mentor, from the soccer coach to the midweek devotional instructor, from your boss to the officer who pulls you over for speeding. Leadership Education is above all a great study of human nature, and everyone you interact with can teach you this core subject. The seasons, turns of the sun and moon, the cycles of history—for those with a classical eye there is much to be learned from everything. The Depth Phases teach that the true test is not so much who your mentors are but what kind of a mentee you are, in all your walks and experiences of life. If the student refuses to settle for anything less than a great Depth Phase, he can find mentors to help.

Leadership Education is all about owning the responsibility to find the opportunities, mentors and resources for your own education—whether formally in college or outside of it. Not every Depth Phase is the same, and no doubt different people should pursue a different course of study than others. Whatever your best Depth Phase, it will likely include many of the greatest classics of our world.

Part IV

....

A Mandate For Service: The Applicational Phases

CHAPTER NINE

Mission Phase

A Leadership Education will naturally be followed by a life of service and leadership. Some of the most transformational events in a person's life will occur during the Applicational Phases of Mission and Impact. During these phases, an individual moves forth from the Educational Phases of Scholar and Depth to adulthood. True, they are "fully grown" by the time they engage the Educational Phases, but after the transition that follows the early phases, the quality of life and the quality of the individual have changed.

There is a metamorphosis of *becoming* that marks a new level of commitment to the primary allegiance, a new clarity and consecration to mission, a more refined ability to affect change in the world and a greater ability to impact the people within the sphere of influence. The catharsis of this adult transition transports the individual to a time when his purpose is to achieve the personal mission and impact for which his Educational Phases have prepared him. The drive to "prepare for greatness" shifts to a drive to *deliver*. In short, the foundational and educational phases brought to fruition demand that an individual inspire greatness in others and move the cause of liberty.

In addition to life experiences, a powerful force constructing the Applicational Phases is the exponential returns of wisdom and understanding yielded from the living of principles derived from hours of study and diligent daily immersion in the individual's central classic. The greatest component of the Applicational Phases is not education *per se*; it is application of one's education and whole soul to improving the world.

Individuals in the Applicational Phases are not finished with the previous phases. Indeed, the important habits of Core, Love of Learning, Scholar and Depth all continue to form the foundation and education upon which they build two towers—a family and an organization. Those in the Applicational Phases continue to live the lessons of good and bad, love learning and develop new skills, engage in passionate study of classics from all genres and invest their time and resources in opportunities that benefit others as well as themselves, their families, their organizations and their communities.

Many books have been written that will be helpful for those in the Applicational Phases. The person with a Leadership Education will know how to find, learn from, and effectively apply needed knowledge and wisdom from such books and other quality materials. Truly, for most who are transitioning into the Applicational Phases, no primer is needed here. Those in Applicational Phases can write the book themselves, so to speak. In addition, they will have the necessary people skills to network and work with individuals in a manner that refines them and allows them to further the causes that matter in society. So, this information is not specifically intended as a guide to those in Mission or Impact; it is a vision of the future for those not yet there, so that as the reader progresses from phase to phase in anticipation of the Applicational Phases they have a vision of the end in mind.

As a people we are too detached in this generation from those who are successfully in Applicational Phases. Either their experience seems too personally specific to apply to us, or they seem to be men and women of another breed, whom we could never hope to emulate. During the last two generations there has been a stong societal reprimand in store for those who sought to rise above the norm. It's not *democratic*; it's not *polite*. Those who did rise above were largely harnessed by political correctness. In order to maintain credibility and effectiveness to accomplish their mission they learned how not to shine in the wrong places, at the wrong times. They learned how not to speak in an authoritative voice; they learned how not to set themselves up as a light. As a result, the benefit of their experience is largely inaccessible to those of us who would follow in their footsteps.

We include this section because it is important for students at all levels of Leadership Education to understand what is ahead in order to give their education today the focus, vision and energy it deserves. Specifically, there are three main parts of the Applicational Phases: Transition to Mission, Mission Phase, and Impact Phase.

Transition to Mission

The shift from the Educational to the Applicational Phases can be painful. Up to this point, the young person has had one major focus in life: preparation for his or her life mission. By the time a student has earned a quality Scholar and Depth Phase education, he has become adept at studying, learning, and applying what is learned. Then, suddenly, he is asked to apply everything he knows in a totally different way.

He is required to actually *be* something very different—not a student, but an adult. But adjusting to adulthood is only half of the challenge. In truth, Leadership Education demands of the adult *two* new things, not just one. He is required to build two towers. This will take everything he has to give, and will push him to his limits. The two towers that he is to build are a family and an organization (as entrepreneur or intrapreneur). Ideally, he will have the help of a true help-meet, a leadership spouse, in building both towers. If not, he is asked to build them anyway.

The brutal reality of how difficult building one of these towers will be, much less two, is frankly shocking to virtually everyone who experiences it. The husband is overwhelmed with the challenges of his career. The wife finds herself fighting depression as she feels so inadequate to the demands of starting a business. The mother gets little sleep and struggles to just meet the basic daily needs of the family. The single individual struggles with where they fit on the continuum and how to commit to a life course without excluding opportunities for finding a mate. There are many examples. At this time in life, everything changes.

The first experience the Leadership Educated person often has at this point is to question everything in her life so far, raising frustrated queries such as: "If this is so incredibly hard, then obviously my education didn't prepare me for it. My parents didn't do it right; my teachers didn't understand. Why didn't my mentors teach me better?" An honest appraisal will demonstrate that the truth is actually the opposite. In reality, everyone is facing this same incredibly difficult challenge—adulthood. Those with a Leadership Education are much better prepared to face life's challenges than those educated in conveyor belt fashion. They have been educated to view their life as a creation of Providence in response to their efforts, rather than looking to others to provide what is needed. They are accustomed to working hard rather than "goofing off" and know that the sweetest fruits are borne of the greatest sacrifices. Those who experienced Leadership Education amidst the perpetual strivings of home and family maintenance and personal improvement will be even better prepared for the struggles of adult life.

Most people without the benefit of Leadership Education have very little chance of building an organization tower and instead just struggle to make ends meet each month. For the conveyor-belt educated, negotiating life as an adult is a process of entrusting their lives to experts and fitting themselves into the conveyor belts of career ladders. This may appear, at the outset, easier than the forgings and strivings of those on the leadership path.

Those educated on a conveyor belt who discover at this point that they wish to live a life of leadership are literally called upon to simultaneously build three towers: a family, an organization, *and their own personal Scholar and Depth Phases.* In other words, it is even harder for them. And they need the help, encouragement and support of those who have been educated according to the Leadership Model.

When these realizations come, when you come face-to-face with just how challenging building towers will be, it is time to launch yourself fully into Mission Phase. The transition between each phase is marked with disorientation, confusion, discontent, yearning for change, and feelings of disconnection from past phases and frustration with life. The transition from the Depth to Mission is the hardest yet, and the transition from Mission to Impact will likely be even harder. Remember what you learned in past transitions: having a vision of the your long-term life mission and a clear plan for what to do *right now* will help you get on the right track right away. You learned how to transition before; apply these lessons again. Get clear on what needs to be done, and get started. As with the transition to Scholar and the transition to Depth, it will get harder before it gets easier—so you might as well begin the forward march.

Mission Phase

Here are a few guidelines that will help you succeed in Mission Phase. We do not know all the answers—not even close!—and we will not list everything you will need; but pretty much everything we list here will be helpful. Together, the following ten items will give you high direction and a number of projects to set you on course. Obviously, you will learn many additional things as you progress, overcome roadblocks, and listen to mentors. As you succeed, a few people will rain on your parade or try to knock down your towers. The following suggestions will help you overcome current challenges and prepare for those that come later:

1. Use the Family Executive Council (FEC) well. If you are single, arrange an FEC with God, yourself and perhaps others (e.g. a parent or parents). If you are married, use the FEC to really

progress. Hold your FEC faithfully. Brainstorm, visualize, discuss, analyze, consider, creatively propose solutions, make decisions and be accountable for carrying them out. Get God's input, follow the Spirit, trust your intuition and the inspiration you feel, and work things out as an FEC team. This is primary, and it is essential.

2. Get to work. As you consider the starting and later steps, go to work. Make good plans, closely consider what needs to be done, but do not get caught in analysis-paralysis. Get started. Work, work, work. You will learn as you go, and some answers (and many more questions) do not become clear until you know the lay of the land a little better.

3. Get Mission Mentors for your organization tower. Seek out, listen to and apply the counsel of mentors who have long and effective experience in your area of mission. You know how to work with mentors, but the Mission Mentor is different in some ways than the Liberal Arts Mentor. A great liberal arts mentor sought to see *your* genius and help you with it, but a mission mentor is looking for protégés—people who share the same or similar genius that *he* has made into a life mission. He wants to know that you are a team player, but with enough independence to be a true leader. He does not want to waste time on people without initiative, ingenuity, integrity, allegiance and the other lessons of Depth Phase. Mostly, he does not want to waste time telling you the same thing over and over. Listen and apply the first time. Again, you already know how to do this; it was central to your Leadership Education. Just because you have come this far does not mean you don't need to submit yourself to a mentor. He has valuable counsel for you. Apply it.

4. Get mentors for your family tower. First of all, identify the very best lessons (both constructive and cautionary) you learned from your parents, grandparents, aunts and uncles, and other informal mentors on family life. Do the same with community and church

leaders that you look up to. Then go deeper. Do a study of great marriage and parenting relationships and teachings in history, literature, modern times and other cultures. You will be amazed at the answers that are there for you! Really learn the best principles, and go to work applying them. Above all, learn from your own experiences—both the successes and the mistakes. Your Leadership Education taught you the value of learning from mistakes. Mentor yourself, and include God as a mentor in this most important tower you will ever build. Remember to put your marriage first, above other family concerns. A great marriage makes up for a lot of other failures.

Too many families make the mistake of neglecting or even giving up on an ailing marriage to try to salvage the kids—and end up losing both. They reason that the current situation is destroying the kids' hope for happiness and their assumptions of how to build a relationship. The reality is that most of the circumstances that made the relationship ill and "beyond saving" (he cannot reach constructive compromise, she always involves others in our problems, he uses the kids against me, she has a personality disorder, he show more allegiance to his parents than to me, etc.) *don't go away* once the divorce is final. It just introduces one more strident voice into the melee. Now the courts determine when and how you may speak to each other, how the kids will be educated, where you may live/travel/vacation, with whom you may socialize, and so forth. Several couples of our acquaintance lament that the divorce didn't remove the issues that most troubled them. It simply made dealing with kids and finances astronomically more difficult. There are circumstances of abuse and extreme neglect that warrant subjecting the family to such intrusion and isolation. They are tragic, and society is right to provide the means for the dissolution of such families. But let us be wise and listen to the urging of those who regret seeking such a solution when it was not their only choice.

5. Keep learning. This is a natural for those who earned a Leadership Education, but you will still need to structure time and do the study.

6. Get passionate about health. Learn about it, live it. Good health is so helpful to building your two towers. It will take an incredible amount of energy to accomplish your mission, and energy flows from health.

7. Be a wise financial steward. Learn and follow true principles of financial management. Like health, this will open doors, increase confidence, and add to your effectiveness. With sound physical and financial health, you will be prepared to take advantage of opportunities that come your way and sustained in times of sacrifice and hardship.

8. Be a generational catalyst. You inherited some bad things from past generations (ideas, health challenges, traditions, etc.) along with the good. These things often seem to be part of you, but they do not have to remain so. What you consider your weaknesses may well be temptations. Identify them and fix them. By so doing, you can heal these challenges for the generations ahead—maybe even for generations past. This is very, very hard work. But it will bless the lives of countless others and help you fully achieve your mission of building your towers. Indeed, it is part of the role of your generation. You have the disposition and the opportunity for self-improvement and introspection that are a costly luxury. This luxury was afforded you by the ones whose sacrifices gave you peace and security in addition to the challenges that you want to purge from your character, from your worldview, and from the legacy you pass on. Neither the generations that directly preceded you nor those that directly follow could or will be able to afford that luxury, due to the generational role that was or shall be theirs of responding in a crisis or rebuilding in the

aftermath. Let go of pride, bitterness and self-pity and seize the opportunity to make a difference in your generational line.

9. Faciliate those in earlier phases. They really need your help, and you really need the energy, peace and additional learning that come from serving them. It may at times seem that you should ignore them and just focus on your towers—but doing so actually slows you down. Buckminster Fuller called this "precession." As you serve others who need you, you will increase your understanding, wisdom and ability to deal with your own challenges.

   Additionally, many people who are starting Mission Phase may unintentionally derail those who are still on the earlier path, especially those in the educational phases. Mission Phase is so demanding, and so different, that a beginning Mission Phaser often thinks everybody should be going through what *she* is experiencing. It is important to know that this is normal, and to help others be effective at the stage they are at. Recognize that the answers you get for your personal progression apply to you personally, not universally. And as a mentor or a friend, do not disrespect the inspiration that impels someone in Scholar or Depth phase to make the necessary sacrifices to carry off that critically important season of *their* progression.

10. Individualize and personalize. Clearly identify your vision, the next few steps to accomplish your mission, and the details of accomplishing them. Go to work, and keep working, reviewing and improving, and working some more. Never give up! But do take time to review and improve, correct mistakes, and change course as needed. Keep building the two towers until it is right to move on.

As you apply these ten guidelines, more lessons and ideas will naturally arise. As you continue to plan, work and serve, you will eventually build your two towers and significantly give to and improve the world. You will also come to realize that the

Foundational and Educational Phases were actually a part of your mission all along. You will see the unity and meaning and integral relationship of all the phases more clearly than ever before. With this new perspective, it seems that all you have ever been doing is building your two towers and fulfilling your mission.

Because of this fundamental shift in your paradigm, you may feel the tendency to downplay the process that brought you to this place. And because of your personal power as a leader in Mission Phase, others may feel confused when you try to communicate your vision to them. Remember that although each of us is genetically programmed to be an adult, infancy is still a time of nurture and milk, and the preceding phases of others must be allowed to run their course. True, we may no longer identify personally with being an infant, but as we quickly learn in dealing with infants, vision does not change fundamental needs or requisite growing experiences.

Likewise, in just this way, you will need to be respectful and patient with the process that others must go through to progress to their own Mission Phase. Mentor them with wisdom and restraint, and help them maximize their experience in the phase they are in. You may feel that you have reached the promised land, but to tell others who are still out in the wilderness to stop and plant their crops is out of touch and does not serve them well.

As a Statesman in Mission Phase there is never really a time when we should not be doing a little from all of the Phases. Still, it is in building our two towers that we expend most of our work in life. As we lose our lives in service to others, we will find that we have become more than we ever imagined possible.

Three Challenges

Nearly every person of this generation who is in Mission Phase faces at least three predictable challenges—we call them 1) seeking for the quick fix, 2) struggling over roles, and 3) setting up a leadership conveyor belt. Let's discuss each of these in order.

The Quick Fix

In the Transition to Mission and all through Mission Phase, we face the temptation to waste a lot of time looking for the "easy" answer, the "quick fix," the pill that solves our concerns. In reality, Mission Phase means you are the expert on your life. There are no quick fixes that will make everything better without hard work.

Women, in particular, tend to think that if we just talk to the right person or meet with the right circle of friends, somebody will give us that secret knowledge that makes everything ideal. This can lead to additional challenges if it displaces other more sound methods of arriving at policy decisions for life, family and relationships. It is imperative to rise to the level of adult and be the expert on your own life and two towers. We each have to face struggles, figure out the answers, apply them and learn from mistakes and successes. It slows us down to spend energy looking for experts or paths or easy solutions—instead, we must face the reality that it is supposed to be hard, and go to work doing what needs to be done.

Everything you learn can help you in this process, but there is no elixir of perfection that will solve everything. In many schools, "good" students learn to play the teacher's game, get the grade and master the secret of the class. Unfortunately, this lesson is a roadblock to success in Mission Phase, because the game is over. In real life, there is no shortcut to success. You have to pay the price to accomplish your mission and build your two towers. Leaders need to help others build their towers, and since adulthood is about leadership, we all have to face the real world and get to work. Once we approach it with the right attitude, accept the new direction of our lives and settle down to the tasks at hand, it is possible to move forward with increased vigor and excitement. As we overcome challenges, creatively solve problems and experience success, we gain confidence and inspire others. Our love of learning and passion are rekindled and we find the onward and upward progression engaging and compelling—and much more rewarding and fulfilling than any other course or life path.

The Family Way

Another challenge in Mission Phase is the struggle to reconcile our roles in life, especially in marriage and career. It seems many people today are trying to understand and improve upon society's expectations of gender. Many are seeking to consciously change their definitions of ideal fathering, mothering, manliness and femininity or how they mentor boys versus girls. The conveyor belt has stripped our society of clear understandings of our basic roles as men and women. It is exciting to see this rapidly growing interest among those striving to revive a deliberate and carefully considered family culture in their homes.

As students of society, history and family culture, one thing we would like to see as part of this trend is for the various groups, writers and promoters of true manhood and womanhood to keep the family central. Those with a Leadership Education should be leaders in this endeavor. This may seem obvious to many, but perhaps it is not as obvious as it should be.

Here is the question we would pose: shouldn't major decisions about such core issues as childbearing, childrearing, nutrition, education, and whether a woman works outside the home be made by wife and husband sitting down together and prayerfully deciding what is right for their family?

The Feminist and Anti-Feminist viewpoints both seem to have a problem with this. For example, if a couple decides that the woman stays home, the Feminists label the man chauvinistic and the woman a victim or a "doormat." If the couple carefully decides for the woman to be in the workforce, the Anti-Feminists call her a Feminist, or at least misguided. They shake their heads, wag their tongues and fear for the children and the marriage.

It is true many Feminists argue that women should *never* be homemakers. According to them, it is degrading to the woman and she is a drain on society. They say she should be a producer, or in some way add value to the economy outside of the home. With the same dogmatic zeal, the Anti-Feminist declares that a godly woman will never work outside of the home. You could substitute a host of other issues that would engender similar results—conflicting points of view, both dictating to the family a strict behavior with a normative value.

Granted that it is good and right to promote motherhood, femininity and homemaking, does it necessarily follow that there is a checklist that such families will adhere to inflexibly? Will such an inspired couple never decide that mother accept employment outside of the home? Or will such a couple always homeschool every child? Will their children necessarily be delivered by a lay midwife at home, and never immunized? Will antibiotics never be administered? Shall such parents never take steps to limit the size of their families? Must they always grind their own wheat? Will every aluminum can be recycled? Will they never eat packaged macaroni and cheese?

We have purposely carried these examples to the extreme (and we dearly hope that these examples seem absurd to the thoughtful reader), to demonstrate that many well-intentioned women, and men, are recommending a standard to families over whom they have no stewardship when they could be recommending a process, or a form, which answers any and all questions of family government.

Many families we respect and admire have not followed checklists such as these. We have no reason to doubt that their choices are right for them. We even like them and their children! We certainly don't follow such a list. We hope that the Feminist "thesis" and Anti-Feminist "anti-thesis" will give rise to the dialectical "synthesis": The Family Way. It is our belief that the basis of our society is the marriage relationship—specifically the sovereignty we give to married couples to wisely determine what is best for their family.

Knee-jerk, one-size-fits-all advice endangers noble parenthood as surely as do those who would confuse the roles of men and women beyond recognition. Danger lurks not because the recommendations are necessarily ill-considered or patently wrong, but because they threaten to unseat the Family Executive Council and thus imperil *all* decisions and roles. In our opinion, this is among the greatest threats facing families today. It is more subtle and insidious than some of the great evils we vigorously guard against: addiction, infidelity, debt, etc. A family where the core unit—the married couple—is not regarded as sovereign has little defense against the things that threaten it, no matter what their source.

Women in particular benefit greatly from supportive friendships wherein they can help and lift each other. But when the confidence and intimacy of these friendships supplant or threaten the communication between spouses, these friendships can be a poor substitute at best—and potentially much worse. Wise women can enjoy healthy friendships that actually strengthen them in the roles as spouse and mother. They can encourage youth in honoring their roles as men and women.

Along with teaching our young men and women the arts of manhood and femininity, shouldn't we teach them The Family Way? The Family Way is: Married couples carefully and prayerfully finding out and implementing what is best for their family, trusting their joint decisions instead of worrying what society thinks, and not second-guessing the sovereignty of someone else's Family Executive Council. We can all do a little better to continually promote The Family Way whenever family topics come up.

The Leadership Conveyor Belt

A third challenge that many people face is to turn Leadership Education into its own type of conveyor belt. It seems that a few people who read the Leadership Education books and articles or attend the seminars resonate with the idea of getting off the conveyor belt, but unwittingly find themselves drawn to a new "Leadership Education Conveyor Belt." This can be a difficult transition, and staying off any conveyor belt is very important.

It is important to understand the general guidelines in this book, and it is vital to follow them or break them when it is best for each individual child. The key is having our own expertise, so that we can with confidence adhere to or ignore the guidelines, and know when to do which.

There is a difference between engaging a mentor for our personal development and seeking an expert to tell us how to run our family or home. Making and keeping commitments even when it is demanding or when we do not understand or value what the mentor is asking of us is critical in late Scholar and into Depth Phase and even beyond. It is another thing entirely to abdicate our role as decision maker for our family. No mentor worth your time would allow himself to be put in that role.

A young mother told Rachel, "I keep feeling like I should sit down on the floor with my five-year-old and read him books a lot more, but that would ruin my scholar phase." By all means, "ruin" your scholar phase—if that is the right thing to do. If not, then do not. Or maybe you read to your five-year-old a lot more and just slow down your Scholar Phase studies. This is one reason why Mission Phase is so challenging: YOU have to decide what to do. One of the hardest things about getting off the conveyor belt is becoming your own expert on matters of family concern. One of the basic assumptions of Leadership Education is that you are the expert on your own home and the education of your children. If the right thing is to sit down and read with the toddler, do it. If you should slow down your Scholar Phase, do it. If you should speed up your Scholar Phase and watch with amazement as other factors enrich your toddler's life in miraculous ways, by all means—do it! Being a leader means being able to ignore all the concerned voices and "good" choices, and to commit to and follow through on the *right* one. Getting off the conveyor belt means that you study the guidelines of Leadership Education and then personalize them to you and your children.

One day a professional teacher called and asked, "How can I apply the 7 Keys when my district won't let me use classics in class?" Oliver responded, "Can you copy a page from Plato or Euclid and hand it out to the class and discuss it?"

"Well, yes, I can do that," he said, "but they won't let me get rid of the textbooks."

"Great, then supplement the textbooks with classics," Oliver suggested. This teacher later told us that it works wonderfully. He includes something from a classic in every class, and the students have started reading even the textbooks differently—with more interest and much more closely.

A mother met with Rachel after a convention and asked if it was possible for her to do her own brand of Leadership Education, or if she had to use the method and books taught by the Commonwealth School in her area. When we told Tiffany Earl and Aneladee Milne, the founders of the Commonwealth School approach, they laughed. "Of course she can," they quickly replied. Tiffany added, "She needs to do what is best for *her* children." That's Leadership Education!

Another group announced that they were not using Leadership Education any more because they disagreed with our religious views. We asked if they were abandoning classics. Their answer was "no." Mentors? "No." In answering our queries, we discovered they were using all the 7 Keys. Whatever name they decide to call it, that's Leadership Education!

Another woman told Oliver she loved the book *A Thomas Jefferson Education* but could not keep coming to seminars because she just did not believe in "Inspire, not Require." Further dialogue revealed that she had two autistic sons and without requirements they did not function well. Oliver recommended that she require, structure content as well as time, and also that she emphasize quantity along with quality. General guidelines combined with specific personalization. That's Leadership Education!

A charter school administrator came to Oliver concerned that the parents really hated the idea of classics and that she was losing valuable recruits. "Can you just train your teachers deeply in the classics and apply the other Keys?" Oliver asked. She implemented it, and it worked! The parents were sold on the other six keys and over time even got excited about the classics.

One parent could not believe we would recommend Saxon math, another questioned why we would suggest the E.D. Hirsch series, and another wondered why we liked Montessori. We recommend that parents and teachers consider any book, program, seminar or curriculum that interests them, learn from it, and then apply what will work with their students or in their home. We do not place any priority on staying abreast of all the new offerings in educational resources that become available every year—you probably know of some wonderful things that we have never heard of. Too many who subscribe to the philosophy of leadership education are shy about embracing something that they feel might benefit their family because it has not been endorsed by some expert somewhere. They need not be! That is what it means to really get off the conveyor belt: to become the expert on your home or classroom. That's Leadership Education!

Leadership Education means general guidelines and principles combined with specific personalization for each student. If it becomes just another conveyor belt, the key element in the whole process is lost. That element, put simply, is this: Leadership Education must have a leader at the helm. There is a *double entendre* here—the facilitator (be that parent or teacher) must be a leader pursuing self-education so that the student or child will be a leader pursuing self-education.

Leadership Education means personalizing for yourself and your student so that everyone will get the best education possible. Since most of us are used to conveyor-belt thinking, this shift in mindset can be challenging to embrace, even when we accept it on an intellectual level. But it is essential to getting off the conveyor belt. The general guidelines are incredibly important and one strays far from them with some risk involved; but they are still just *guidelines*. Leadership Education requires us to pay the price in order to personalize whatever is needed to help each student get the ideal education for them. That's Leadership Education!

The Price of Leadership

Every person with a Leadership Education will face challenges in the transition to Mission Phase and in building his or her towers. In addition to the struggles mentioned here, each person will face individual trials. Success will come as you clearly identify that you are now in Mission Phase, understand that you are the expert on your towers, and go to work until the towers are built. This is incredibly hard work, but it is the purpose of a leadership life.

Leaders will remember lessons of Core and "trust the process," knowing that its fruits are worth its labors. And in the process, they will enjoy life, have a lot of fun, and learn to bring the best feelings and experiences into their lives. Leadership can be challenging, but it should also be joyful.

CHAPTER TEN

Impact Phase

There will come a time when your two towers are mostly completed. They will never be fully completed, but you will arrive at a place where most of your tower work is done and you have time for other endeavors. In the career world this is called retirement, but on the leadership path there is no such thing as retirement. Instead, you have entered a new era of your life in which the valuable wisdom and experience you have gained must be shared and communicated to those who will follow. You are now in Impact Phase.

Impact Phase

There are at least thirteen roles that leaders take on later in life. As they do, they naturally experience the transition to Impact Phase. Much of Impact Phase overlaps with Mission Phase and building your two towers, but it also includes spending significant time fulfilling these thirteen roles. Note that some people emphasize a certain few of these roles, while others put a little time into each. Also note that we are not listing these in any order of priority or chronology. They are all important roles of impact, and each person must personally choose which to emphasize at certain times, with certain people, in certain situations. But ideally, leaders will spend some time in each of these Impact Phase roles.

As you read the list, please take a moment to write down your vision of how you would like to fulfill each of the roles at some point in your life. Only you can write what your true impact in life will be.

Whatever phase you are currently in, taking the time to do this well will significantly benefit your life. If you are in Scholar or Depth Phase, it will increase your passion and excitement for learning and help you put in the hard work. If you are in Mission Phase or one of the adult transitions, it will ease the challenge of new adulthood, mid-life crisis, or the prospects of aging. It will increase your understanding of your mission and vision and help you get a better education. Please do not skip this section. It will provide purpose, direction and impetus for you to persist in your growth and strivings. If you are not exactly sure what one of the following roles entails, spend some time researching the words and brainstorming how you might fulfill each role according to your understanding. We have purposely given no commentary, so that you can creatively envision in your own mind how you could best carry them out personally.

We recommend that you spend at least one hour on each role—preferably on separate days. Go to a place where you can quietly visualize and think, and where you will not be interrupted. Look at the role you are brainstorming about and spend some quality time thinking about how you can fully fulfill this role in your life. Fill at least a page per role with your thoughts, impressions, ideas and musings.

You may want to record the whole process in your journal. In seminars when we do this exercise, we request that participants not take their cell phones or anything that might interrupt their focus as they visualize how they can fully accomplish each role.

You were born for these roles; your purpose is to detect who you really are and record your feelings, thoughts, ideas, goals and possibilities within each role. Take the time to enjoy this exercise by doing it well. We know that this book is not a workbook, but it is so valuable for each reader to go through this exercise that we're including a page for each brainstorming session. If you choose to use a notebook or other place to write your thoughts on each of these thirteen roles, that's fine. But we hope you can look past this generation's training to not "write in the book" and really fill in your feelings and thoughts about your life in these thirteen arenas. The results will be worth it!

1. MENTOR: BUILD PROTÉGÉES

2. SCHOLAR: FILL IN GAPS IN YOUR EDUCATION, AND GO DEEPER IN YOUR AREAS OF EXPERTISE

3. CITIZEN: INCREASE FREEDOM

4. ENTREPRENEUR: ADD VALUE

5. SENTINEL: WARN UPCOMING GENERATIONS

7. PHILANTHROPIST: SELFLESSLY INCREASE HAPPINESS

8. DISCIPLE: LET GO OF BAGGAGE AND DISCIPLINE YOUR LIFE

9. ARTIST: CREATE BEAUTY

10. STATESMAN: CHANGE THE WORLD FOR GOOD

11. HEALER: CHANGE THE ONE

12. ELDER: NEVER RETIRE, BUT GET OUT AND SERVE, SERVE, SERVE

Be sure to take the time to do this exercise with all thirteen roles before you read on in this book. This work will be very helpful to you, whatever phase you are currently in. You will likely want to rewrite it and study it more as the years pass.

Live Your Mission

Whatever your two towers and thirteen roles, we invite you to educate yourself accordingly. This is Leadership Education. It takes a lifetime, but it is worth it. It is why each of us was born; it is our reason for living.

The Leadership Path is the life each of was born to live. It starts with a Leadership Education. Every person is a genius. Our purpose in life is to find out our genius, the mission God gave us, and to accomplish it. During the Foundational Phases, the key people on our path are parents and siblings. During the Educational Phases, the key people are parents, mentors and friends. And during the Applicational Phases, the key people are spouse, children, family, colleagues and the community networks we build. Throughout our lives the emphasis should be others—loving them, serving them, helping them. That is why leaders were born. And we were all born to be leaders.

Nothing will have more impact on the future of the world than for each of us to find out why we were born and to do it. Human beings tend to do this when parents, teachers and other mentors invite us to it. Our invitation to each reader is to become the genius you were born to become, by getting and applying a leadership education and using it to serve and impact others. Our hope is that you will pass this invitation along to everyone you meet and serve. If you do, you will live a life of far-reaching and long-felt impact.

CODA

Grandparenting

The true test of leadership is grandparenting. Everything else falls short. And it is not enough to grandparent just your posterity. Grandchildren get married; superb grandparents know that they need to grandparent potential spouses long before their grandchildren are married. Grandchildren work; superb grandparents know that they need to grandparent potential bosses, managers, colleagues and employees long before their grandchild enters a career. The same is true for everyone your grandchild will meet in life, and everyone who will impact your grandchild's life. This is what community means: grandparents teaching and raising everyone in their grandchildren's world.

In short, grandparenting is perfecting all thirteen roles of Impact Phase—leaving the world better than what you inherited. Some generations get this right, while others fail miserably. The impact on happiness and prosperity, or the lack of it, is huge. In short: a grandparent generation can change anything in the world.

This is not limited to people who are over sixty years old. Far from it. All of us need to start grandparenting as soon as we are in Scholar Phase. Puberty is the call to grandparenting, to begin preparing a better world for your future grandchildren. The call to grandparenting is the impetus to Scholar Phase, to "put away" childish things as Paul of Christendom taught and "seek for a better country."

A life spent making the world better for your future grandchildren is a life of service, leadership, and greatness. It takes a full lifetime to really make change. This is the message and purpose of life and the most important thing any of us can ever do. It is the reason for our lives. We better get started on it early, or as soon as we realize what it is all about.

Lee Pitts tells the wonderful story of a farmer in the Great Depression who is busily working on his farm in the summer heat. His friends gather at the local coffee shop and worry about him. Doesn't he know that prices are too low for him to make a profit on his crop? Doesn't he know that if he plants a crop he can't get government subsidies? It's hot, it's humid, his planting will actually lose him money—has he gone crazy?

One of the farmers agrees to go ask him these questions. It turns out that this hard-working farmer is aware of all of the many reasons that may justify others not to plant, but he keeps working. His friend finally asks him, exasperated, what he is planting. "Oak trees," he says.

You can imagine what his friend must think: "What? Oak trees? You've gone 'round the bend! Your work will have no value until at least fifty years have passed!"

The farmer replies that the oak trees aren't for him. *They are for his grandchildren.*

Our purpose in life is to plant, nurture and become oak trees, and to help others do the same. That is grandparenting: planting oak trees! We are growing the oak trees of the future *today*.

All of us should realize our true purpose and mission—to make the world better for our grandchildren and their children. This is Leadership Education. This is what it really means. This is true even in the midst of struggle and challenge, financial depression or world war. During the most trying times, it is even more crucial.

What if the fourteen-year-old knew this? How would it change his education? Or the eighteen-year-old college student? Questions of "what are you majoring in?" or "what will your career be?" would take on whole new dimensions. If the twenty-four-year-old knew this, he would approach dating, courting, commitment and marriage differently than many do in our modern world. What if the thirty-three-year-old mother knew this, and her husband? Making a living would be just that—a way to pay the bills while you work on what is really important. Making a living is a waste unless we also make a life—a great life, a leadership life, one which transforms the world of our grandchildren to something really, truly better.

What if the fifty-four-year-old knew this? Those grey hairs would indicate that the time is getting close: "The time for my real purpose is almost here! What else do I need to do to be ready? How must I change things in the next twenty years so my grandchildren inherit the world I envision for them?" The eighty-one-year-old would say: "How can I change the whole world so my great-grandchildren have someone worthy of them to marry? To employ or work for? To enjoy freedom and community with?"

Grandparenting changes everything. In our modern world people often introduce themselves as "a doctor," "a teacher," "a mechanic." A few who really get it say, "Hi, I'm Lyle, and I'm a dad," or "I'm Vicki Jo, and I am a wife and mother." We are always uplifted when we meet such people. What if all of us took it to an even higher level: "Hi, I'm Bob and my mission in life is to be a superb grandfather," or "I'm Mary and I want to be the best grandmother ever. I can't wait for grey hair!"

Okay, maybe that's too much. But the sentiment is profound. For almost all of us, Grandparenting is the fulfillment of our lives, it is who we were meant to be. We believe that the real meaning of the word "father" is grandfather. At the deepest level, when we really seek fathering, what we want is true grandfathering. Same with mother. If we grandparent our own children, we will be truly great mothers and fathers. When we all grandparent, for the whole society, everything in the world improves. And understand, please, what we hope is obvious: your marital, maternal or paternal status has nothing to do with your obligation to future generations. You are a beneficiary of the legacy left by those who went before, most of whom were wholly unrelated to you. And the legacy you leave will be for those that follow, regardless of the genes you do or do not pass on. The children of the future are *your* grandchildren. That's Leadership. That's Leadership Education.

The following poem written by Rachel in tribute of a beloved father and grandfather demonstrates what matters most, and the important roles filled by grandparents who assume their important place in society:

Gingerly he turns the key and
guides the pendulum's flight,
Replaces, then, the key inside
and beds down for the night.

While others love to hear the chime
that says the day's begun,
'Tis father's hand that marks the time
and gives it pow'r to run.

When desert sun would scorch and burn
the shoots and buds so tender,
All through the night he takes the turn
that green life it may render.

Though it were sandy desert soil
unwillingly to yield
He lays his hand to work and toil
and lo — a verdant field.

With tenderness he looks on as
the lambs find mother's side,
And watches as they nurse and feed,
his face aglow with pride.

But then he sees the small one who
has not a mother there,
"Come, Lamby, here," and in his hand
he takes him in his care.

When hearts are filled with gratitude
or lifted up with love,
He voices our emotions in
his praise to God above.

The words of loved, sacred hymns
in tenor sing so true,
And Father's hand can make the old
piano praise Him, too.

As with the fields and flocks,
and the piano when he sings,
As with the antique, wind-up clocks,
and other treasured things,

His touch has given life and care
and sustenance and power,
To grandchildren who've gladly come
to earth in this great hour.

A hand of friendship, discipline,
of comfort, guidance, love,
To men and women here for God,
just come from up above.

And when he speaks with faith and power,
God's will we understand.
How great the blessings wrought beneath
the touch of Father's hand.

When was the last time you did something hard, *really* hard, specifically for your grandchildren and their children?

What should you do for them—right now? Who do you need to be—in the years ahead? What price are you willing to pay? What lesser things can you sacrifice? What efforts will you invest to become the grandparent that will ensure the opportunity of meaningful lives to future generations? Your decisions now—today—will help determine their destiny. We each have a unique and personal mission of impact that no one else can do as well. When we discover this and give our lives to it, we are leaders. This is the Path of Leadership. Whatever our age or phase of life, we must enter and stay on the Path of Leadership. The future of the world depends upon it—upon you.

Free Audio!

Check out edits, updates
and upgrades to this book
and download a free audio!

TJEd.org/New-7-Keys